Hiking Indiana

HELP US KEEP THIS GUIDE UP TO DATE

Every effort has been made by the author and editors to make this guide as accurate and useful as possible. However, many things can change after a guide is published—trails are rerouted, regulations change, techniques evolve, facilities come under new management, and so on.

We would appreciate hearing from you concerning your experiences with this guide and how you feel it could be improved and kept up to date. While we may not be able to respond to all comments and suggestions, we'll take them to heart, and we'll also make certain to share them with the author. Please send your comments and suggestions to the following address:

Globe Pequot Press
Reader Response/Editorial Department
P.O. Box 480
Guilford, CT 06437

Or you may e-mail us at: editorial@GlobePequot.com

Thanks for your input, and happy trails!

Hiking Indiana

A Guide to the State's Greatest Hiking Adventures

Second Edition

Phil Bloom

FALCONGUIDES

GUILFORD, CONNECTICUT
HELENA, MONTANA
AN IMPRINT OF GLOBE PEQUOT PRESS

FALCONGUIDES®

Copyright © 2000, 2010 by Morris Book Publishing, LLC

ALL RIGHTS RESERVED. No part of this book may be
reproduced or transmitted in any form by any means,
electronic or mechanical, including photocopying and
recording, or by any information storage and retrieval
system, except as may be expressly permitted in writing
from the publisher. Requests for permission should be
addressed to Globe Pequot Press, Attn: Rights and Per-
missions Department, P.O. Box 480, Guilford, CT 06437.

FalconGuides is an imprint of Globe Pequot Press.

Falcon, FalconGuides, and Outfit Your Mind are registered
trademarks of Morris Book Publishing, LLC.

All interior photos by Phil Bloom.

Project editor: Gregory Hyman
Layout artist: Kevin Mak
Maps: Trailhead Graphics Inc. © Morris Book
Publishing, LLC

Library of Congress Cataloging-in-Publication Data
Bloom, Phil.
  Hiking Indiana : a guide to the state's greatest hiking
adventures / Phil Bloom. – 2nd ed.
     p. cm. – (Falcon guides)
  Includes bibliographical references and index.
  ISBN 978-0-7627-3843-4 (alk. paper)
  1. Hiking–Indiana. 2. Trails–Indiana. I. Title.
  GV199.42.I6B56 2010
  796.5109772–dc22
                                    2009046680

Printed in the United States of America

10 9 8 7 6 5 4 3 2 1

Contents

Overview Map viii
Acknowledgments ix
Introduction 1
    Ecology 3
    Geology.. 4
    Human History 5
    Fundamentals.. 6
    Clothing 8
    Weather and Seasons 9
    Animals 10
    Bugs 11
How to Use This Guide... 11
Map Legend 12

The Hikes
Dunelands
  1 Long Lake Loop 14
  2 Dune Succession Trail 17
  3 Cowles Bog 20
  4 Little Calumet River Trail, Bailly Homestead, and Chellberg Farm 22
  5 Beach Trail... 26
  6 Heron Rookery Trail 30
  7 Mount Baldy Trail.. 32

Glacial Lakes
  8 Bicentennial Woods: Eagle Trail 37
  9 Crooked Lake Nature Preserve.. 39
 10 Merry Lea Environmental Learning Center.................................... 41
 11 Chain O'Lakes State Park... 44
 12 Edna W. Spurgeon Woodland Nature Preserve 48
 13 Olin Lake Nature Preserve 51
 14 Pokagon State Park 54
 15 Wing Haven Reserve: Trillium Woods Trail 59

Wabash Valley
 16 Fox Island Park 64
 17 Ouabache State Park... 67
 18 Kekionga Trail.. 71
 19 Salamonie Reservoir: Bloodroot Trail 76
 20 Salamonie Reservoir: Switchgrass Marsh and Tree Trails.............. 79
 21 Boy Scout Trail 82

22 Kokiwanee Nature Preserve 85
23 Hathaway Nature Preserve at Ross Run 88
24 Delphi Canal Trails 91
25 Wabash Heritage Trail 94
26 Portland Arch Nature Preserve 99

Central Plain

27 Mounds State Park 103
28 Fort Harrison State Park: Fall Creek Trail 106
29 Pine Hills Nature Preserve 108
30 Shades State Park: Ravine Trails 111
31 Shades State Park: Pearl Ravine 115
32 Turkey Run State Park 119
33 Big Walnut Creek Nature Preserve: Tall Timbers Trail 122

Southeast

34 Muscatatuck National Wildlife Refuge 127
35 Versailles State Park 130
36 Clifty Falls State Park 132
37 Charlestown State Park 137
38 Adventure Hiking Trail 140
39 Shaw Lake Loop 144
40 Starve Hollow State Recreation Area 146
41 Knob Lake Trail 150

Hill Country

42 Morgan–Monroe State Forest: Low Gap Trail 154
43 Morgan–Monroe State Forest: Three Lakes Loop 158
44 Scarce O'Fat Trail 161
45 Brown County State Park: Trail 8 164
46 Ogle Hollow Nature Preserve: Trail 5 167
47 Twin Caves Trail 170
48 Spring Mill State Park: Village Trail 174

Southwest

49 Harmonie State Park 179
50 Shakamak State Park 181
51 McCormick's Creek State Park: Falls Canyon Trail 185
52 McCormick's Creek State Park: Wolf Cave Trail 188
53 Patoka Lake: Main Trail 192
54 Lincoln State Park 196

Hoosier National Forest

55 Cope Hollow Loop 202
56 Peninsula Trail... 206
57 Sycamore Loop.. 208
58 Pioneer Mothers Memorial Forest 213
59 Hemlock Cliffs National Scenic Trail...................................... 215
60 Two Lakes Loop 218
61 Tipsaw Lake Trail.. 223
62 Saddle Lake Loop... 226
63 Mogan Ridge East 228
64 German Ridge Lake Trail... 232

Knobstone Trail

65 Deam Lake to Jackson Road.. 236
66 Jackson Road to New Chapel... 238
67 New Chapel to Leota 241
68 Leota to Elk Creek 244
69 Elk Creek to Oxley Memorial 246
70 Oxley Memorial to Spurgeon Hollow...................................... 249
71 Spurgeon Hollow to Delaney Park... 252

Appendix A: Suggested Reading 255
Appendix B: Additional Resources 256
Index.. 259
About the Author 261

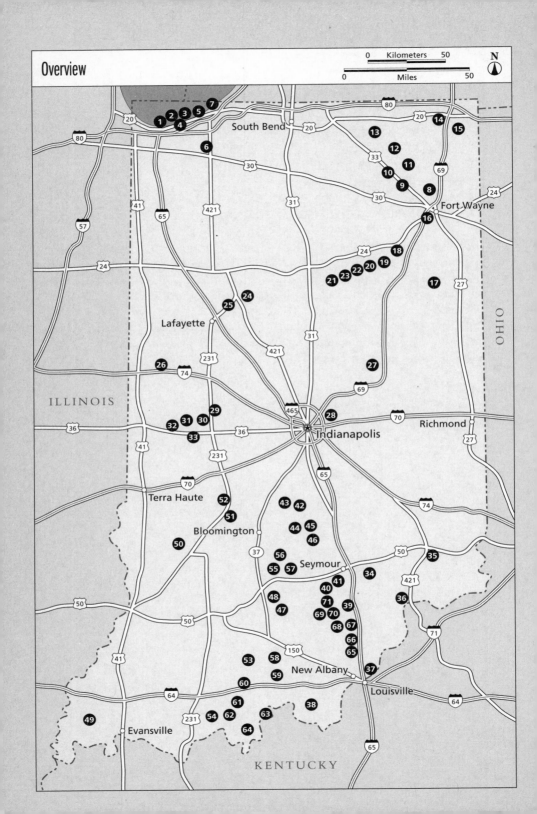

Acknowledgments

Hiking can be a solitary endeavor. Sometimes it is the best way to enjoy nature. Researching and writing a hiking book, however, requires considerable help, and there are several people to whom I am grateful.

To begin with, my parents, Mike and JoAnne Bloom, deserve credit for giving me my first taste of the outdoors. I am sure my siblings remember the times Mom and Dad would take us for hikes along the banks of the Salamonie River or in some other state park.

The late Bill McArdle, scoutmaster of Boy Scout Troop 20 at Queen of Angels Grade School, taught me and hundreds of other boys the basic hiking skills that helped make those 20-milers endurable.

Years later I met Judy Esterline and Judy Deimling, hiking buddies who showed me a new way to hike—going slower and with eyes wide open to what was at your feet. They made the woods come alive with their knowledge of wildflowers and native plants.

A special thanks to Kay Ellerhoff, formerly of Falcon Publishing, who helped make the professional connection that allowed those past influences to be transformed into this work.

This project took time—the first edition as well as this revised version. Thanks to the many editors at FalconGuides and Globe Pequot Press who exhibited patience throughout—beginning with Randall Green and including David Lee, Molly Jay, Bill Schneider, and finally Scott Adams.

A long-distance acknowledgment goes out to Tracy Salcedo in California, whose attention to detail in the editing process was remarkable. Through phone calls and e-mails, she helped keep me on the right path.

Special thanks go to Jessica Haberman and Paulette Baker of Globe Pequot who edited this edition of *Hiking Indiana*.

Thanks also to the editors at the *Fort Wayne Journal Gazette,* where I worked for twenty-eight years, for their support in allowing me time away from the office to complete the first edition of this book.

Special credit for double-checking information for this second edition goes to Shane Perfect with ACRES Land Trust, Bruce Rowe at Indiana Dunes National Lakeshore, Les Wadzinski and Nancy Myers with the Hoosier National Forest, and Indiana Department of Natural Resources staff—Jill Vance at Spring Mill State Park, Brad Bumgardner (Indiana Dunes), Jeff Cummings (Fort Harrison), Fred Wooley (Pokagon), Barbara Cummings (Turkey Run and Shades), Dick Davis (Clifty Falls), Angie Manual (Mounds), Michael Crews (Lincoln), Bob Greiner (Ouabache State Park), Ted Tapp (Versailles), Andrea Logsdon (Charlestown), Brad Schneck (Jackson-Washington State Forest), and Walt Zak (Clark State Forest).

Thanks also to the many coworkers, friends, and family whose interest in how "the book" was progressing contributed regular reminders that I needed to stick with it or let them all down.

It can get lonely out there on the trail, so I particularly enjoyed the time shared with special people. Thanks to my brother-in-law, Dr. John Herber, with whom I spent a splendid day on the Lakeview and Boundary Trails, the last hike taken in the first edition marathon.

Thanks to my children, Jacob and Jennifer. I hope you always remember our time on the trails in the same special way that I remembered those spent with my parents, brothers, and sisters.

To my grandchildren—Benjamin, Claire Marie and Matthew—this revised edition is as much for you as it is for anyone. I hope you come to think of it as a doorway to nature.

The person who deserves the most praise is Jessie, my wife. Without her this book would not exist. Her encouragement was constant. Her personal sacrifices were many; her love, sustaining. She is the best hiking partner I've ever had. Jessie, I'll go hiking with you . . . anywhere, anytime. Always.

Finally, this updated guide is dedicated to the memory of my late sister, Martha.

> When I walk through sunlit meadows
> or down a woodland trail,
> I will pause sometimes near wildflowers,
> and think sweet thoughts of you

Introduction

God crowned her hills with beauty,
Gave her lakes and winding streams,
Then He edged them all with woodlands
As the settings for our dreams
　　　　　—From the official state poem,
　　　　　"Indiana," by Arthur Mapes

This is a hiking guide to Indiana. Why Indiana? Why not?

After all, it was from here that renowned hiker and conservationist John Muir began his exploration of nature and wilderness. Following recovery from a work accident in Indianapolis, Muir walked 1,000 miles from Indiana to the Gulf of Mexico. He later went west to California, founded the Sierra Club, and was instrumental in establishing several national parks.

It is only by coincidence that Muir is connected to Indiana, but within the state boundaries are the kinds of natural wonders he might have appreciated had he stuck around.

The Hoosier State is far more than steel mills, the Indianapolis 500, nine of the ten largest high school basketball gymnasiums in the world, and flat fields of corn and soybeans. Yet Indiana's natural treasures are unknown or underappreciated by many people, including a lot of Hoosiers.

Indiana has richly diverse offerings—from Indiana Dunes National Lakeshore on Lake Michigan to the rolling hills of Brown County State Park, from the banks of the Wabash River to the Charles C. Deam Wilderness in Hoosier National Forest.

Indiana's mix of wild places and civilization may be exemplified best by the outline of the state. Except for a dip in the northwest corner where Lake Michigan intrudes, much of the western, northern, and eastern boundaries are as straight as a surveyor's ruler. In contrast, the hand of nature carved out the rest, as shown in the twisting course of the Ohio River to the south and the Wabash River along the lower third of the west boundary.

Publicly held land—where most hiking trails are located—accounts for less than 5 percent of Indiana's 36,185 square miles. Large cities dominate the state—Indianapolis with more than one million residents; Fort Wayne, Gary, South Bend, Evansville, and Terre Haute all with more than 100,000 residents.

The demand for green spaces is being met by the state's Department of Natural Resources. Since 1995 the DNR has opened four state parks—Falls of the Ohio, Fort Benjamin Harrison, Charlestown, and Prophetstown—and added thousands of additional acres with acquisitions like Goose Pond Fish and Wildlife Area.

The DNR manages twenty-four state parks, nine reservoirs, seventeen fish and wildlife areas, thirteen state forests, and more than 200 nature preserves. Hiking opportunities exist at nearly every location—from routes of 0.25 mile or less to the 58.0-mile Knobstone Trail, Indiana's scaled-down version of the Appalachian Trail. Some trails have historic significance, like the Wabash Heritage Trail. Others, like the Knobstone, have geologic significance. Most are just fun to hike.

Yet it's sometimes hard to escape the rush of the modern world, even on a trail. Consider, for example, a spot on the Wabash Heritage Trail. At this point alongside Burnett's Creek, the dirt path converges on a paved county road, a railroad track, and a four-lane interstate passing overhead. There may not be another location in the state where as many avenues of transportation intersect.

The DNR completed an inventory of hiking opportunities in 1996 for its Indiana Trails 2000 initiative, a project intended to promote and enhance hiking opportunities across the state. The inventory charted 392 trails covering 950 total miles that are designated specifically for hikers. Other trails cater to mountain bikes, snowmobiles, off-road vehicles, and equestrians, but hikers can also use most of these trails.

In 2006 a state-issued report titled "Hoosiers on the Move" listed 870 hiking trails totaling more than 2,400 miles, with plans to expand the inventory even more through a cooperative effort between the DNR, the Indiana Department of Transportation, the Governor's Council for Physical Fitness and Sports, Indiana Department of Tourism, and the Indiana Economic Development Corporation. Spearheaded by

Trail sign.

Governor Mitch Daniels, the goal of "Hoosiers on the Move" is to put a trail within fifteen minutes of every Indiana resident by the year 2016.

Obviously the hikes included in this book offer only a sample of all that Indiana has to offer. Additional trails worth considering are the Tecumseh Trail, a 48.0-miler in south-central Indiana; Wolf Creek Trail, which skirts the west shores of Brookville Reservoir; Pate Hollow Trail in the Hoosier National Forest; and the Ten O'clock Line Trail, which runs between Brown County State Park and Yellowwood State Forest.

In summary, just about anywhere you go in Indiana, there's a trail to be traveled.

ECOLOGY

Before European settlers arrived in Indiana, the state was a blanket of trees—huge trees. More than 85 percent of Indiana—about twenty million acres—was forested, primarily with hardwood species such as beech, hickory, maple, oak, sycamore, tulip poplar, and walnut. Trees in this dense forest towered 150 to 200 feet high and measured as much as 9 or 10 feet in diameter. Settlers managed to cut down almost all those trees as they cleared the way for farming. The work proceeded at such a pace that Indiana led the nation in lumber production in 1899.

Ironically, much of the rocky soil in southern Indiana proved unsuitable as cropland. As agriculture gave way to industry, many farms were abandoned, paving the way for establishment of the Hoosier National Forest—a patchwork covering almost 200,000 acres in southern Indiana.

What wasn't forest in pre-settlement Indiana was either prairie or wetland, and both suffered a fate similar to the woodland.

Before the Kankakee River was reduced to a drainage ditch, the Grand Kankakee Marsh was to the Midwest what the Everglades are to southern Florida. Including Kankakee Marsh, nearly two million acres of wetlands dotted the state, but only a fraction remains today. The marshes, along with the prairielands that were home to bison, also were plowed under for farmers and industry.

But Indiana is not a wasteland. Despite such runaway efforts to subdue the land, pockets of natural splendor remain due to steadfast efforts to safeguard or restore their integrity.

Examples of rare or endangered flora in Indiana and their locations include Canada blueberry and Forbe's saxifrage at Portland Arch Nature Preserve; yellowwood trees at Brown County State Park and Yellowwood State Forest; Deam's foxglove on the Knobstone Trail; black cohosh at Harmonie State Park; and eastern hemlock at Turkey Run State Park, at Hemlock Bluff Nature Preserve, and Hemlock Cliffs in the Hoosier National Forest.

The fauna of Indiana includes thousands of species, from the smallest insects to white-tailed deer. Aquatic insects, freshwater mussels, Karner blue butterflies, crawfish, salamanders, bluebirds, bald eagles, bobcats, coyotes, wild turkeys, river otters, ruffed grouse, largemouth bass, and catfish are just a few of the species that inhabit the state. But there are other species that no longer exist in Indiana. Among those that have been lost are elk, bison, wolves, mountain lions, and black bears.

GEOLOGY

Like giant bulldozers, ancient glaciers shaped nearly the entire Indiana landscape, which was part of a giant sea in the Paleozoic era, about 250 to 750 million years ago.

The Pleistocene epoch began almost two million years ago and ended about 10,000 years ago. The glacial advance scraped southward across Indiana but never reached the Ohio River. As a consequence, southern Indiana is distinguished from the rest of the state by hilly terrain with deep ravines, lowland areas, and underground streams that have carved out caves in the limestone bedrock in a landscape known as karst topography.

The most recent glacier—the Wisconsin lobe—moved no more than one-third of the way through the northern part of the state. As it retreated about 10,000 years ago, its meltwaters created rolling hills, rivers and streams, and hundreds of small lakes. The deposits of gravel, sand, and soil known as moraines are another glacial feature of the northern lakes region. A morainal deposit appearing as a long, narrow ridge is referred to as an esker.

In between the northern lakes region and southern hills and lowland region is a relatively flat expanse known as the Central Till Plain, which draws its name from the mixture of glacial deposits. It is the largest geographic region in the state, bounded by the Wabash River to the north and the farthest advance of the Wisconsin glacier to the south. Despite the region's flat appearance, the highest point in the state—1,257 feet above sea level near Richmond in Wayne County—is located here.

Two of the most recognizable features of Indiana lie at its borders—a sliver of Lake Michigan in the northwest corner and the Ohio River, which forms the entire southern boundary of the state.

Numerous rivers crisscross the state, but none has greater influence than the Wabash, which appropriately is designated as the official state river. From its headwaters just across the Ohio border, the Wabash cuts across the northern half of Indiana and meanders 475 miles south to join the Ohio west of Evansville. The Wabash watershed drains two-thirds of the state.

Other major rivers include the St. Joseph and St. Marys, which meet in Fort Wayne to form the Maumee, which flows eastward into Lake Erie; a different St. Joseph River, which dips down from Michigan through South Bend before heading back through Michigan to Lake Michigan; and the White River system, which drains much of central and southern Indiana.

Two minerals have played important roles in Indiana industry—limestone and bituminous coal. Limestone cut from central Indiana was used in the construction of several famous buildings, including the Empire State Building and Rockefeller Center in New York City, and the National Cathedral and the Pentagon in Washington, D.C.

HUMAN HISTORY

Indiana's name means "Land of Indians," and while there is evidence of prehistoric inhabitants from 160 B.C., the greatest influence of Native American culture came less than 200 years ago.

Nomadic cultures from the Paleo-Indian and Archaic eras may have roamed part of Indiana as far back as 10,000 B.C., but the earliest significant influence of Native Americans came during the Early, Middle, and Late Woodland periods, which extended from about 500 B.C. to A.D. 1000. The mound-building Adena (Early Woodland) and Hopewell (Middle Woodland) cultures gave way to Late Woodland–era peoples and eventually to the Mississippian culture, which lasted from A.D. 1000 to 1450.

Native populations probably peaked during the early 1700s. Numerous tribes inhabited the state at that time, the largest being three northern tribes—the Miami, the Potawatomi, and the Delaware. Members of all three tribes were descendants of the Early Woodland peoples. At one time or another, the area was also home to such tribes as the Chickasaw, Huron, Kickapoo, Menominee, Mohican, Piankashaw, Shawnee, and Wea.

French explorer Robert Cavalier was the first known white man to enter Indiana, passing through in 1679 in search of a passage to the Pacific Ocean. French fur traders soon followed, setting up trading posts near present-day Fort Wayne, Lafayette, and Vincennes. The first permanent European settlement was established at Vincennes in 1731.

Competition between the expansion-minded French and British over fur trade with Indians was a factor leading to war between the two countries over rights to American soil. The British won, and France surrendered its claim to Indiana in 1763.

The British began military occupation of Indiana during the Revolutionary War. Fort Sackville at Vincennes became a focal point in the conflict, but George Rogers Clark and his Virginia troops seized it from the British for good in 1779. Eleven years later, Congress established the Indiana Territory, which included present-day Indiana, Illinois, Wisconsin, and parts of Michigan and Minnesota.

As settlers gained greater control of the territory, Indian resistance increased. Tecumseh, a Shawnee leader, was attempting to build a confederacy of fourteen tribes, but those forces were defeated at the Battle of Tippecanoe in 1811 by Gen. William Henry Harrison, who was later elected U.S. president. Tecumseh, meanwhile, sided with the British in the War of 1812.

When Indiana became the nineteenth state on December 11, 1816, its population was about 64,000.

In 1838 nearly 700 members of the Potawatomi tribe were forced out of the state at gunpoint and marched hundreds of miles to a reservation in Kansas.

Lavish road and canal construction projects drove the state to bankruptcy by 1840, but railroads brought economic improvement prior to the Civil War. However, it wasn't until the 1880s that the discovery of natural gas and development of the automobile paced an industrial boom.

By 1900 the state's population had reached 2.5 million. Today it is almost 6.4 million.

Following is a listing of other noteworthy dates in Indiana history:

1816–30: Abraham Lincoln spends his boyhood and young adult years on an Indiana farm.

1824: Indianapolis is established as state capital.

1841: William Henry Harrison, winner of the Battle of Tippecanoe, dies after only thirty days in office as U.S. president.

1867: Scottish-born John Muir leaves Indiana, eventually to become one of the country's leading conservationists and founder of the Sierra Club.

1889: Benjamin Harrison, grandson of William Henry Harrison, the only U.S. president elected from Indiana, is sworn into office.

1906: U.S. Steel builds a factory in Gary.

1909: Gene Stratton-Porter's novel *Girl of the Limberlost* is published.

1911: The first Indianapolis 500 auto race takes place.

1916: The Indiana state park system is established with the dedication of McCormick's Creek as Indiana's first state park.

1935: Hoosier National Forest is created.

1966: Indiana Dunes is designated as a national lakeshore, and land acquisition for Muscatatuck National Wildlife Refuge begins.

1982: Congress approves Charles C. Deam Wilderness in the Hoosier National Forest.

1994: Patoka River National Wildlife Refuge is established.

2000: Big Oaks National Wildlife Refuge is established on 50,000 acres of the former Jefferson Proving Grounds, a military munitions test facility.

2005: Indiana Department of Natural Resources acquires the 8,000-acre Goose Pond and Beehunter Marsh complex and establishes the state's fourth-largest largest fish and wildlife area.

2008: Indiana DNR allocates $19 million to trail enhancement projects statewide and doubles ownership of abandoned rail corridor property for future trail projects.

FUNDAMENTALS

Hiking really is a simple activity, which perhaps explains its popularity. In most instances hiking does not require specialized gear, although all sorts of gadgets are available. Hiking does not require special training. Nevertheless, there are some basic guidelines that all hikers should follow.

First choose the right hike. Figure out what you want to accomplish with a hike. Do you want to discover new places? Explore nature? Simply get some exercise?

Understand your limitations, and do not overdo it. Figure out how physically fit

Smokey Bear offers a safety reminder.

you are and what you can handle before charging off on longer, more demanding hikes.

Take a map whenever possible, even if it's only the brochure available at the park gate or nature preserve registration box. For longer hikes, or hikes in remote areas like the Hoosier National Forest, take a compass or a handheld Global Positioning System (GPS) unit, grab a U.S. Geological Survey (USGS) topographic map, and learn how to use them.

Stay on designated trails. Taking shortcuts, especially on switchbacks, contributes to erosion and may disturb or damage sensitive areas.

Pack water, even for short hikes. Water is essential to keeping the body hydrated. A rule of thumb is to drink sixteen ounces before embarking on a hike, then pause every half hour for another four to six ounces. If you must use water from a lake or stream, be sure to purify it first with a filter or iodine tablets or by boiling it.

Avoid crowds by planning your hike for midweek. State parks draw their biggest crowds during the summer months, especially on weekends.

Be aware of stream conditions. Some trails, particularly those through the ravines of southern Indiana, cross streams that can be dangerous during periods of heavy rain. Do not attempt to ford a stream unless you are sure you can make it safely across.

Practice the zero-impact outdoor ethic: Pack it in; pack it out. This is a mandatory policy in the Charles C. Deam Wilderness, but it is a good approach to adopt for all situations. Pack out everything, including gum wrappers, cigarette butts, and twisty ties. Avoid building campfires unless absolutely necessary. Leave the place you have visited looking as if you were never there.

Avoid making needless noise. Nothing disturbs the solitude of nature more than hearing boisterous people tromping down the trail.

Most of all, enjoy.

CLOTHING

Seasons and weather conditions usually dictate proper attire on the trail, but so will each hike.

Begin at the bottom by properly outfitting your feet. Most trails can be hiked in tennis or gym shoes, but longer hikes and hikes in rugged terrain require a good pair of hiking boots. And don't forget socks. I prefer to start with a thin pair of socks, over which I wear heavier wool socks. For me this combination helps prevent blisters. Pack an extra pair of socks for longer hikes; changing them along the way can be refreshing.

Pack rain gear. Weather changes can occur rapidly in Indiana, so it is best to be prepared. A light jacket will suffice on short hikes, but a full outfit of water-repellent, breathable material is a must for longer trips.

The rest is personal preference, but make sure your clothing is appropriate for the season. Some people wear long pants and long-sleeved shirts even in warm weather; others prefer shorts and T-shirts. Be assured, the latter will be uncomfortable on the hottest of days if the trail leads through heavy brush or areas with mosquitoes.

In cooler weather, dress in layers. It is easier to remove a layer if you get too hot than it is to add something you do not have.

WEATHER AND SEASONS

Indiana has a varied climate, but it can usually be described as humid in summer and cold in winter. Temperatures in winter can dip well below zero, and summer days can be unbearably hot and humid.

Weather conditions can be unpredictable, especially in early summer, when powerful storms can pop up on short notice. Average June temperatures range from a low of 60 degrees Fahrenheit to the mid-80s for central Indiana, with variances to the north and south. Average January temperatures range from the low 20s to the upper 30s. Annual rainfall averages about 38 to 40 inches, with additional precipitation coming from snow that varies from 10 inches in the south to around 40 inches in the north.

Some areas of the state have become synonymous with certain seasons—Brown County State Park for fall foliage, Pokagon State Park for cross-country skiing and a refrigerated toboggan run that carries sledders downhill at speeds reaching 50 miles per hour; and Indiana Dunes State Park for summer fun on the sandy beaches of Lake Michigan. But the attraction of those locales is not limited to one season. Brown County is just as beautiful in spring for wildflowers, as is Pokagon, Olin Lake Nature Preserve, and a host of other areas.

Spring: If you like wildflowers, consider a hike at this time of year. It is easy to find woodlands carpeted with Virginia bluebell, large-flowered trillium, wild columbine, Jack-in-the-pulpit, Dutchman's breeches, or Solomon's seal. Spring also is a good time for watching wildlife, especially migrating birds like Canada geese, ducks, sandhill cranes, and certain songbirds.

Indiana springs are known for erratic weather patterns and are prone to violent storms that can spawn tornadoes. It is a good idea when hiking at this time of year to pack rain gear and perhaps a sweater or fleece to ward off sudden temperature changes. Some trails may be messy because of spring thaw or even impassable due to rain or flooding.

Summer: June, July, and August can be among the toughest months to hike in Indiana. It's not only a time when weather can be stifling but also a time when trails, campgrounds, and parks are frequently packed with vacationers. Although the weather can reach extremes, it is also more stable in summer than in other seasons, allowing for extended periods of good hiking. Be alert for quickly developing thunderstorms with dangerous lighting. Summer is also the season for bugs—mosquitoes, bees, wasps, hornets, flies, and gnats.

Fall: If there is a better time of year to hike in Indiana than spring, it is during the fall. Temperatures begin to drop in September and October, especially at night, when it can get quite chilly. Daytime temperatures often are still warm enough for shirt-sleeves, even shorts. With schools back in session, trail traffic diminishes and campsites are more available after the Labor Day weekend. But the real beauty of autumn is the rich display of color presented by the hardwood forests and woodlands across the state. Oak, maple, tulip, hickory, and other trees switch color schemes from uniform green to orange, red, and yellow. Since hunting seasons begin in autumn, it is a good idea to make yourself more visible by wearing one or more piece of blaze-orange clothing.

Winter: If solitude is your desire, this may be the time to consider a hike, especially in the southern half of the state, where snow is a less-frequent obstacle. Daytime temperatures can be almost mild, and traffic along the trails is definitely at its low point. Even in the deepest woods, it is often easier to see wildlife because the sight lines are so clear with the absence of vegetation. If there is snow on the ground, wildlife tracks can be easily spotted. Trails can be slippery, though.

ANIMALS

You don't have to worry about bears or wolves in Indiana, although both once roamed the state. The largest mammal in the state today is the white-tailed deer, which is abundant in most parts of Indiana. Canada geese are almost as plentiful as deer, especially in the northeastern lakes region and in urban areas. Other common animals are squirrels, rabbits, raccoons, and wild turkeys, as well as foxes, coyotes, and opossums.

Bobcats and badgers also are present. No longer on the state's endangered species list, they still have protected status as species of special concern.

There are poisonous snakes in Indiana, the copperhead being the most common. It usually is found in southern Indiana, where timber rattlesnakes and cottonmouths (water moccasins) also are found, but only rarely. The eastern Massasauga rattlesnake is found in swampy areas of northern Indiana, but in such small numbers that it is considered endangered by the state.

Snakebites are rare and almost always nonfatal, but play it safe by steering clear of snakes. Timber rattlesnakes live in high, rocky terrain and are often found on ledges. A timber rattler will usually, but not always, send a warning by raising and rattling its tail. Copperheads frequent the same habitat as timber rattlers, but they are not as easy to detect. Its copper-red head and brown bands allow the snake to blend into fallen leaves. Copperheads offer no warning before striking, so be careful walking over fallen logs. Cottonmouths have an especially aggressive nature, but this aquatic species is the least common of the state's poisonous snakes and lives only in a few isolated areas. The simplest way to avoid poisonous snakes and their dangerous bites is to be alert and watch your step.

Indiana has played an active role in restoration efforts involving raptor species like the bald eagle, peregrine falcon, and osprey. Another restoration success story is the reintroduction and establishment of a self-sustaining population of river otters.

BUGS

Hikers in Indiana need to be aware of only a few pesky bugs. The most serious concerns have to do with ticks and stinging insects such as bees, hornets, and wasps.

Ticks often carry diseases that can cause serious problems for humans. More than a dozen species of ticks have been found in the state, but the two of particular concern are wood ticks, which carry Rocky Mountain spotted fever, and deer ticks, which carry Lyme disease. Consequently, hikers should check themselves for ticks, particularly after a hike in brushy or grassy areas where ticks reside.

Two spiders—the black widow and brown recluse—have bites that can be life threatening, but such occurrences are not common.

Mosquitoes and gnats are more of a nuisance, especially during warm, wet seasons. They generally can be dealt with by using insect repellents.

HOW TO USE THIS GUIDE

Hiking Indiana is organized largely by geographic regions, beginning in the northwest corner of the state with the Dunelands and working southward to finish with the Knobstone Trail.

Within each section, the hikes are presented in sequence, which changes from area to area. For instance, hikes in the Dunelands are presented from west to east, beginning with the Long Lake Loop near Gary and working east toward Michigan City. Hikes in the Hill Country head north from Bloomington in a clockwise sweep.

If you are familiar with other Falcon guidebooks, you may notice the absence of elevation charts in *Hiking Indiana*. That is because very few of the hikes have significant elevation changes, and those that do rarely change more than 250 feet. However, some of these hikes, particularly those in southern Indiana, can provide even the most avid hiker with a pretty good workout.

Map Legend

Transportation

Interstate Highway	══⟨55⟩══
U.S. Highway	──⟨61⟩──
State Road	──⟨22⟩──
County/Forest Road	⊏CR 1⊐⊏FR 1⊐
Unpaved Road	======
Railroade	┼─┼─┼─┼
Featured Trail	━━━━━
Other Trail	---------
Boardwalk/Steps	‖‖‖‖‖

Hydrology

Lake/Reservoir	
River/Creek	～～
Intermittent Stream	–·–·–
Marsh/Swamp	
Sand Bar	
Waterfall	⫰
Spring	⟡

Symbols

Airport	✈
Boat Ramp	⫸

Symbols (cont)

Bridge	≍
Campground	▲
Capital	⊛
Cave	∩
City/Town	○
Gate	•—•
Mountain/Peak	▲
Parking	🅿
Picnic Area	🛆
Point of Interest/Structure	▪
Restroom/Latrine	♨
Tower	♙
Trailhead (Start)	⓫
Viewpoint/ Overlook	◄
Visitor Center	❓
Scale	0 Kilometer 1 / 0 Mile 1

Land Use

State Boundary	–·–·–·–
National Forest	▭
Local Park/State Park/ Wildlife Area/Preserve	▭

Dunelands

One word defines the Dunelands of northwest Indiana—conflict. Whether it has been by the natural forces that originally shaped the area or the social forces of modern times, conflict has been at the heart of the Dunelands story.

Lake Michigan—the first of the Great Lakes—was formed by glacier movement more than 14,000 years ago. Left behind when the glacier receded was the residue that makes up the dunes, which in some instances are still being formed today. Mount Baldy at the east end of the Indiana Dunes National Lakeshore and Smoking Dune at the West Beaches are "living" dunes—in other words, they continue to grow and move as they are reshaped by the wind that created them.

Mount Baldy creeps inland at the rate of 4.5 feet per year, gobbling up trees in its path. At Smoking Dune, further evidence can be seen where a boardwalk has been rerouted over a section now buried in sand.

As magnificent as the dunes are—including bogs, marshes, ponds, and varied forests—the area remains in conflict because of competing forces. The Indiana Dunes National Lakeshore, established by Congress in 1966, is fragmented by private residences and smokestack industry over its 23-mile stretch. The older Indiana Dunes State Park, which lies almost in the center of the national lakeshore, is less affected by the same forces but has its own problem—high visitation. Most of the annual one million visitors congregate at the beach or explore the nearby dunes.

Although most of the hikes in this section are in proximity to the dunes, some are not. One of the more remote hikes is the Heron Rookery Trail, located about 10 miles southeast of Chesterton but still part of the national lakeshore complex supervised by the National Park Service. Others are the Bailly Homestead and the Chellberg Farm site near the Little Calumet River.

The dunes have long been an area of discovery. In fact, they are the birthplace of the science known as ecology—the study of how living things relate to one another and their environment. Henry Cowles, father of this scientific field, was intrigued by the mystery of the dune environment, first as a graduate student and later as head of the botany department at the University of Chicago in the early 1900s. Cowles was puzzled by the coexistence of plant species usually found in different environments—arctic bearberry and prickly pear cactus, northern jack pine and dogwood. The more important discovery was the progression of plant life from the beaches to inland areas—sand stabilized by grasses, followed by shrubs, and then trees.

Trails in this section are presented starting near Gary to the west and moving east to Michigan City.

1 Long Lake Loop

This loop trail skirts a lake and passes over and through dunes, ponds, and woodlands.

Location: Near Gary, northwest Indiana
Distance: 2.0-mile loop
Elevation change: 85 feet
Approximate hiking time: 1 hour
Difficulty: Moderate
Jurisdiction: Indiana Dunes National Lakeshore
Fees and permits: Entry fee to West Beaches Memorial Day through Labor Day
Maps: USGS Portage; National Park Service brochure

Special attractions: Prickly pear cactus and dune-vista views of Long Lake
Camping: No camping at West Beaches; 140 modern campsites at Indiana Dunes State Park; 79 drive- or walk-in sites at Indiana Dunes National Lakeshore's Dunewood Campground, open Apr 1 through Oct 31
Trailhead facilities: Parking lot at the Long Lake Trail trailhead; beach house with restrooms and drinking fountains at the West Beach Trail trailhead

Finding the trailhead: From Interstate 80/94 southeast of Gary, go north 1 mile. Turn right onto US 20, go 0.9 mile to County Line Road. Turn left and go 1.2 miles north, crossing US 12 to the WEST BEACHES sign. Turn right (east) to enter the park. From the gatehouse, drive east for 0.4 mile to a parking lot on the right (south) side of the main road. To begin the hike, walk south from the parking lot toward the lake.

Prickly pear cactus found along the Long Lake Trail is an example of the diversity of plant species at the Indiana Dunes National Lakeshore.

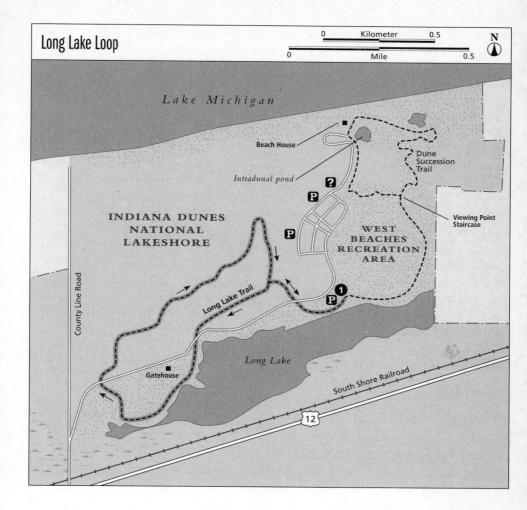

Long Lake Loop

Lake Michigan

Beach House

Intradunal pond

Dune
Succession
Trail

Viewing Point
Staircase

INDIANA DUNES
NATIONAL
LAKESHORE

WEST
BEACHES
RECREATION
AREA

County Line Road

Long Lake Trail

Long Lake

Gatehouse

South Shore Railroad

12

The Hike

Most visitors to this western edge of the Indiana Dunes National Lakeshore come for the sandy beaches and a chance to swim in Lake Michigan on hot summer days. They don't know what they are missing—an ecological mix of trees, shrubs, and plant life, some that seem completely out of place in this part of the country. For instance, the early part of the trail is lined with prickly pear cactus, a species most people would associate with the deserts of Utah, Arizona, or New Mexico. But here they are.

The trail begins on the south side of the parking lot toward Long Lake at a green sign noting that this is a Chicago Region Birding Trail Site.

Turn right (northwest) for a flat walk that goes back across the main road. After crossing the road, follow the trail northwest toward the distant tree-covered dune.

At the base of the dune, turn left (southwest) at the trail juncture and begin the outbound loop that leads to the main road at 0.4 mile. Cross the road and climb a wooden staircase to the top of a dune, where a wooden deck overlooks Long Lake.

Continue southwest off the staircase, crossing a wooden bridge and beginning a downhill stretch that skirts the west edge of a small pond on the right before returning to the main road. Cross the road to reach a chain-link fence at 0.9 mile. Turn right (northeast) and walk along the fence. You may see signs for the Marquette Trail, a bicycle trail, on the other side of the fence.

After about 50 yards, the Long Lake Loop passes a service building and picks up on the opposite side of a paved access road. There are no trail markers here; the easiest way to find the trail is to look for it on the inside elbow of a bend in the road.

The trail goes north through a heavily wooded area adorned with ferns. A wooden staircase leads to a hairpin turn in the trail and around another pond. Continue northeast and uphill as the trail cuts through a valley with high, wooded dunes on both sides to reach the high point of the trail—85 feet higher than the trailhead parking lot—at 1.7 miles. From here you can see the West Beaches parking lot, picnic shelters, and the massive wooden staircase of the Dune Succession Trail.

Walk down the sandy face of the dune to pick up the trail at the base of the hill. Turn right (south) and at 1.9 miles return to the trail juncture that begins the outbound leg of the loop. Turn left here and return to the parking lot while taking one more look at the prickly pear cactus.

Miles and Directions

0.0 Begin at the trailhead.

0.1 Turn left (southwest) at a trail juncture.

0.4 Cross the main road and climb a wooden staircase.

0.9 Cross the main road and turn right (northeast) at a chain-link fence.

1.7 Descend from a dune and turn right (southwest).

1.9 Return to the trail juncture for the outbound loop; turn left (south).

2.0 Arrive back at the trailhead.

2 Dune Succession Trail

This interpretive hike highlights the stages of dune development through plant succession.

Location: Near Chesterton, northwest Indiana
Distance: 1.0-mile loop
Elevation change: 100 feet
Approximate hiking time: 45 minutes
Difficulty: Moderate
Jurisdiction: Indiana Dunes National Lakeshore
Fees and permits: Entry fee to West Beaches Memorial Day through Labor Day
Maps: USGS Portage; National Park Service brochure

Special attractions: Intradunal pond, dunes, viewing platform
Camping: No camping at West Beaches; 140 modern campsites at Indiana Dunes State Park; 79 drive- or walk-in sites at Indiana Dunes National Lakeshore's Dunewood Campground, open Apr 1 through Oct 31
Trailhead facilities: Visitor center and a beach house with restrooms and drinking fountains

Finding the trailhead: From IN 49 go west 9 miles on US 12 to a four-way stop. Turn right onto County Line Road, cross the railroad tracks, and continue to the WEST BEACHES sign. Turn right (east) to enter the park. From the gatehouse, drive east for 0.8 mile to the visitor center parking lot. To begin the hike, walk from the parking lot to the beach house and on through to the beach.

The Hike

From the parking lot follow the paved road for 0.25 mile to the beach house and beach, which can be a very busy area on hot summer days. Walk through the beach house and turn right (east) to pick up the trail by finding the marked posts that correspond to the interpretive brochure. Along the trail you will discover how dunes are built by elements of nature—wind, sand, and vegetation. Part of the hike is on loose sand; the rest is on boardwalks and staircases designed to reduce dune erosion.

Pause for a moment on the wood deck at 0.3 mile to view the intradunal pond, created when strong winds blasted through an opening in the dune and scooped out sand to beneath the water table. Plants found here—horned bladderwort and Kalm's lobelia—differ from plants along the nearby dunes.

These are fairly new dunes, perhaps formed in the past 5,000 years. Marram grass is one of the first "dune builders" and is evident along the beach and on the beginning section of the hike. Marram grass stabilizes the sand through an underground network of roots and rhizomes. Another important plant is the cottonwood tree, which appears on the leeward side of the first dune. Although these cottonwoods appear short, they are just the tips of much taller trees buried in the sand. Protected from the wind, the leeward area hosts little bluestem grass, sand cherries, hop trees, and more wildflowers, such as puccoon and sand cress.

At the midway point of the hike there is a stand of jack pines, which provides shelter for arctic bearberry. Both are northern plant species, uncommon this far south, that were carried here by ice age glaciers.

Jump onto a boardwalk at 0.5 mile to continue the hike, which continues through a steep-sided valley. This valley was created by a blowout that occurred when strong winds carved out an opening in the dune. A portion of the old boardwalk has been buried, evidence of how the dune continues to wander under the force of wind. The extensive boardwalk and staircase system leads uphill on a wooded dune featuring black oak, hickory, basswood, dogwood, and sassafras trees. Such trees indicate how protected this area is from the wind and storms coming off Lake Michigan. The

The staircase on the south side of the dune on the Dune Succession Trail.

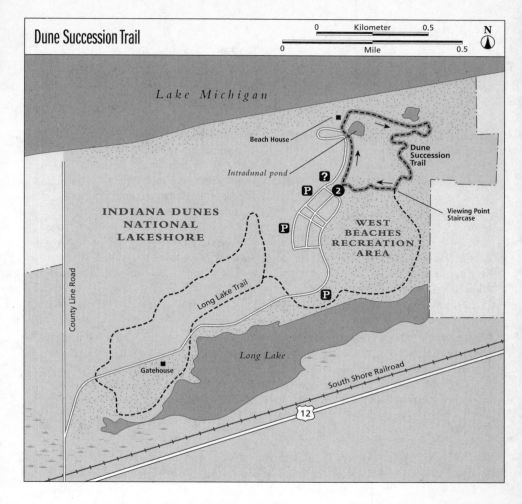

staircase system helps reduce erosion as well as makes the climb easier. Atop the hill at 0.7 mile is an overlook, followed by a 169-step stairway to the bottom of the dune and a soft, sandy hike back to the parking lot at the 1.0-mile mark.

Miles and Directions

0.0   Begin at the trailhead.

0.2   Reach the beach.

0.3   Arrive at the viewing platform near the intradunal pond.

0.5   Follow the boardwalk.

0.6   Climb the staircase to the inner dune and tree graveyard.

0.7   Reach the viewing platform atop the highest inner dune.

1.0   Arrive back at the trailhead.

3 Cowles Bog

A loop hike around a bog, through wooded dunes, past marshes, and along the Lake Michigan shoreline.

Location: 12 miles east of Gary, northwest Indiana

Distance: 5.0-mile loop

Elevation change: 100-foot dune climbs near beach

Approximate hiking time: 3 hours

Difficulty: Easy to moderate, except for strenuous dune climbs near the beach

Jurisdiction: Indiana Dunes National Lakeshore

Fees and permits: No fees or permits required

Maps: USGS Dune Acres; Dunes National Lakeshore map

Special attractions: Cowles Bog and Lake Michigan shoreline

Camping: No camping at Cowles Bog; 140 modern campsites at Indiana Dunes State Park (1.5 miles east); 79 drive-in or walk-in sites at Indiana Dunes National Lakeshore Dunewood Campground (6 miles east), open Apr 1 to Oct 31

Trailhead facilities: Small parking area and a portable toilet at the trailhead; no water available

Finding the trailhead: Drive 2 miles north from Chesterton on IN 49 to US 12 and turn left (west). Drive 1.4 miles and turn right (north) onto Mineral Springs Road. Cross the tracks of the Chicago South Shore Railroad, drive 0.6 mile, and turn right (east) on a dirt road just short of the security post for Dune Acres. Drive 0.1 mile on the dirt road to a parking lot and then walk back down the dirt road to the Cowles Bog trailhead on the west side of Mineral Springs Road.

The Hike

Cowles Bog is a historically significant site. It was here in the early 1900s that Dr. Henry Cowles, a professor at the University of Chicago, did much of his scientific research on plant ecology. The area was designated a National Natural Landmark in 1965. Access to the bog is restricted, but it can be seen from a distance while hiking the trail. This trail is well defined with marked intersections, although windblown sand can obscure the inbound marker along the beach.

This is an easy stroll at the start. Walk back along the parking lot entry road before crossing to the west side of Mineral Springs Road to the actual trailhead. The trail begins fairly straight and level, and a boardwalk splits a marshy area on the north side of the bog. Sprays of ferns coupled with duckweed and skunk cabbage provide a rich green backdrop, and wildflowers give the area a sweet aroma. Dune ridges rise and fall along the right side of the trail.

At 0.9 mile you will reach a juncture with a shortcut trail that goes left (south) around the bog. Turn right (north) instead. Climb a sandy hill and begin a meandering stroll over humps and ridges of the wooded inner dunes, which are dotted with occasional ponds.

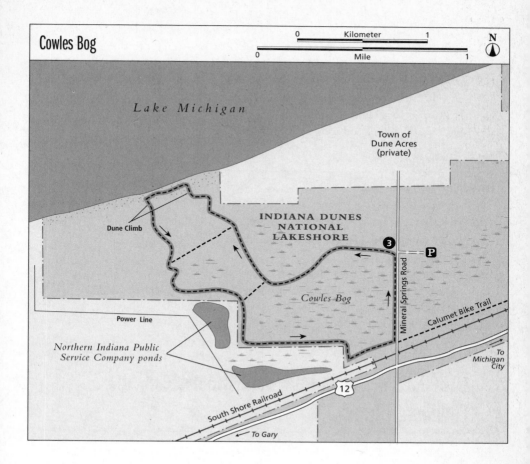

Cowles Bog

0   Kilometer   1

0   Mile   1

N

Lake Michigan

Town of
Dune Acres
(private)

Dune Climb

**INDIANA DUNES
NATIONAL
LAKESHORE**

3

P

Cowles Bog

Mineral Springs Road

Calumet Bike Trail

Power Line

*Northern Indiana Public
Service Company ponds*

To
Michigan
City

12

South Shore Railroad

← *To Gary*

At 1.5 miles there is another shortcut. Again, stay right (north). Near the 2.0-mile mark, climb a steep crest of the outer dune, which provides a clear view of downtown Chicago to the west. Immediately to the west is a coal-fired power plant, an ironic contrast to the serenity of the Cowles Bog area. Descend the dune to the beach and turn left (west), walking about 0.25 mile before turning inland. The trail marker sometimes is nearly buried by blowing sand and can be difficult to find. If the marker is not distinguishable, head southeast toward the dune; the path up the dune will become visible.

It is another steep climb on a soft, sandy trail to the top of the dune, which drops off sharply to the right. Walk 30 to 40 yards on a level grade before heading downhill. With each stride it will seem as though you're sliding an extra foot in the loose sand.

Cross several dips and rises over sand hills that form the inner dunes of the property. Keep to the right (south) as you pass both of the connecting shortcut paths from the outbound trek. Before reaching the second connecting path, you'll pass a small pond at the edge of the NIPSCO power company property that forms the southern boundary of Cowles Bog.

Just past the 3.6-mile mark, reach a service road with the bog on the north side and large NIPSCO ponds on the south. The road is arrow-straight to the east for 0.75 mile, then bends right for 100 yards and connects to a crushed-stone roadway. Walk 0.25 mile to a parking lot that serves as the starting point of the Calumet Bike Trail. Turn left out of the parking lot at 4.5 miles and walk 0.5 mile north along Mineral Springs Road to the trailhead. Although the trail concludes along this paved stretch of roadway, you'll get a good look at the bog on both sides.

Miles and Directions

0.0   Begin at the trailhead.

0.1   Pass Cowles Bog.

2.0   Reach Bailly Beach and Lake Michigan; turn left.

2.2   At a trail marker that may be buried by sand, turn left.

2.3   Climb the dune.

3.6   Reach the Northern Indiana Public Service Company (NIPSCO) pond.

4.5   Reach the Calumet Bike Trail trailhead and Mineral Springs Road. Turn left out of the parking lot.

5.0   Arrive back at the trailhead.

4 Little Calumet River Trail, Bailly Homestead, and Chellberg Farm

This loop hike begins near the historic Bailly Homestead, continues along the Little Calumet River through marsh and meadow, and concludes at the Chellberg Farm.

Location: Four miles west of Chesterton in northwest Indiana

Distance: 3.1-mile loop

Elevation change: Minimal

Approximate hiking time: 1 to 2 hours

Difficulty: Moderate

Jurisdiction: Indiana Dunes National Lakeshore

Fees and permits: No fees or permits required

Maps: USGS Chesterton and Dune Acres; Dunes National Lakeshore brochure

Special attractions: The Bailly Homestead, Little Calumet River, Chellberg Farm

Camping: No camping allowed on-site; 140 modern campsites at nearby Indiana Dunes State Park; 79 drive-in or walk-in sites at Indiana Dunes National Lakeshore Dunewood Campground, open Apr 1 through Oct 31. Both are located east of the homestead.

Trailhead facilities: Small visitor center and gift shop; restrooms located just off the parking lot; water available in the restrooms

Finding the trailhead: From the I-94/IN 49 intersection in Chesterton, drive 1.6 miles north on IN 49 to US 12. Go west 1.4 miles on US 12, following the brown National Park Service signs to

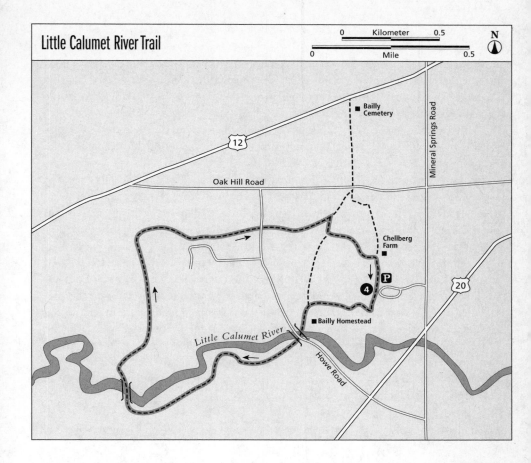

Mineral Springs Road and turn left (south). Travel 0.5 mile on Mineral Springs Road to a four-way stop. Pass through the intersection and continue another 0.3 mile on Mineral Springs Road to a right turn into the Bailly and Chellberg parking lot.

The Hike

In 1822 Honore Gratien Joseph Bailly de Messein, a French–Canadian, chose this site for a trading post because the Little Calumet River offered a canoe route that intersected two major land routes used by Native Americans. Bailly gained wealth by selling furs for as much as $5 apiece to the American Fur Company, which was owned by Jacob Astor. When beaver hats became unfashionable in Europe, Bailly switched to the tavern business. A devout Catholic, Bailly often entertained visiting priests, who held Mass at the family home. Bailly's death in 1835 ended his plans to develop a town at what is now the site of Bethlehem Steel.

Almost four decades later, in 1872, Swedish immigrants Anders and Johanna Kjellberg purchased forty acres from their former employer, Joseph Bailly's son-in-law.

They took up farming and later changed the spelling of their name to Chellberg.

These days the Bailly site, which is designated a National Historic Landmark, includes the main house, kitchen/chapel, a two-story cabin, a brick house, and a fur-trading cabin. Volunteers bring to life the nineteenth-century Chellberg farm by dressing in period clothing and tending to the daily chores of planting, harvesting, cooking, and caring for livestock.

Although the area carries the Bailly and Chellberg names, they weren't the first inhabitants. There is evidence that prehistoric people lived and hunted along the Little Calumet River as far back as 200 B.C.

The areas around the Bailly Homestead and Chellberg Farm are heavily used; the back part of the trail along the Little Calumet River is more remote and scenic. The hike begins at a visitor center near the parking lot and follows a well-manicured trail of wood chips as it descends into a ravine, crosses a footbridge, and climbs the other side of the ravine into a clearing at the site of the Bailly Homestead at 0.3 mile.

Continue the hike by going west from the Bailly Homestead. Cross Howe Road at 0.4 mile to a portion of the trail that follows the Little Calumet River for about 1.0 mile. The trail is a well-worn dirt path; plastic trail signs with red arrows point the way.

The trail passes through gullies and over three footbridges as it meanders southwest along the river. At 1.3 miles you will reach a bridge that crosses back over the Little Calumet. On the other side of the river, the trail follows a boardwalk through a swampy edge of the river bottom that in spring and summer puts on a flowery show. Off the boardwalk the trail heads north, ascending the left (west) side of a gully before crossing a footbridge to the right (east) side.

Hikers cross the bridge over the Little Calumet River at Indiana Dunes National Lakeshore.

At 1.8 miles the trail enters a meadow and alternates between woods and meadows as it heads north and then east to cross Howe Road again at 2.3 miles. At 2.5 miles the trail splits; you can go left (northeast) to the Bailly family cemetery or right (south) to the Chellberg Farm. Go right for 0.1 mile to another split in the trail and turn left (east) to reach the farm. The trail descends into a ravine at 2.8 miles and crosses a foot-bridge at the bottom. Climb the other side of the ravine to reach the farm.

After visiting the Chellberg Farm, complete the hike by picking up the trail on the south side of the farmhouse, passing the maple sugarhouse and walking 0.2 mile back to the parking lot.

Miles and Directions

0.0 Begin at the trailhead.

0.3 Reach the Bailly Homestead.

0.4 Cross Howe Road to the Little Calumet River.

1.3 Arrive at a bridge over the Little Calumet River.

2.3 Cross Howe Road.

2.5 Reach the junction with a side trail to the Bailly family cemetery.

2.8 Drop into the ravine below the Chellberg Farm.

2.9 Reach Chellberg Farm. Pick up the trail on the south side of the farmhouse.

3.1 Arrive back at the trailhead.

A hiker enters the meadow on the Little Calumet River Trail part of the Indiana Dunes National Lakeshore.

5 Beach Trail

A loop trail through woods and along Lake Michigan, concluding with a climb through dunes.

Location: 3 miles north of Chesterton in northwest Indiana
Distance: 7.0-mile loop
Elevation change: About 200 feet from Lake Michigan shore to Mount Tom
Approximate hiking time: 3 hours
Difficulty: Strenuous
Jurisdiction: Indiana Department of Natural Resources, Division of State Parks & Reservoirs
Fees and permits: Park entry fee; season passes available
Maps: USGS Dune Acres; Indiana Dunes State Park brochure

Special attractions: Lake Michigan shoreline and the three tallest dunes in the area—Mount Tom, Mount Holden, and Mount Jackson
Camping: 140 modern campsites plus a youth tent area at Indiana Dunes State Park; 79 drive-in or walk-in sites at Indiana Dunes National Lakeshore's Dunewood Campground, open Apr 1 through Oct 31
Trailhead facilities: Large parking lot and a nature center at the trailhead; water available at the nature center and other locations throughout the park

Finding the trailhead: From Chesterton drive 3 miles north on IN 49 to the Indiana Dunes State Park gatehouse. From the gatehouse drive 0.1 mile to a roundabout; take the first right (southeast) and go 0.6 mile to the nature center parking lot. The trailhead for Trails 8 and 10 is clearly marked at the south side of the nature center.

The Hike

Established in 1925, Indiana Dunes State Park is one of the oldest parks in the state system. The park features a combination of sand dunes, woods, and marshes nestled within the boundaries of the Indiana Dunes National Lakeshore. The dunes are home to a diverse variety of plant species.

The park has a network of seven trails that can be hiked separately or in combination. The best way to get a good feel for the park and the dune environment is a hike that includes all or part of Trails 10 and 8. This hike is best taken in the morning for two reasons: (1) White-tailed deer and other wildlife are more visible just after sunrise, and (2) on hot summer days the sand has not yet been toasted by the sun.

The route can be walked either clockwise or counterclockwise, but I prefer the latter. Hitting the high, sandy dunes right off might discourage you from completing the rest of the hike, which is worth the effort. On the leeward side of the dune, the trail is easy to follow. So is the beach portion, but hikers along the beach must be alert to markers to connect with Trail 8 near the swimming beach. The trails in the park are busiest on weekends and holidays.

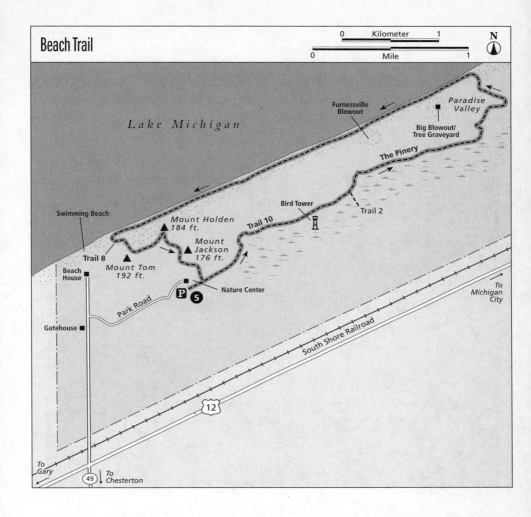

Note: Due to the fragile nature of the dune ecosystem, it is important to stay on park trails.

Begin the hike at the nature center. There is a slightly tricky maneuver at the outset when the path from the nature center reaches a crossroads with Trails 8 and 10. Go straight about 10 yards to where the trail splits and take the right (northeast) fork to stay on Trail 10. It is a gentle stroll between heavily wooded older dunes on the left and an extensive marsh on the right. Unlike the much younger dunes toward the lakeshore, these back dunes are an established forest of oak, hickory, sassafras, and maple trees, along with an abundance of ferns and wildflowers.

Just before the 1.0-mile mark, a short spur trail on the right (south) leads to a bird observation tower that overlooks an extensive marsh stretching a couple miles through the heart of the park.

At 1.3 miles things begin to change. Pass a junction with Trail 2, which comes in from the right. Go straight (east) and within 0.25 mile reach an area called The Pinery—the last stand of virgin white pine in the area.

Just beyond the 2.0-mile mark, cross a boardwalk and enter Paradise Valley, a flat expanse that swings through a splash of wildflowers and ferns. This is the turning point

The tree graveyard along Lake Michigan shoreline at Indiana Dunes State Park.

of the hike, as the trail curves to the northwest over a small dune to reach the shore of Lake Michigan. On most days you can see the Chicago skyline from here. Take note of the zipping sound as your feet sweep through the loose sand. Quartz crystals combine with moisture, pressure, and friction to create "singing sand." Few beaches in the world have this type sand. If it is too difficult to walk through the loose sand, slip down to the shoreline, where pounding waves have packed the sand tighter.

While hiking the lakeshore, be alert for tall signposts on the sandy ridges that identify the Big Blowout/Tree Graveyard, the Furnessville Blowout, and the Beach House Blowout. Blowouts occur when strong winds carve out large chunks of established dunes, sometimes exposing graveyards of dead trees previously buried in the sand.

Plants are plentiful along the shoreline side of the dunes—Kalm's St. John's wort, spiderwort, marram grass, and little bluestem are common. Also watch for places where swallows have built nests into the compacted sand.

Nearing the supervised beach at the west end of the park at 5.5 miles, look for the signpost for Trail 8. Wild lupine, a host plant for the federally endangered Karner blue butterfly, grows along Trail 8. So does low-bush blueberry, which offers a tasty treat in July.

At the TRAIL 8 signpost take a left turn to begin climbing Mount Tom. It will not be easy, so pause atop Mount Tom for a couple reasons—to catch your breath and to take in the view. Mount Tom provides great opportunities to see such rare birds as summer tanagers, black-throated green warblers, and black-and-white warblers.

A wooden staircase descends Mount Tom to the left (east) as the trail crosses a saddle to Mount Holden (184 feet above Lake Michigan). The trail turns south as it descends from Mount Holden before beginning a more gradual climb of Mount Jackson. Go down the wide, sandy swath off the southwest side of Mount Jackson. Pick up the trail and follow its lengthy downhill path to a crossroads where Trail 8 meets up again with Trail 10. Turn right (west) and walk 100 yards to return to the nature center parking lot.

Miles and Directions

0.0   Begin at the trailhead.

0.1   At the junction with Trail 8 and 10, go right (northeast) on Trail 10.

0.9   Arrive at the junction with a side trail to a marsh and bird observation tower.

1.3   Reach the junction with Trail 2; go straight.

3.0   At the beach go left.

5.5   Reach the junction with Trail 8; go left.

6.8   Arrive at the crossroads of Trails 8 and 10. Go right to return to the nature center parking lot.

7.0   Arrive back at the parking lot and trailhead.

6 Heron Rookery Trail

This linear trail along Little Calumet River includes a stop at a heron rookery.

Location: Southeast of Chesterton
Distance: 2.4 miles out and back
Elevation change: Minimal
Approximate hiking time: 1 hour
Difficulty: Easy
Jurisdiction: Indiana Dunes National Lakeshore
Fees and permits: No fees or permits required
Maps: USGS Michigan City West and Westville; Dunes National Lakeshore brochure

Special attractions: Heron rookery
Camping: No camping allowed on-site; 140 modern campsites at Indiana Dunes State Park (1.5 miles east); 79 drive-in or walk-in sites at Indiana Dunes National Lakeshore's Dunewood Campground (6 miles east), open Apr 1 through Oct 31
Trailhead facilities: Portable toilet; no water available

Finding the trailhead: Go 2 miles west on US 20 from its intersection with US 421 on the south side of Michigan City. Turn left (south) onto LaPorte/Porter County Line Road and go 2 miles to Porter CR 1500 North. Turn right (west) and drive 1 mile to Porter CR 600 East. Turn left (south) and go 0.7 mile to the Heron Rookery Trail parking lot on the right.

The Hike

From the northwest corner of the east-end parking lot, walk about 15 yards before coming to a fork in the trail. The right (north) fork leads to a spot on the south bank

The parking lot sign at Heron Rookery Trail, part of the Indiana Dunes National Lakeshore.

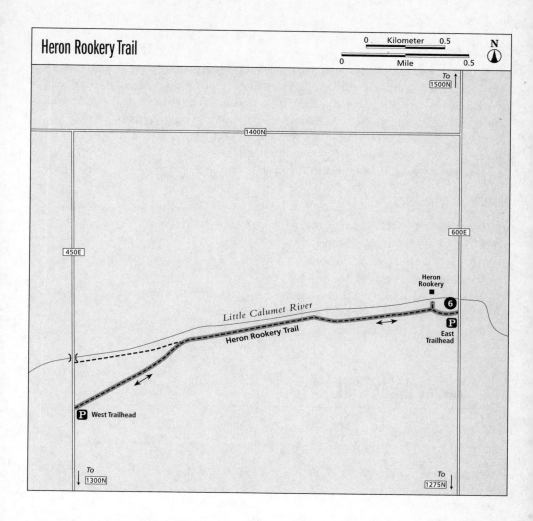

Kilometer 0.5
0
Mile 0.5
N

To
1500N

1400N

600E

450E

Heron
Rookery

6

Little Calumet River

Heron Rookery Trail

East
Trailhead

P West Trailhead

To
1300N

To
1275N

of the Little Calumet River from which you can see the heron rookery—a protected area on the north bank where great blue herons return annually to a colony of nests high in the treetops.

Herons are storklike wading birds with long legs and pointed bills. There are about fifty species of herons worldwide, and the great blue heron is the largest American species. An adult great blue heron stands 4 feet tall and has a 7-foot wingspan.

Back at the trail juncture, the left (west) fork leads to a peaceful walk along the Little Calumet, a small but vital river for both Native Americans and early European settlers. The trail is very narrow, and on wet days this can be a sloppy, slippery hike. Footing can be a little tricky at places where the river has washed out the bank. This portion of the hike begins in a meadow and then reaches a fence and a short set of steps down to the river. The trail hugs the riverbank more closely beyond this point.

At times it is right at the water level and at other times 10 to 15 feet above the water. The area is rich in wildflowers.

Three small footbridges along the trail cross feeder streams at 0.4, 0.8, and 0.9 mile. After the third bridge, the trail widens a bit. Look for a bridge over the Little Calumet as a sign that you are nearing the trail's end. The trail splits at 1.0 mile, with the left fork leading to the west-end parking lot and the right fork hugging the riverbank to the bridge on Porter CR 450 East. If you choose the right fork, turn left (south) at the county road and go about 0.1 mile to the west-end parking lot.

Retrace your steps to return to the main lot at the east end.

Miles and Directions

0.0 Begin at the trailhead. Bear right at the fork to view the heron rookery.

0.4 Cross the first small footbridge.

0.8 Cross the trail's second footbridge.

0.9 Cross a third footbridge.

1.0 Reach the junction with the trail to the west-end parking lot. Bear left.

1.2 Arrive at the west-end parking lot. Retrace your steps.

2.4 Arrive back at the trailhead.

7 Mount Baldy Trail

A steep climb up a "living" sand dune to a scenic view of Lake Michigan.

Location: On west edge of Michigan City in northwest Indiana

Distance: 0.8-mile out and back

Elevation change: 126 feet

Approximate hiking time: 45 minutes

Difficulty: Strenuous

Jurisdiction: Indiana Dunes National Lake Shore; National Park Service

Fees and permits: No fees or permits required

Maps: USGS Michigan City West; Dunes National Lakeshore brochure

Special attractions: Sunset on Lake Michigan with the Chicago skyline as a backdrop

Camping: No camping permitted on-site; 140 modern campsites at Indiana Dunes State Park (1.5 miles west); 79 drive-in or walk-in sites at Indiana Dunes National Lakeshore's Dunewood Campground (6 miles west), open Apr 1 through Oct 31

Trailhead facilities: Restrooms and picnic tables; small parking lot for 10 to 15 vehicles; water available in the restrooms

Finding the trailhead: From the intersection of IN 35 and US 12 in downtown Michigan City, go 2 miles west on US 12 to the Mount Baldy entrance of the Indiana Dunes National Lakeshore. Turn right off US 12 and follow the entry road 0.1 mile to the parking lot. The trailhead is off the southeast corner of the parking lot near a wooden staircase adjacent to the entrance road.

The Hike

The popularity of climbing Mount Baldy—an estimated 400,000 people per year—contributed to a recent rerouting of this trail in an effort to slow the dune's advance.

The back side of Mount Baldy, now closed off to foot traffic to stem erosion.

Pushed by wind off Lake Michigan, the giant dune is moving inland about 4 feet each year, swallowing up trees in its path. Two factors have accelerated the movement in recent years: a shortage of dune grass atop Mount Baldy (enabling the wind to more easily move sand) and too many visitors climbing the fragile south side of the dune. Until a permanent solution is developed, park officials hope that diverting traffic off the traditional route will allow vital dune grasses to take hold.

The new trailhead begins at a three-tiered wooden staircase southwest of the parking lot and adjacent to the entry road.

From the top of the staircase, turn right (north) to hike through a forested area to a trail juncture at 0.2 mile. Going straight (north) will take you to a wooden staircase and the Lake Michigan Beach. Instead turn right (east) and go uphill toward Mount Baldy. At 0.3 mile pass a blocked-off boardwalk that was part of the original trail.

A portion of the trail is stabilized by wooden slats, but the last 50 yards to the summit is a strenuous trudge through soft sand. The end result is a breathtaking view of Lake Michigan's seemingly endless blue waters. Other dune-top sights include a converted nuclear power facility and Michigan City to the east; the Indiana Dunes National Lakeshore below and west; and far in the distance to the west, the skyline of Chicago. This is a splendid place to watch a sunrise or sunset.

Scores of people frolic up and down the sandy face of Mount Baldy to the beach, which also is "starving"—erosion robs it of more sand than the natural current can supply due to a breakwater built for the nearby Michigan City Harbor. To offset the

Marram grass blows in the wind atop Mount Baldy on the Lake Michigan shoreline. The grass is known as a "dune builder" because its root system helps stabilize sand.

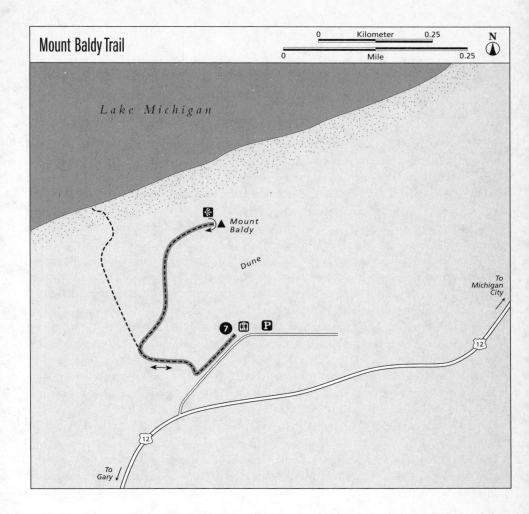

Lake Michigan

Mount Baldy

Dune

To Michigan City

To Gary

imbalance, the U.S. Army Corps of Engineers has fed the beach by trucking in tens of thousands of cubic yards of sand four times since 1974.

From the top of Mount Baldy, retrace your steps to the parking lot.

Miles and Directions

0.0 Begin at the trailhead.

0.1 Turn right (north).

0.2 Turn right (east) at the trail juncture. (**Option:** Go straight, north, to a wooden staircase that leads to the Lake Michigan beach.)

0.3 Pass a boardwalk that was part of the previous trail.

0.4 Reach the summit of Mount Baldy. Retrace your steps.

0.8 Arrive back at the parking lot and trailhead.

Glacial Lakes

People who move to northeast Indiana frequently are confused when they hear locals talk about going to "the lake" on summer weekends. They begin to think they may have moved closer to one of the Great Lakes than first imagined. True, Lake Michigan and Lake Erie are only a few hours or less away from most of northeastern Indiana. In reality, though, what the locals call "the lake" actually is a generic reference to any body of water where they, a relative, or close friend have a cottage.

There are more than one hundred natural lakes in Steuben County; a few hundred more form a beltway connecting LaGrange, Noble, and Kosciusko Counties. Some are small ponds only a few acres in size. Others represent the largest natural lakes in the state, including 3,000-acre Lake Wawasee in Kosciusko County; 1,900-acre Lake Maxinkuckee in Marshall County; and 1,000-acre Lake James in Steuben County.

Regardless of size, nearly all the lakes that grace this area of the state were created by glaciers that last passed through Indiana about 10,000 years ago. But the ten largest lakes pooled together pale in comparison to long-lost Beaver Lake, which was situated in northwest Indiana. At 28,500 acres, this shallow lake was the largest in the state until drainage of the nearby Kankakee River eventually dried it up.

When ancient glaciers bulldozed across the state, they pushed along tons of debris in the form of rocks, mud, and sand. As the glaciers retreated, blocks of ice were left behind in the pockets and depressions. As the ice blocks melted, lakes were formed. A common type of lake in northeast Indiana is the kettle lake—a deep hole with steeply contoured shorelines. A prime example is Lake Lonidaw at Pokagon State Park. The lake is only a few acres in size, but it is more than 40 feet deep.

Lake Lonidaw is protected as part of a state nature preserve, but nearly every other lake in northern Indiana is highly developed—ringed by summer cottages, year-round homes, trailer courts, campgrounds, marinas, or golf courses. The "lake" season typically runs from Memorial Day weekend through Labor Day weekend, a time during which the nearby small towns experience population explosions with the influx of vacationers.

Nevertheless, it is possible to find pockets of nature that provide an escape from the hubbub. Olin Lake and Crooked Lake Nature Preserves are two such sites. Olin Lake is the largest undeveloped lake in the state; at more than 100 feet, Crooked is the deepest. Hikers can reach the scenic shorelines of both lakes, as well as other glacial lakes, by hiking along the trails listed in this section. Trails are presented in a clockwise direction from the north at the Eagle Trail in Bicentennial Woods toward Angola.

8 Bicentennial Woods: Eagle Trail

A short loop along a wooded trail by quiet creek, with a side trek to a secluded marsh.

Location: North of Fort Wayne
Distance: 1.4-mile loop; optional loops totaling 1.0 mile
Elevation change: Minimal
Approximate hiking time: 1 hour
Difficulty: Easy
Jurisdiction: ACRES Land Trust
Fees and permits: No fees or permits required

Maps: USGS Huntertown
Special attractions: Several gigantic oak, maple, and sycamore trees, some estimated to be 200 to 250 years old
Camping: No camping permitted
Trailhead facilities: Small parking lot at the trailhead; no potable water or restrooms

Finding the trailhead: Go north from Fort Wayne for 8 miles on IN 3 from the I-69 interchange to Shoaff Road and turn right (east). Go another 1.5 miles to the Bicentennial Woods parking lot, passing West and Kell Roads. The parking lot is on the right (south) side of the road.

The Hike

Although this hike is not exactly in "lake country," it is close enough. Impacted by ancient glaciers, the area is certainly worthwhile. As the city of Fort Wayne approached its 200th anniversary in 1994, a local land preservation group—ACRES Land Trust—looked for an appropriate property to commemorate the historic occasion. The group selected this eighty-acre tract because the gigantic trees growing here are representative of what much of the area looked like before it was settled.

Only a few trees were ever removed from the property, which is believed to be the last stand of virgin timber in Allen County. Stately oak trees with trunks 4 feet in diameter and huge sycamores dominate a small, heavily wooded area that is bisected by Willow Creek, a quiet tributary of scenic Cedar Creek. The property has two designated hikes—the Dogwood Trail and the Eagle Trail, which is described here. This is a very secluded area with little traffic.

To begin the hike, locate the path on the south edge of the parking lot. Walk 70 yards to a T intersection where the Eagle and Dogwood Trails begin. Turn left (south) onto the Eagle Trail and make a gradual descent along the face of a low ridge that slopes to the right. Reach another T intersection at 0.1 mile. Here you can turn left (east) to access the Willow Creek footbridge or go right (northwest) to Arnold's Oaks. The right turn is a one-way walk of only 20 yards that leads to a view of half a dozen gigantic trees that have been named in honor of the family that preserved the area before it was purchased by ACRES.

Turn left at the T and walk 50 yards to the footbridge over Willow Creek. Cross the footbridge and take an immediate right (southwest) turn; walk along the edge of

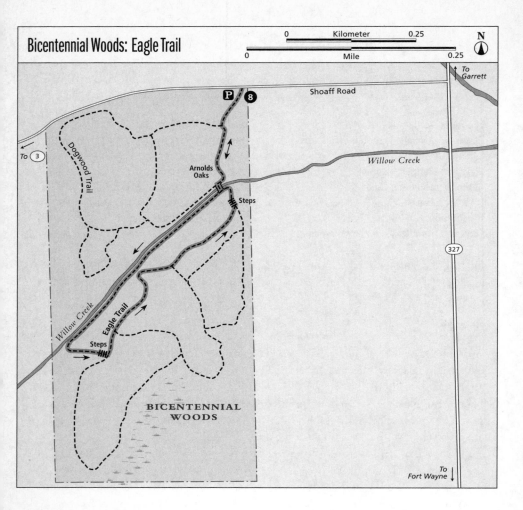

Bicentennial Woods: Eagle Trail

the creek for 0.3 mile before turning left (southeast). Go 200 feet to a wooden stair-case. Climb the steps and go about 100 yards to a T intersection. Turn right (south) to begin a counterclockwise loop that leads back to the inbound trail and connects to two optional loops of 0.3 mile each.

The trail leads back to another wooden staircase at 1.3 miles. Go down the steps to reach the Willow Creek footbridge. Cross the bridge and return to the parking lot.

Miles and Directions

0.0 Begin at the trailhead.

0.1 Reach the Eagle Trail/Dogwood Trail juncture; turn left (east). (**Option:** Turn right and walk 20 yards to view Arnold's Oaks.)

0.2 Cross the Willow Creek footbridge and turn right (southwest).

0.6   Turn left (southeast).

0.9   Climb a wooden staircase to reach a trail juncture and turn left (northeast) at the T intersection. (**Option:** Turn right for an optional loop past a wetland.)

1.0   Pass the first of two more optional loops connecting from the right.

1.3   Arrive at a wooden staircase that leads back to the Willow Creek footbridge.

1.4   Arrive back at the trailhead.

⑨ Crooked Lake Nature Preserve

A double–loop trail through old fields, along a bluff, and along the lakeshore.

Location: North of Columbia City on Crooked Lake

Distance: 2.0-mile double loop

Elevation change: A 45-foot decline from the trailhead to the lakeshore

Approximate hiking time: 45 minutes

Difficulty: Easy

Jurisdiction: Indiana Department of Natural Resources, Division of Nature Preserves, in association with ACRES Land Trust

Fees and permits: No fees or permits required

Maps: USGS Merriam; Crooked Lake Nature Preserve brochure

Special attractions: Phil M. McNagny Jr. Tall Trees Memorial Grove; Leaman cemetery; Crooked Lake

Camping: No camping permitted

Trailhead facilities: Parking space for 6 to 8 vehicles; no potable water available

Finding the trailhead: From US 30 in Columbia City, go north on IN 9 for approximately 7 miles to the Whitley-Noble county line. Turn left (west) onto Noble CR 600 South and go 0.5 mile. The nature preserve parking lot is on the left (south) side as the road curves sharply to the right (north) and becomes Noble CR 250 West.

The Hike

It is practically impossible to find a lake in northern Indiana that is not completely encircled by either summer cottages or year-round homes. This state–designated nature preserve protects about 3,500 feet of the north shoreline of Crooked Lake. The spring-fed lake is one of the most pristine in Indiana and, at 105 feet, one of the deepest.

It was on the shores of Crooked Lake that the Leamans, a pioneer family, were forced to interrupt their westward journey when a teenage daughter became ill. The daughter died, and legend has it that the mother was so distraught at her tragic loss that she wouldn't resume travel. The Leamans buried their daughter on a hillside overlooking the lake and built a home nearby. Over time, several other family members were buried in the small cemetery that lies on the east loop through the nature preserve.

The hundred–acre preserve features old farm fields, ridges, hardwood forests, a pine plantation, and a 0.5-mile walk along the shore of Crooked Lake. The woodlands

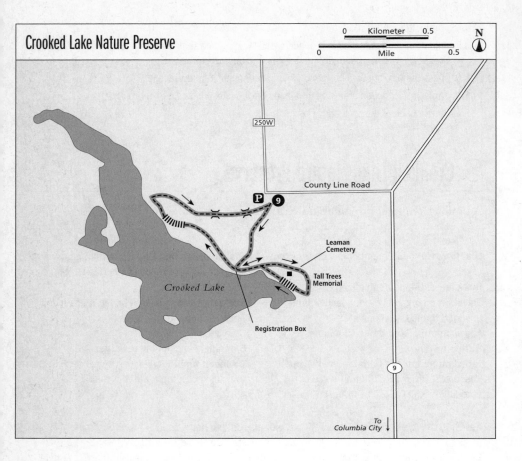

0   Kilometer   0.5

0   Mile   0.5

N

250W

County Line Road

P 9

Leaman
Cemetery

Tall Trees
Memorial

Crooked Lake

Registration Box

9

To
Columbia City

feature green ash, beech, dogwood, hickory, ironwood, red oak, white oak, and sassafras trees.

Begin the hike by passing through the entry at the small parking lot. Pick up an interpretive brochure and walk the mowed path through fields that were farmed until the late 1970s. Already the natural progression of vegetation is taking place as small trees pop up among the Queen Anne's lace, goldenrod, wild berries, and prairie grasses. It is about 0.3 mile from the trailhead through the fields and down a gradual slope to a registration box near the lakeshore. The preserve's east and west loops begin here, and together they make a pleasant hike.

Start with the east loop to keep in sequence with the numbered signs along the trail. Walk the shoreline for about 0.25 mile, crossing boardwalks in two marshy areas before curving left for an uphill climb. Along the right side of the trail is a broad ravine featuring a winding creek and the Phil N. McNagny Jr. Tall Trees Memorial Grove, which is at the top of the ridge at 0.6 mile. Turn left (west) and at 0.7 mile pass what remains of the Leaman Cemetery along the left (south) side of the path.

Continue along the ridgetop, which features large red oak trees, before descending toward the lake and to the registration box at 0.9 mile, where you will start the west loop. The path winds along the lakeshore, crossing two ravines and one boardwalk before turning right (east) and heading uphill at 1.4 miles. Cross a footbridge at the back end of a ravine before passing a pine plantation on the left (north). Just past the pines, cross another footbridge and then reenter the old farm fields. At 1.9 miles link up with the main path and turn left to return to the parking lot.

Miles and Directions

0.0 Begin at the trailhead.

0.3 Pass the registration box at the start of the east loop. Turn left onto the loop.

0.6 Reach the Phil M. McNagny Jr. Tall Trees Memorial Grove.

0.7 Pass the Leaman Cemetery.

0.9 Arrive at the registration box and the start of the west loop. Turn left onto the loop.

1.4 Reach the west end of the west loop trail.

1.9 Return to the juncture with main trail; turn left.

2.0 Arrive back at the trailhead.

10 Merry Lea Environmental Learning Center

A network of trails through meadows and forests, past Bear and Cub Lakes, and circling a large wetland.

Location: North of Columbia City
Distance: 4.7 miles of interconnecting loops
Elevation change: Minimal
Approximate hiking time: 2.5 hours
Difficulty: Easy
Jurisdiction: Merry Lea Environmental Learning Center
Fees and permits: No fees or permits required
to use trails; donations encouraged
Maps: USGS Ormas; Merry Lea map sheet
Special attractions: Peaceful meadows and wetlands
Camping: No camping permitted
Trailhead facilities: Nature displays, reference books, water fountain, and restrooms at the learning center

Finding the trailhead: From Columbia City drive north 10 miles on IN 109, passing between Crooked and Big Lakes, to a directional sign pointing west to Merry Lea at Whitley CR 350 South. Turn left (west) and go 1 mile to Whitley CR 500 West. Turn right and go 0.4 mile to a T intersection with Whitley CR 300 South. Directly across from the intersection is the entrance to Merry Lea—a 1,150-acre complex managed and partly owned by Goshen College. Go 0.3 mile down the main lane to a parking lot near the learning center. The hike begins on a mowed path southwest of the learning center.

The Hike

Nearly forty years ago Mary Jane and Lee A. Rieth were inspired by their love of nature to establish the Merry Lea Environmental Learning Center as a way of preserving habitat and creating a site for environmental study. Twenty years later the Rieths began turning over the 1,150-acre property to Goshen College, which manages Merry Lea for educational and scientific purposes.

The area includes bogs, marshes, fields, meadows, and forest environments that are ideal for quiet hikes, wildlife watching, or plant study. The trails are generally well groomed but sometimes can be confusing to follow in spots where trails have been cleared by mowers. Merry Lea is a popular location for school trips, so weekdays can be quite busy.

Begin the hike by walking west from the South Trailhead parking lot past the learning center to a mowed path behind the building. Go about 0.1 mile to an intersection with a signpost marked with an "A." This signpost, the first of many on the hike, is located in the southeast corner of Mary's Meadow. Take the left path and swing around the southwest corner of the meadow, turning north to enter the Maple Bottom at post E. The path can be muddy in wet weather.

At 0.4 mile reach signpost H and turn right (east) onto Hickory Ridge. Walk to post C and turn left (north) to wind through Rieth Woods toward Shrew Meadows. At 0.7 mile (post D), turn right (east) and go to signpost O (0.8 miles), where the trail splits. Stay straight (east) as a gravel path winds between two drastically different environments—dry and sparse Bear Lake Prairie on the left and Onion Bottom, a large wetland and pond, on the right.

At 1.1 mile (post M) turn left (east) and walk along the north side of Wilmer Meadows for a little more than 0.3 mile to post P, on the north shore of Cub Lake. Several paths merge here. Go left (east) from Cub Lake and cross a bridge over a drainage ditch between Cub and Bear Lakes. Continue east to post Q, where the trail splits again at the southwest corner of Wysong Meadow. Turn left (north).

At 1.9 miles cross a footbridge over Thumma Ditch to signpost R, turn left (northwest), and split South Kesling Meadow by going slightly uphill. At 2.1 miles (signpost S), turn left (west) and make a clockwise loop around Kesling Wetland to signpost T (2.5 miles). At the trail juncture, turn left (north) to the East Trailhead parking lot to the right (southeast) toward the Kesling Farmstead.

Turn right (south) at signpost T and complete the loop around the wetland to return to signpost S (2.7 miles) and signpost R (2.9 miles) before returning to Wysong Meadow. Turn left (east) and take the outside loop of the meadow back to signpost Q at 3.2 miles.

Continue retracing the outbound path past Cub Lake, now on the left (south), to return to signpost P (3.6 miles). Turn left (southwest) to cover the south edge of Wilmer Meadows, reaching signpost N and a gravel road at 4.0 miles. Cross over the road and through a picnic area to enter the woods and continue the westbound trail.

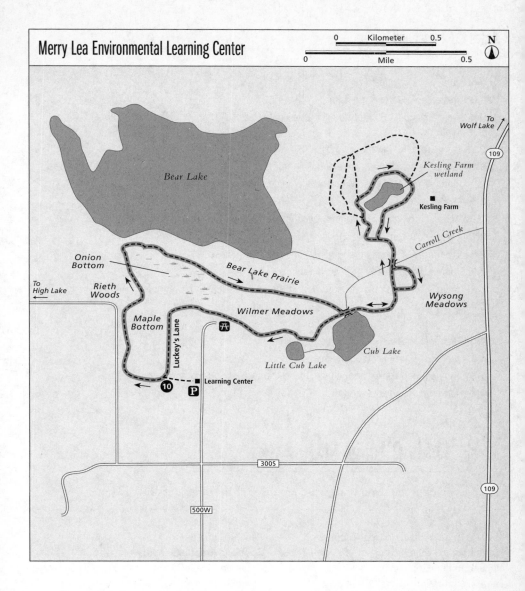

Shortly after entering the woods, a side trail on the right leads to a two-tiered observation deck overlooking Onion Bottom. It's worth a stop.

After returning to the main trail, turn right (west) and go 0.1 miles (signpost J) and turn left (southwest), going another 0.1 miles to signpost G at Luckey's Lane (4.3 miles). Turn left (south) and follow the old roadbed to signpost B (4.5 miles). Turn left (east) and make a clockwise arc through the woods to return to the South Trailhead parking lot and the learning center at 4.7 miles.

Miles and Directions

0.0 Begin at the trailhead.

0.1 Turn left at signpost A.

0.3 Pass Maple Bottom (post E).

0.4 Reach signpost H and turn right (east) onto Hickory Ridge. Turn left (north) at post C for Rieth Woods.

0.7 Come to a boardwalk (signpost D).

0.8 Signpost O; skirt Bear Lake and Onion Bottom.

1.1 Turn left (east) at post M and walk along meadow to signpost P.

1.4 Arrive at Cub Lake.

1.9 Cross footbridge over Thumma Ditch to post R; turn left (west).

2.1 Signpost S; turn left (west).

2.5 Signpost T; go straight (southeast) to Kesling Farmstead.

2.7 Return to signpost S; go straight (south).

2.9 Signpost R; go straight to northwest corner of Wysong Meadow; turn left.

3.2 At signpost Q retrace your steps west past Cub Lake to signpost P.

3.6 Signpost P; turn left to pick up trail running along the south side of a meadow.

4.0 Signpost N; cross picnic area and pick up the trail on the other side.

4.2 Signpost J; turn left (southwest).

4.3 Turn left onto Luckey's Lane (signpost G) and walk to post B; turn left.

4.7 Arrive back at the trailhead.

11 Chain O'Lakes State Park

A network of connecting trails wind around a chain of glacier-formed lakes.

Location: Near Albion in Noble County
Distance: 3.3-mile loop
Elevation change: Minimal
Approximate hiking time: 1.5 hours
Difficulty: Easy
Jurisdiction: Indiana Department of Natural Resources, Division of State Parks & Reservoirs
Fees and permits: Park entry fee, higher for nonresidents; season passes available
Maps: USGS Merriam; Chain O'Lakes State

Park brochure
Special attractions: Kettle lake system
Camping: Chain O'Lakes State Park—413 modern to primitive campsites; youth tent areas
Trailhead facilities: Nature center located in the Old Stanley Schoolhouse, a one-room brick schoolhouse built in 1915, open daily Memorial Day through Labor Day; drinking fountain outside the nature center and other water sources throughout the park

Finding the trailhead: Chain O'Lakes State Park is located midway between Albion and Churubusco. From Albion go 4 miles south on IN 9 to the park entrance; turn left (east) and drive 1 mile to the park gate. From the gate go 1 mile on the main park road; turn left (northeast) and drive another 1.25 miles. The nature center is on the right (west) side of the road; the parking lot is on the left (east) side. The trail begins at the TRAIL 8 sign near the northeast corner of the nature center.

The Hike

Chain O'Lakes State Park is exactly what the name implies—a park featuring a series of eleven small lakes connected to one another by channels. The trails are wide, well maintained, and well marked. There are a few potentially muddy spots near the lakes. The amount of traffic on the trails varies.

The lakes are what remain of the Pleistocene ice age, whose glaciers retreated from this area between 13,000 and 14,000 years ago. Beneath the melting glacier, streams deposited sand and gravel, while detached blocks of ice formed steep depressions that became the park's kettle lakes. Miami Indians settled here on the north shore of what now is Bowen Lake—named for William Bowen, one of the first white settlers in the area in the 1830s.

The hike begins near the east end of the park, at the nature center housed in a former one-room schoolhouse. First built in 1915, the Stanley Schoolhouse is the fourth school building at this site. Students attended the school until it closed in the early 1950s.

Begin the hike on the north side of the nature center at Trail 8, an interpretive nature trail that forms a loop around Big Finster Lake. Walk around the north side of Big Finster Lake and at 0.2 mile turn right onto a path that leads across and down a ridge overlooking Dock Lake to the left (south).

At 0.4 mile the path drops off the ridge and connects with Trail 2. Turn right (north) and walk counterclockwise around the shore of Bowen Lake. At the southwest corner of the lake, cross a footbridge and turn right (east) at the Trail 7 post. Go 20 yards and take another right (east) turn that leads along a flat ridge through upland woods to the main park road. Cross the road and continue hiking through a meadow as the path curves to the left (south). A creek is on the right side of the path and a small ridge on the left.

The path makes a gradual climb up to an overlook above the channel that connects Sand and Weber Lakes. Drop off the ridge and walk toward the channel to reach the intersection of Trails 7 and 5 at 1.7 miles. Turn left (south) onto Trails 7 and 5, walking along the north shore of Sand Lake, the largest of the eleven lakes in the park.

At 1.9 miles the path reaches a small parking lot near a fishing pier. From the pier walk on the gravel road to the paved park road and cross the road to pick up Trail 7 and reenter the woods. A channel between Sand and Bowen Lakes runs along the right side of the trail.

Chain O'Lakes State Park

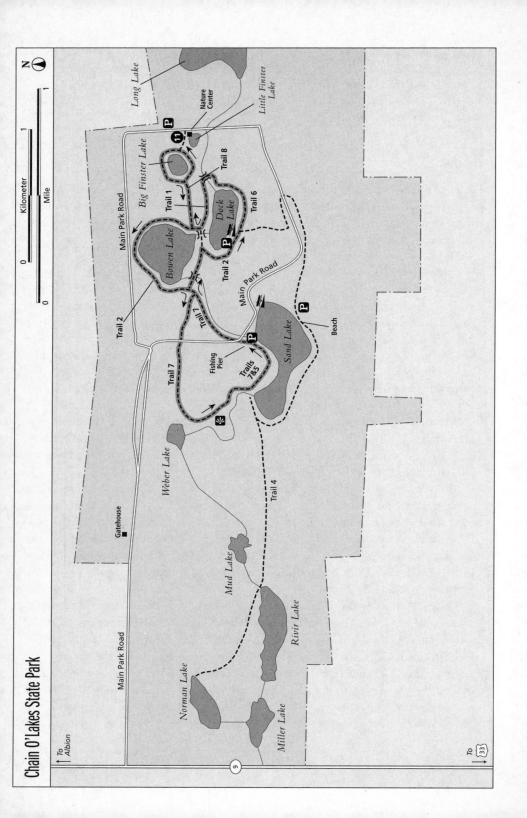

At 2.2 miles Trail 7 ends as it connects with Trail 2. Turn right (east) onto Trail 2 and cross a footbridge over the Sand–Bowen channel. At 2.4 miles turn right (south) off Trail 2 and onto Trail 1 as it skirts the west shore of Dock Lake. There is a boat launch on the south shore of Dock Lake. Walk through the parking lot toward pit toilets to pick up the marked trail. When Trail 1 joins Trail 6, turn left and follow Trail 6 around the south and east shores of Dock Lake to a footbridge that rejoins Trail 1 as it crosses the channel between Dock and Long Lakes. Cross the bridge and turn left (west) along the north shore of Dock Lake. Take the path back to a footbridge over the Dock–Bowen channel. About 10 feet before the footbridge, make a 180-degree turn to head back uphill to the nature center. Approaching Big Finster Lake at 3.1 miles, turn right as the path reconnects with Trail 8 and reaches the nature center at 3.3 miles.

Miles and Directions

0.0 Begin at the trailhead.

0.2 Turn right on path to ridge.

0.4 Trail 2 junction; turn right (north) to circle Bowen Lake.

1.7 Turn left (south) onto Trails 7 and 5 and reach Sand Lake.

1.9 Pass a small fishing pier; cross the park road to Trail 7 and reenter the woods.

2.2 Turn right (east) onto Trail 2 and cross footbridge over channel between Sand and Bowen Lakes.

2.4 Turn right (south) onto Trail 1 and arrive at Dock Lake.

2.6 Turn left onto Trail 6 around Dock Lake.

2.8 Cross footbridge and turn left (west) to rejoin Trail 1.

3.1 Reach Big Finster Lake; turn right onto Trail 8.

3.3 Arrive back at the nature center and the trailhead.

12 Edna W. Spurgeon Woodland Nature Preserve

This trail loops up, over, and through rolling glacial kames.

Location: West of Kendallville in Noble County, northeast Indiana
Distance: 1.3-mile loop
Elevation change: Minimal
Approximate hiking time: 45 minutes
Difficulty: Easy
Jurisdiction: ACRES Land Trust
Fees and permits: No fees or permits required

Maps: USGS Ligonier
Special attractions: Glacial kames, vernal pond, large tulip poplar trees
Camping: No camping permitted
Trailhead facilities: Gravel parking lot for about a dozen vehicles; no drinking water or restrooms

Finding the trailhead: From I-69 north of Fort Wayne, take exit 134 and drive west on IN 6 for 25 miles, passing through Kendallville, Brimfield, and Wawaka. Turn right (north) onto Noble CR 600 West and go 2.2 miles to the ACRES Land Trust parking lot on the right (east).

The Hike

In 1961 Edna W. Spurgeon donated this sixty-five–acre piece of real estate to a new organization called ACRES Land Trust. Since then, ACRES has added sixty more sites to its inventory totaling almost 4,000 acres across fourteen counties and two states (Indiana and Ohio).

This preserve was the first plot donated, and it does not take long to encounter its special characteristics.

Known by locals as "The Knobs," the area is a remnant of the glacial age that shaped much of Indiana's terrain, especially northeast Indiana. What appear to be a series of irregular, rolling hills are actually kames, or sediment deposits. Sand, gravel, and till were collected by glacial meltwater and deposited on the ice in kame deltas. As the glaciers continued to melt, the kame deltas collapsed onto the land below to form these hilly knobs. State nature preserve status ensures the land will remain this way.

The hike begins at the northeast corner of the parking lot. Go through the fence opening and walk along a flat stretch for about 200 yards before going downhill and then uphill to reach a trail juncture at 0.2 mile. Turn right (southeast) and start what becomes a roller-coaster stroll up, down, and through the kames in a counterclockwise direction.

Along the way you will pass by some of the biggest tulip poplar trees in the state. Large beech and maple trees also grace the woodland, which is home to an array of wildflowers, including bloodroot, trillium, Dutchman's breeches, and blue-eyed Mary.

At 0.7 mile reach a trail juncture. Take the right (northeast) fork and follow a ridge that curls around a vernal pond before reconnecting with the main trail at 0.9 mile. Turn right (west) and return to the parking lot.

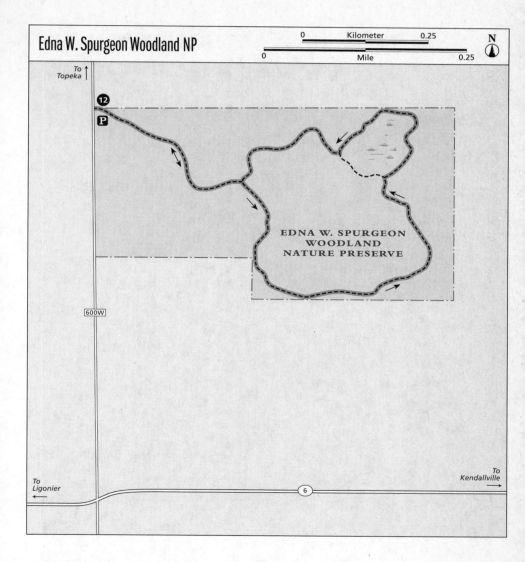

Edna W. Spurgeon Woodland NP

0 ⎯⎯ Kilometer ⎯⎯ 0.25
0 ⎯⎯⎯⎯ Mile ⎯⎯⎯⎯ 0.25

N

To Topeka

12

P

EDNA W. SPURGEON
WOODLAND
NATURE PRESERVE

600W

To Ligonier

To Kendallville

6

Miles and Directions

0.0   Begin at the trailhead.

0.2   Reach a trail juncture; turn right (south) to begin the main trail outer loop.

0.5   Cross a boardwalk.

0.7   Arrive at a trail juncture; turn right (northeast) to begin the Vernal Pool Loop.

0.9   Reach a trail juncture with the main trail; turn right (east).

1.0   Arrive at the first trail juncture; turn right (northeast) to return to the parking lot.

1.3   Arrive back at the trailhead.

Tulip poplar is the official state tree of Indiana. Edna W. Spurgeon Woodland, the first nature preserve of the local land trust group ACRES, features some of the tallest tulip poplars in the state.

13 Olin Lake Nature Preserve

An interlocking loop trail through mixed woods to a lake with undeveloped shoreline.

Location: North of Kendallville in LaGrange County, northeast Indiana
Distance: 1.8-mile figure eight
Elevation change: Minimal
Approximate hiking time: 1 hour
Difficulty: Easy
Jurisdiction: Indiana Department of Natural Resources, Division of Nature Preserves
Fees and permits: No fees or permits required

Maps: USGS Oliver Lake; Olin Lake Nature Preserve brochure
Special attractions: Olin Lake, the largest undeveloped lake in the state
Camping: No camping permitted
Trailhead facilities: Gravel parking lot for about a dozen vehicles; no drinking water available

Finding the trailhead: From Kendallville drive west for 4 miles on IN 6 to IN 9. Turn right (north) onto IN 9 and go north 7 miles, passing through Rome City and Wolcottville. Turn left (west) onto LaGrange CR 660 South and go 2 miles to a T intersection with LaGrange CR 125 East. Turn right (north) and go 0.5 mile to LaGrange CR550 South. A parking lot for the nature preserve is on the right as the road curves to the left (west).

The Hike

Olin Lake is a rarity in Indiana because not one single cottage can be found on its entire shoreline. Although this 103–acre lake is 82 feet deep in one spot, its low, marshy shore contributes to its being the largest undeveloped lake in the state. State nature preserve status will keep it that way.

Olin is one of several lakes in a glacial chain connected by channels. To the northeast is tiny Martin Lake; to the northwest is Oliver Lake, a popular fishing lake stocked annually with brown and rainbow trout and home to a remnant population of lake trout.

The hike begins at the east end of the parking lot. Picture a figure eight on its side for a mental image of the trail layout. The east loop of the figure eight is lightly used, since the main attraction, Olin Lake, is near the midpoint of the trail. Traffic is minimal, with the most use coming in spring, when wildflowers put on an early show.

Walk between the fence posts to a registration box, where you can pick up a copy of the interpretive brochure. The preserve is abundant with wildflowers—large-flowered trillium, false rue anemone, trout lily, Dutchman's breeches, bloodroot, spring beauty, hepatica, cut-leaved toothwort, and Jack-in-the-pulpit. At 0.3 mile the trail crosses a boardwalk through a mucky area where two other plants are prominent— jewelweed, also called touch-me-not, and skunk cabbage. Look for a small tree that has smooth, gray bark with ripples. It's called musclewood. Many other trees grow in the low, wet soil, including basswood, red maple, black ash, and red elm.

After crossing a footbridge, the trail splits at signpost 2, at 0.4 mile. Turn right (southeast) and walk through an upland woods featuring large beech, sugar maple, tulip, walnut, and oak trees.

At 0.6 mile a crossroad marks the center point of the figure-eight trail. Turn right (southeast) and follow the east half of the figure eight as it loops counterclockwise

Trillium.

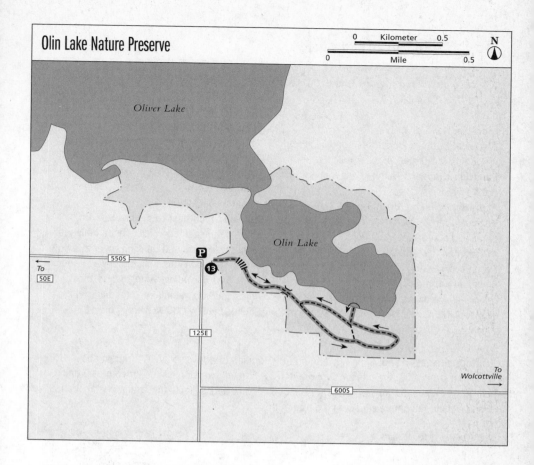

through more upland woods before reconnecting near the crossroads at 1.0 mile. Turn right (north) and walk less than 0.1 mile through a thick zone of shrubs to Olin Lake. Retrace your steps to the crossroads one more time and turn right (west) to walk the west loop of the figure eight in a counterclockwise direction.

At 1.4 miles come to signpost 2 again. Turn right (northwest), heading back over the footbridge and the boardwalk to the parking lot.

Miles and Directions

0.0   Begin at the trailhead.

0.3   Cross a boardwalk.

0.4   Cross a footbridge and reach the juncture with signpost 2; turn right (southeast).

0.6   Center point of figure eight; turn right (southeast).

1.4   Return to the juncture with signpost 2; turn right (northwest).

1.8   Arrive back at the trailhead.

14 Pokagon State Park

A hike over varied terrain that skirts the outer perimeter of Pokagon State Park.

Location: North of Angola

Distance: 8.0-mile loop; three optional loops of 1.8 miles, 1.0 mile, and 1.7 miles

Elevation change: 135 from Lake James to Hell's Point

Approximate hiking time: 3 hours

Difficulty: Mostly moderate, except for distance and stairway at Hell's Point

Jurisdiction: Indiana Department of Natural Resources, Division of State Parks & Reservoirs

Fees and permits: Park entry fee, higher for out-of-state vehicles; season passes available

Maps: USGS Angola West; Pokagon State Park brochure; Pokagon Trail brochure

Special attractions: Hell's Point, Lake Lonidaw, Potawatomi Inn, many historical structures built in the 1930s and 1940s by the Civilian Conservation Corps (CCC)

Camping: Pokagon State Park—273 modern to primitive campsites

Trailhead facilities: Large paved parking lot at the nature center, which is open daily year-round; restrooms and drinking water at nature center. There are numerous other water sources in the park, including campgrounds, picnic areas, the Potawatomi Inn, and the Spring Shelter, built by CCC workers in the 1930s.

Finding the trailhead: From exit 154 on I-69, turn left (north) onto IN 127 and go about 100 yards to a stoplight at the intersection with IN 727. Turn left (west); pass underneath I-69 and follow IN 727 about 1 mile to the park gatehouse. Follow park signs to the nature center. The trail begins behind the nature center on a paved path.

The east end of the Pokagon Trail is spotted with wetlands like this.

The Hike

At 1,460 acres Pokagon State Park may be one of the smallest parks in Indiana, but it is also one of the most popular. More than a million annual visitors partake of its various attractions, including hiking trails, camping, horseback riding, cross-country skiing, an 1,800-foot refrigerated toboggan slide, the Potawatomi Inn and cabins, and one of the largest natural lakes in the state—Lake James. The park was established in 1925, and most of its early buildings were constructed by the Civilian Conservation Corps in the 1930s and 1940s.

The park is named for father and son Leopold and Simon Pokagon, the two most recent leaders of the Potawatomi Indian people. The Potawatomi sold about one million acres in northern Indiana, southern Michigan, and northeast Illinois to the U.S. government for 3 cents an acre, including a deed to the site of present-day Chicago.

The park owes its geographic legacy to the most recent ice age, which left in its tracks piles of rocky debris known as glacial till and the many lakes that dot the Steuben County landscape. Two of the most noticeable glacial remnants in the park are Hell's Point, located in the park's northeast corner, and Lake Lonidaw, named for Simon Pokagon's wife.

The hike described visits both locations and covers all or part of Trails 1, 2, 3, 4, 5, and 6. Hikers have the option of an additional 1.8-mile loop on Trail 7, a 1.0-mile loop on Trail 8, and a 1.7-mile option on Trail 9.

A young hiker traps the water spraying from a spring along the Pokagon Trail. The spring is tested weekly for water quality.

The park trails are heavily used and thus easy to follow. Some trail segments— around the nature center, campgrounds, and Lake Lonidaw—can be busy, but other areas can seem remote. Major holiday weekends are the busiest.

To begin the hike walk around to the back side of the nature center and down a paved path that joins a dirt trail marked trail 1. Turn right and hike south and then north as the trail parallels privately owned cottages that line Lone Tree Point on Lake James.

Just beyond the 0.5-mile mark, hike uphill into a clearing that at one time was a fenced pen for bison and elk, which no longer exist in the wild in Indiana. Various trails converge on Trail 1 as it continues north to the Apple Orchard Picnic Area; ignore these and remain on Trail 1.

You will reach the picnic area at 1.3 miles. Cut northeast diagonally across the picnic area to a path that leads downhill to a bridge passing over the main park road. Go under the bridge to find a paved bicycle trail that parallels the paved road leading to the park campground area. Continue north, passing the campground gatehouse at 1.8 miles, and walk about 50 yards to Trail 4.

Someone made the most of this tree stump at Pokagon State Park.

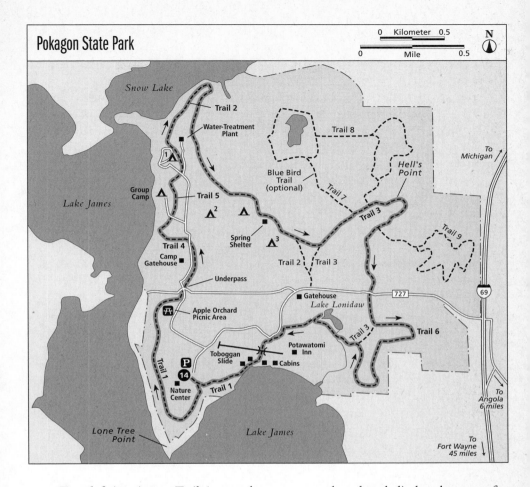

0   Kilometer   0.5

0   Mile   0.5

N

Snow Lake

Trail 2

Water-Treatment Plant

Trail 8

To Michigan

Blue Bird Trail (optional)

Hell's Point

Trail 7

Trail 3

Trail 9

Group Camp

Trail 5

Λ^2 Λ

Lake James

Spring Shelter

Λ^3

Trail 4

Camp Gatehouse

Trail 2   Trail 3

Underpass

Gatehouse

727

69

Lake Lonidaw

Apple Orchard Picnic Area

Trail 3

Trail 6

Toboggan Slide

Potawatomi Inn

Cabins

Trail 1

P

14

Nature Center

Trail 1

To Angola 6 miles

Lone Tree Point

Lake James

To Fort Wayne 45 miles

Turn left (west) onto Trail 4, cross the campground road, and climb a short set of wooden steps. Walk northwest on the trail, crossing a path that connects the group camp to the park's general store. Trail 4 heads downhill and twice connects with other paths. Stay to the right each time and connect with Trail 5 near the shore of Lake James. Turn right (north) and go uphill, cross a paved road, and pass along the east edge of a string of small cabins that are the group camp. Trail 5 ends at a paved road leading to Campground 1.

Cross the road and pick up Trail 2 on a gravel road that passes the park's water-treatment plant and swings out to a point overlooking Snow Lake, one of a handful of smaller lakes in the James chain of lakes. When Trail 2 turns south away from Snow Lake, you are about 3.0 miles into the hike. Continue along Trail 2 as it slips behind the tent camp area. At 5.0 miles reach the Spring Shelter, a small shelter built by the CCC in 1938 next to a natural spring that produces drinkable water. (Park personnel check the water for purity each week.)

Southeast of the shelter, Trail 2 forks; take the left fork, which leads to Trail 3. Turn left (northeast) onto Trail 3 and walk about 0.25 mile to the intersection with Trail 7. Another 50 yards on Trail 3 takes you to a crossroads with Trail 8 to the left and Trail 9 to the right.

Go straight (east) on Trail 3 for another 0.25 mile to Hell's Point, the highest point in the park and the third-highest point in the county. A wooden staircase of eighty-three steps makes the climb easier, plus cuts down on erosion of the hill. This hill is actually a glacial deposit of sand and stone known as a kame. The elevation change from the top of Hell's Point to the shore of Lake James is 135 feet.

From Hell's Point hike south as Trail 3 descends into a series of small marshes and streams that dot the eastern area of the park. Cross IN 727, the entry road to the park, and walk less than 0.25 mile to the intersection with Trail 6. Turn left (east) and take Trail 6 as it skirts the park border for 1.0 mile before rejoining Trail 3. Turn left (west) onto Trail 3 as the trail enters the Potawatomi Nature Preserve, a 256-acre preserve featuring cattail marshes, sedge meadows, and a tamarack–black ash swamp. The high glacial ridges that surround this area feature stands of red and white oak, shagbark hickory, and maple trees.

Lake Lonidaw, at 7.3 miles, is a deep glacier-formed kettle lake. From Lake Lonidaw walk southwest and then west to the main park road. Turn left (south) and walk along the road past Potawatomi Inn to a parking lot entrance with a boat rental sign. Turn left (south) and cross the parking lot to a bridge across the toboggan slide. Cross the bridge to a set of cabins. Walk between Cabins 64 and 65; cross the parking lot and pick up Trail 1 behind the parking space for Cabin 73. Turn right (southeast) and follow Trail 1 for a little more than 0.25 mile along the shore of Lake James to the paved path that leads back to the nature center.

Options

The first of three optional loops off Trail 3 is Trail 7, also known as the Blue Bird Hills Trail (1.8 miles). Trail 7 leads to a large hillside meadow, loops around a wetland area, and returns to its trailhead on Trail 3. There's also a short spur on the northeast side of the Trail 7 loop that connects with Trail 8.

A short 50 yards up Trail 3 from the Trail 7 trailhead is the start of Trail 8. Turn left (northwest), cross a paved county road, and followed a 1.0-mile trail that winds through open, rolling terrain and probably the best example of an oak savanna eco-system in the park.

Trail 9, the third option, begins across from the Trail 8 trailhead. If you choose this option, prepare for lots of hills over a 1.7-mile loop that takes you to the far eastern border of the park.

Miles and Directions

0.0 Begin at the trailhead at the nature center.

0.5 Hike uphill into a clearing.

1.3 Reach the Apple Orchard Picnic Area. Cut across the picnic area to pick up a path; head downhill to a bridge over the park road.

1.8 Pass the campground gatehouse. Walk 50 yards and turn left (west) onto Trail 4. Stay to the right at two trail junctions.

2.0 Turn right (north) onto Trail 5.

2.5 Pick up Trail 2 on a gravel road.

5.0 Reach the Spring Shelter.

5.4 Turn left (northeast) onto Trail 3; stay on Trail 3 at junctions with Trails 7, 8, and 9.

5.8 Climb to Hell's Point; continue right (south) on Trail 9.

6.2 Cross IN 727.

6.3 Turn left (east) onto Trail 6.

7.3 Arrive at Lake Lonidaw. Walk southwest and then west to the main park road and turn left (south) onto the road.

7.7 Turn left (south) at a parking lot and cross bridge to a group of cabins. Pick up Trail 1 behind Cabin 73 and turn right (southeast).

8.0 Arrive back at the trailhead.

15 Wing Haven Reserve: Trillium Woods Trail

A short stroll through upland and lowland woods to a secluded lake, then back through a quiet ravine along a stream.

Location: On the north outskirts of Angola, northeast Indiana
Distance: 0.9-mile loop
Elevation change: 65 feet
Approximate hiking time: 30 minutes
Difficulty: Easy
Jurisdiction: ACRES Land Trust
Fees and permits: No fees or permits required
Maps: USGS Angola East; Wing Haven Reserve information sheet
Special attractions: Little Gentian Lake, one of seven small lakes in the Seven Sisters chain; log cabin; possibility of seeing rare sandhill cranes
Camping: No camping permitted
Trailhead facilities: Parking area at the trailhead but nothing else; no drinking water source available

Finding the trailhead: Take exit 154 from I-69 near Angola and turn right (south) onto IN 127 toward Angola. At the first road, Steuben CR 400 North, turn left (east). Drive about 0.4 mile to the parking lot on the left (north) side of the road.

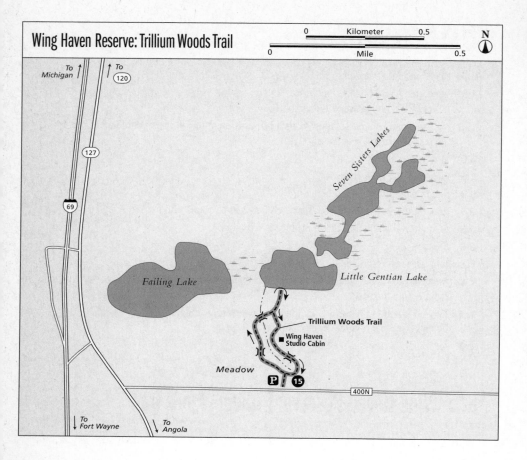

Kilometer
0 0.5
Mile
0 0.5

N

To Michigan
To 120

127

69

Seven Sisters Lakes

Failing Lake

Little Gentian Lake

Trillium Woods Trail

Wing Haven Studio Cabin

Meadow

P 15

400N

To Fort Wayne

To Angola

The Hike

Wing Haven Reserve is a 160-acre holding of the ACRES Land Trust, a private preservation group that received the land as a gift from the estate of Helen Swenson. The
property is about half the size of the original Wing Haven Resort, opened in 1950 by
Swenson and her husband, Ben. The resort closed in 1970, and part of the property
was sold and converted to a conference/retreat center and later a church camp. In
2007 benefactors donated that portion of the original site to the state for development as an extension of nearby Pokagon State Park.

There are three short trails at Wing Haven, including the Trillium Woods Trail
described here.

Begin the hike at the east end of the parking lot near a kiosk that displays information about Wing Haven and ACRES. The well-maintained, well-marked trail skirts
the eastern edge of the meadows as it curls northward. At 0.1 mile the trail splits, with
the left fork continuing along the meadow's edge and the right fork slipping into the

woods. Either option will do, since the forks rejoin after a very short distance. The trail then crosses a footbridge and heads north and uphill into an upland woods featuring a blend of oak and hickory.

At 0.3 mile Little Gentian Lake becomes visible as the trail curves right and drops downhill to cross another footbridge at 0.4 mile. Just past the footbridge, come to a T intersection. Turn left (north) and walk less than 0.1 mile to an observation pier on Little Gentian Lake. It is worth a moment to pause here and soak up the solitude. Fishing is prohibited. Canada geese and other waterfowl frequent the tiny lake, which is part of the Seven Sisters chain. In recent years, sandhill cranes have begun to nest in the area—the first time that has happened in this corner of Indiana since 1929.

From the lake head south to the T intersection and continue uphill to the rustic log cabin that Helen Swenson used as an art studio. Today it serves as a gathering place for ACRES events and as a visitor center during open houses held the first Sunday of each month. Reach the cabin at 0.6 mile and walk to the right (west) side to locate the trail as it descends into a ravine. Crisscross the stream four times on footbridges before coming to a stairway out of the ravine at 0.8 mile. Turn left (south) upon reentering the meadow and return to the parking lot.

Miles and Directions

0.0 Begin at the trailhead.

0.1 Trail splits; take either fork.

0.4 Cross a footbridge and reach a T; turn left (north).

0.5 Reach Little Gentian Lake and observation pier.

0.6 Pass the Wing Haven log cabin.

0.8 Leave the ravine and reenter meadow. Turn left (south) to return to parking lot.

0.9 Arrive back at the trailhead.

Wabash Valley

Oh, the moonlight's fair tonight along the Wabash,
From the fields there comes the breath of new-mown hay;
Through the sycamores the candle lights are gleaming,
On the banks of the Wabash far away.

With these lines, Paul Dresser celebrated the Wabash River with his 1913 song, "On the Banks of the Wabash," which was named the official state song the same year. The river, on the other hand, endured years of neglect. That changed in 1996 when Indiana's General Assembly declared the Wabash the "official state river," a deserving title for a variety of reasons.

From its origin just over the Ohio border, the Wabash cuts a swath across north-central Indiana to its western border and then flows south past Terre Haute and Vincennes to merge with the Ohio River. The third-longest tributary of the Ohio River, the Wabash covers 475 miles from start to finish. The Wabash watershed drains nearly two-thirds of the state and forms almost 200 miles of the border with neighboring Illinois.

The river has played an integral role in Indiana history. Long before the French and British arrived, Native Americans were drawn to the fertile river valley, home to bountiful wild game, including buffalo and deer. The Miami, Shawnee, Wea, Piankashaw, Kickapoo, Pepikokia, and Osage all established villages along the Wabash. They were not the first. Archaeological evidence indicates Native Americans lived along the Wabash as far back as 10,000 years ago.

The name given to the river by local indigenous peoples, *Wah-bah-shik-a,* means "water flowing over white stones." The French, who had arrived as fur traders by 1700, altered the name, calling it Ouabache (pronounced *WAU-bash*). Later on, pioneer settlers kept the French pronunciation but changed the spelling to Wabash.

Because the river provided an obvious transportation route, the French established trading posts and military forts at Kekionga (now Fort Wayne), Ouiatenon (near Lafayette), and Sackville (near Vincennes). Replicas of those forts remain today as historic sites where the past is celebrated. One of the biggest annual events is the Feast of the Hunter's Moon at Fort Ouiatenon, held each October, which re-creates an eighteenth-century gathering of French and Native Americans.

Over time, more than two dozen towns were located along the Wabash, including Harmonie near the southern terminus. Harmonie was established in 1814 as a religious commune.

About the same time, state leaders embarked on their own dream—a statewide network of canals for transporting farm goods as well as people. It was several decades before work actually began in 1832 in Fort Wayne, and it took more than thirty years to finish. Areas that were completed flourished, but soon after the Wabash & Erie Canal was completed, it was rendered obsolete by the development of railroads.

The river has not always been a friendly neighbor. Massive floods wreaked havoc on river towns, but flooding is minimized today by three dams. One forms J. Edward Roush Lake; the others are on tributaries of the Wabash—the Mississinewa and Salamonie Rivers.

Impacted by agricultural and industrial runoff, the Wabash River has become a focal point of a different sort in recent years. The Wabash River Heritage Commission is a coalition of groups working to develop recreational opportunities along the river, including hiking trails.

In 2002 the Department of Natural Resources opened Prophetstown State Park, restoring hundreds of acres of native prairie bordered by the Wabash and the town of Battle Ground. It was in this area in 1811 that the Battle of Tippecanoe took place—a confrontation between Native Americans assembled by Tecumseh and U.S. troops under the direction of Gen. William Henry Harrison. Harrison's soldiers fought off an ambush and in the process spoiled Tecumseh's plan to form a tribal confederation to battle the westward movement of white settlers.

Today the area is a 2,000-acre state park featuring camping, hiking, and bicycle trails wrapped around a rolling tallgrass prairie.

Trails in this section are presented from Fox Island County Park near Fort Wayne, south to the Ouabache Trail near Bluffton, then west to the Portland Arch Nature Preserve near Lafayette.

16 Fox Island Park

Loop trail along a wooded dune to a marsh overlook and back.

Location: Southwest side of Fort Wayne
Distance: 2.6-mile loop
Elevation change: A minor elevation increase at the upper dune
Approximate hiking time: 1.5 hours
Difficulty: Easy
Jurisdiction: Allen County Parks & Recreation Department

Fees and permits: Gate entry fee per vehicle; additional fee to hunt mushrooms
Maps: USGS Fort Wayne West; Fox Island Park trail sheet
Special attractions: Bog, marsh
Camping: No camping permitted
Trailhead facilities: Nature center with restroom and drinking fountains

Finding the trailhead: From Fort Wayne go 0.4 mile west from I-69 on US 24 to the third stoplight. Turn left (south) onto Ellison Road, following the directional signs pointing to Fox Island Park and the state police post. Follow Ellison Road for 1.9 miles as it parallels I-69, crosses over the interstate, and becomes Yohne Road. Go another 0.8 mile to the park entrance and turn left (north). From the gatehouse turn right (east) to the nature center parking lot.

The Hike

When the Wisconsin Glacier began its retreat more than 10,000 years ago, wind shaped a sand dune rising 40 feet high in the heart of a sluice that carried away glacial meltwaters. Today that dune is at the heart of Fox Island Park.

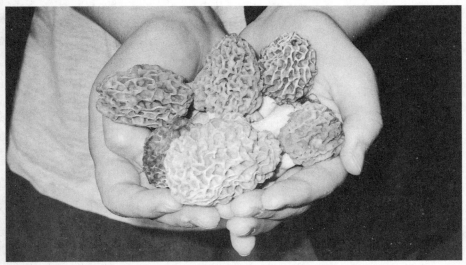

Morel mushrooms are a coveted prize in springtime.

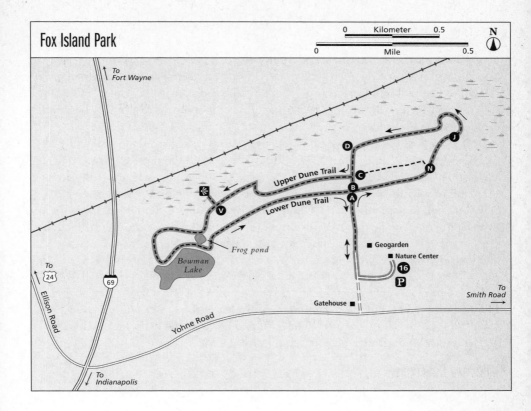

Fox Island Park

0 Kilometer 0.5

0 Mile 0.5

N

To Fort Wayne

Upper Dune Trail

Lower Dune Trail

D

C

B

A

N

J

V

Frog pond

Bowman Lake

To 24

To Indianapolis

Ellison Road

69

Yohne Road

Gatehouse

Geogarden

Nature Center

16

P

To Smith Road

The dune served as a training area for U.S. Army reserves in the 1940s. In 1975 the area opened as a county park at just under 400 acres. Today the park covers more than 600 acres and is the largest continuous block of woodlands in Allen County.

Almost half the park is protected as a state nature preserve. A marsh, wetlands, meadows, a peat bog, and the surrounding dune forest create varied habitat for wild-life and an abundance of wild plants. Nearly 200 species of birds have been seen at Fox Island. The forest features black oak trees along the upper dune; white oak, walnut, and black cherry trees along the dune slopes; and cottonwood, sycamore, and willow trees in the bottomland near marshes and bogs. Fox Island has well-groomed and well-marked trails, which get a lot of use during the summer season.

Go west from the nature center for a about 100 yards on a paved pathway past a bird-observation building; turn right (east) to reach the park's geogarden and a picnic shelter. The rock garden was made using granite, basalt, gneiss, and quartzite samples found in the park or donated by nearby stone companies. Most of the rocks on display were formed one to three billion years ago during the Precambrian era and carried here by glaciers.

From the geogarden walk north along the wide pathway that leads to the dune trail. Know the alphabet for this hike, because all trail junctures are marked by letters.

Pass the A signpost on the left (west) and the nature preserve sign on the right (east) to reach post B at 0.24 mile. Turn right (east), following the Lower Dune Trail for about 0.25 mile before reaching a trail juncture. Turn left (north) and climb to pass a NATURE CENTER sign at the top of the dune. Go straight (north) and downhill, veering left at the first trail split to reach post K at 0.6 mile and post J at 0.7 mile.

At post J turn right (northeast) to make a short loop down to the peat bog, and continue counterclockwise to posts H and G, the latter at .84 miles. Turn right (west) at post G to hike through a forest of walnut and oak trees, passing posts E and F to reach post D at 1.1 miles. Turn left (south), walk back up the dune to post C at 1.2 miles, then turn right (west) to walk the Upper Dune Trail as it gradually slopes downhill toward the marsh in the northwest corner of the park. Pass post X at 1.4 miles and continue to post W at 1.5 miles. Turn right, looping counterclockwise for a little less than 0.25 mile to post V. Turn right (north) to a long pier and an observation deck at the marsh, an excellent place for bird watching. Retrace your steps to post V and turn right (south), crossing a boardwalk to reach a Y-intersection at post U at 1.9 miles. Turn left (east) and go a short distance, passing Frog Pond and post R at 2.0 miles. Continue straight, reaching a trail split at post Q at 2.1 miles. Go right (east), passing post P at 2.2 miles to pick up the return leg of the Lower Dune Trail, which leads to post A at 2.4 miles. Turn right (south) and follow the main trail back to the geogarden and the nature center at 2.6 miles.

Miles and Directions

0.0 Begin at the trailhead.

0.1 Turn right (north) at the geogarden.

0.2 Turn right (east) at the Lower Dune crossroads and post B.

0.6 Reach the post N intersection and go straight (north) past posts O and K.

0.7 Go right (northeast) at post J to the bog.

0.8 Turn right (west) at post G.

1.1 Go left (south) at post D.

1.2 Go right at post C onto Upper Dune Trail.

1.4 Pass post X.

1.5 Go right at post W.

1.7 Go right to the marsh observation deck at post V.

1.9 Reach post U; turn left (east).

2.1 Reach post Q; turn right (east).

2.2 Pass post P.

2.4 Go right at post A.

2.5 Return to the geogarden; go straight and then left to the nature center.

2.6 Arrive back at the trailhead.

17 Ouabache State Park

A combination of park trails forming a perimeter loop through reforested sections in various stages of regrowth.

Location: East of Bluffton, northeast Indiana
Distance: 6.0-mile loop
Elevation change: Minimal
Approximate hiking time: 3 hours
Difficulty: Easy
Jurisdiction: Indiana Department of Natural Resources, Division of State Parks & Reservoirs
Fees and permits: Park entry fee, higher for out-of-state vehicles; season passes available
Maps: USGS Linn Grove; Ouabache State Park brochure

Special attractions: Small herd of bison kept in a twenty-acre pen
Camping: Ouabache State Park—124 modern campsites
Trailhead facilities: Gravel parking lot on the south edge of Kunkel Lake for two dozen vehicles; no drinking water at trailhead; water fountains around Kunkel Lake and near the swimming pool at the midway point of the hike

Finding the trailhead: From IN 1 in Bluffton go east 2 miles on IN 124 to the junction of IN 201. Turn right (south) onto IN 201 and drive a little more than 0.5 mile to a four-way stop. IN 201 turns left (southeast) and goes directly into Ouabache State Park. It is 0.8 mile from the park gatehouse to a parking lot on the south edge of Kunkel Lake. Facing the lake levee, the trail begins on the right (east) side of the parking lot.

One of the bison on exhibit at Ouabache State Park. The small herd is a popular drawing card at the park.

The Hike

The area around Ouabache State Park was once the home of Miami Indians, whose villages flanked the banks of the nearby Wabash River. Ouabache is the French Jesuit spelling of the Miami pronunciation of Wabash, but some people today mispronounce it *Oh-BA-chee*.

The present property was acquired by the state in the 1930s and established as the Wells County State Forest and Game Preserve. The area had been stripped of its mature timber and was heavily eroded, but the Civilian Conservation Corps (CCC) and the Works Progress Administration (WPA) reforested the area. Other projects included construction of buildings and development of a game preserve, considered the "greatest wildlife laboratory in the United States," in which pheasant, quail, rabbits, and raccoons were raised for release elsewhere in the state.

The state phased out the game-raising program in the early 1960s and eventually converted the property to a state park. Remnants of the game pens can still be seen along some portions of the trail. Another key attraction is a twenty-acre wildlife exhibit pen near the midway point of the trail. The pen is home to American bison, an animal that years ago roamed freely across Indiana.

From the Kunkel Lake parking lot, pick up Trail 5 at the east edge of the lot and walk east. The flatness of the trail that greets the hiker does not change much over the next 6.0 miles, but the trail surface does—sometimes gravel, sometimes crushed stone, sometimes grass, and sometimes just dirt.

Almost immediately you come to the first of several footbridges, but most are not as elaborate as this one. In the first 0.5 mile there are three spur trails that join the main trail from the left (north). Disregard them and keep to the right. At 0.3 mile cross the main park road and pick up Trail 5 on the other side. At 0.5 mile the trail passes an area where some of the old game-farm pens were located; look to the right of the trail for wooden posts about 7 feet tall with short boards angled at the top.

At 0.8 mile the trail crosses another paved road, which leads to the youth camping area. At 1.0 mile the trail turns north and squeezes between Campground B and the east boundary of the park.

At 1.3 miles Trail 5 takes a right (east) turn and merges with Trail 3 as both trails swing out and back through a stand of mature hardwood trees. At 1.8 miles the trail turns right (north) as it reaches another intersection—Trail 5 drops Trail 3 and picks up Trail 2. Trails 5 and 2 continue due north along the park boundary to the northeast corner of the park; turn left (west).

At 2.4 miles the trail reaches an open field just north of the park swimming pool. At this point Trail 2 turns left. Trail 5 continues on with two options—go straight and take more than 0.5 mile off the hike, or turn right (north) as the trail takes a wide sweep through the open field along a wide, grass pathway. This is another place to look around for concrete or metal remnants of the former game-rearing operation. The open field is also a good area to spot white-tailed deer if you are on an early morning hike.

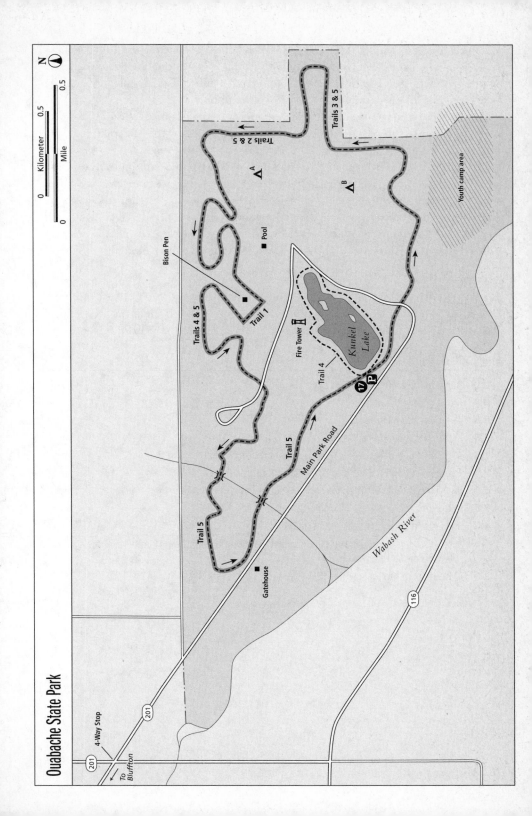

Ouabache State Park

N

0   Kilometer   0.5

0   Mile   0.5

To Bluffton

4-Way Stop

201

201

Gatehouse

Trail 5

Trail 5

Main Park Road

Trails 4 & 5

Bison Pen

Trail 1

Pool

Trails 2 & 5

Trails 3 & 5

△ A

△ B

Fire Tower

Kunkel Lake

Trail 4

17

P

Wabash River

116

Youth camp area

The outer loop will pass the 3.0-mile mark before connecting with the shortcut trail again. At 3.1 miles Trail 5 hooks up with Trails 1 and 4 at the wildlife exhibit pen, home to about a half dozen American bison. Trail 1 makes a 0.75-mile circle of the pen, providing an opportunity to track down the bison.

Trails 5 and 4 continue at the northwest corner of the bison pen, heading west on a winding course through periodic stands of pine trees. Near the 4.0-mile mark the trail crosses a paved road that was the park entry road until 1995.

At 4.2 miles Trail 4 breaks off to the left (south) as Trail 5 continues toward the west boundary of the park; stay straight on Trail 5. The trail crosses a creek at 4.5 miles, swings left (southeast) to parallel the main road as it passes the gatehouse, crosses the creek again, and continues toward the parking lot. At 5.5 miles Trail 5 links again with Trail 4. Trail 4 then breaks off to the left (north) near the parking lot and makes a 1.0-mile loop around Kunkel Lake. Stay on Trail 5 to return to the parking lot.

Option

A 2.75-mile asphalt bike/hike trail begins across the main park road from the trailhead. The bike/hike trail connects with Bluffton's Rivergreenway Trail at the west end of the park on Wells CR 450 East and hugs the south bank of the Wabash River.

Miles and Directions

0.0 Begin at the trailhead and go right.

0.3 Cross the main park road.

0.8 Cross the youth camp road.

1.3 At the junction of Trails 3 and 5, go right (east).

1.8 At the junction of Trails 2, 3, and 5, go right (north) on Trails 5 and 2.

2.4 At the junction of Trails 2 and 5, go right (north) on Trail 5.

3.1 Trail 5 meets Trails 1 and 4. Go straight (south) around bison pen.

3.8 At the junction of Trails 1, 4, and 5, go left on Trails 4 and 5.

4.2 Trails 4 and 5 split; go straight on Trail 5.

5.5 At the junction of Trails 4 and 5, go straight. (**Option:** Turn left (north) onto Trail 4 for a 1.0-mile loop around Kunkel Lake.)

6.0 Arrive back at the trailhead.

18 Kekionga Trail

A loop trail around J. Edward Roush Lake, a flood-control reservoir on the Wabash River.

Location: 3 miles south of Huntington, northeast Indiana

Distance: 11.0-mile loop

Elevation change: No more than 50 feet from trailhead to bottom of some ravines

Difficulty: Moderate

Approximate hiking time: 5.5 hours

Jurisdiction: Indiana Department of Natural Resources, Division of Parks & Reservoirs

Fees and permits: No fees or permits required

Maps: USGS Majenica; Huntington Reservoir bike trail pamphlet

Special attractions: Ravines, Tah-Kum-Wah Creek, scenic views of Roush Lake

Camping: 130 sites at two campgrounds (Kil-So-Quah on the north side of the reservoir; Little Turtle on the south side); youth tent area

Trailhead facilities: Restrooms, a water fountain, and a picnic shelter

Finding the trailhead: From I-69 take exit 86 and go west on US 224 for 5.7 miles to the intersection of US 224 and IN 5. Turn left (south) and go about 1 mile to the Observation Mound picnic area on the left. The trailhead sign is about 100 yards east of the picnic shelter.

Trail sign and overlook of Roush Lake.

The Hike

After opening in 1970 as Huntington Reservoir, the lake has since been renamed in honor of former U.S. Congressman J. Edward Roush, who served the northeast Indiana district. The earthen dam was built as a U.S. Army Corps of Engineers flood-control project on the Wabash River. It is smaller than two other flood-control projects in the Upper Wabash Valley, but the 870-acre lake and surrounding 7,400-acre property provide a variety of recreational opportunities.

The Kekionga Trail initially was established for hikers, but mountain bikers were granted access in 1995. Hikers still have the right-of-way on the trail, but be alert for these faster trail users. An additional trailhead for bikers is located in the Little Turtle State Recreation Area. Disregard mileage posted on trail markers, which is measured from the bike trailhead.

Kekionga also has become home to an annual long-distance trail race—the Huntington Ultra Frigid Fifty, or HUFF, which takes place in late December. This three-lap competition draws hundreds of individual runners and three-person relay teams from a dozen or more states in a race that goes off regardless of weather conditions.

High water can block sections of this trail, so check conditions at the reservoir office. The trail is well marked, although it can be confusing at the trail juncture near Kil-So-Quah and Little Turtle Campgrounds. Just remember to stay right (northwest). Traffic is heaviest near the two campground areas.

From the Observation Mound parking lot, walk back to IN 5, turn left (south), and hike along the left side of the road to cross over the dam. The road is not very scenic (except for the view of the lake from the dam) and requires caution because of vehicular traffic, but the 1.1-mile trail section along the road provides a good warm-up for the rest of the hike.

At the Little Turtle State Recreation Area entry road, turn left (east) and follow the orange trail markers that veer southeast away from the road to a wooded ravine. Continue to skirt the edge of the ravine as the trail alternates between wooded areas and open fields for the next mile. Reach the model airplane field at 2.5 miles. Cut across the gravel road and walk along the left (north) side of a fencerow that bisects two farm fields. Locate a trail marker at the east end of the field and turn left (north).

Go about 0.5 mile before turning right and crossing a deep gully. Near the 3.0-mile mark, pass a marker that points left. Cross another gully before coming to a paved road that leads to the Little Turtle boat ramp.

The trail resumes across the road, turning left at 3.2 miles and descending into a broad ravine that crosses a creek at 3.5 miles. Here you can catch a glimpse of Roush Lake to the left. Head uphill out of the ravine to reach an old roadbed. Turn left and continue to switch between gullies, open fields, and woods over the next mile. Several old Boy Scout trail markers can be seen along the way.

A ravine shows its greenery along the north shore of Roush Lake.

After crossing the north end of an open field, turn right (south) at 4.4 miles and follow an old road back into a stand of older trees. The trail leaves the roadbed and turns left to take a winding course along a couple of ravines before exiting the woods onto Division Road at 5.2 miles. (Again, disregard the mileage on the trail marker.)

Cross to the south side of the gravel road and locate an orange trail sign, then turn left to hike through an old field. Pine trees form a barrier between the field and the road to the left (north). Come to a gravel road at the east end of the field and take the road right (south) as it passes a pond and descends into a wide ravine. Climb up the other side of the ravine to paved Huntington CR 200 East. Star of Hope Cemetery is to the right.

Turn left (north) and cross the bridge that essentially is the barrier between the lake and the Wabash River. It is also the halfway point of the hike. Walk on the left side of the road for a little more than 0.5 mile before turning left to begin the west-bound leg of the hike. Drop into another broad ravine before hiking back uphill and into the woods.

At 7.2 miles come to a large pond and stay to the left. The trail takes a winding course before reaching a footbridge at 7.6 miles. Just beyond the footbridge is a trail juncture with the exercise trail. Turn right (northwest) and follow the trail marked for bikers to avoid having to walk through the Kil-So-Quah Campground. At about 8.0 miles come to Tah-Kum-Wah Creek, which enters the reservoir property from the northeast. Turn left (west) and follow the creek for about 0.5 mile before passing through another ravine.

Just past the 9.0-mile mark cross the paved road that leads to the Kil-So-Quah Campground and turn right (north). Walk along the road a short distance and turn left (west) at the trail sign marked "8." Cross two more ravines before entering a prairie grass restoration project that was begun in 1992. The area straddles a north-south paved road leading to a boat ramp.

Cross the road to resume the trail with less than 1.0 mile remaining. Over the next 0.25 mile you can catch glimpses of the lake to the left (south) and the Huntington Municipal Airport to the right before taking the steepest drop of the hike—about a 50-foot descent into and out of a ravine. There is one final ravine to cross over the last 0.25 mile before ending up at the Observation Mound trailhead.

Miles and Directions

0.0   Begin at the trailhead; turn left (south).
1.1   Pass the Little Turtle State Recreation Area entrance.
2.5   Reach the model airplane field.
3.2   Turn left and descend into a ravine.
3.5   Cross a creek.

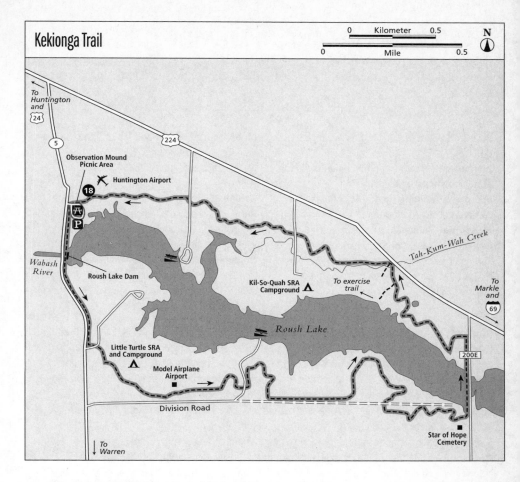

Kekionga Trail

To Huntington and 24

5

224

Observation Mound Picnic Area

Huntington Airport

18

Wabash River

Roush Lake Dam

Kil-So-Quah SRA Campground

To exercise trail

Tah-Kum-Wah Creek

To Markle and 69

Roush Lake

Little Turtle SRA and Campground

Model Airplane Airport

200E

Division Road

Star of Hope Cemetery

To Warren

4.4   Exit an open field and turn right (south) onto an old road.

5.2   Cross Division Road.

6.0   Arrive at Huntington CR 200 East and the Star of Hope Cemetery; turn left.

7.2   Reach a large pond; keep left.

7.6   Turn right at the juncture with the exercise trail.

8.0   Reach Tah-Kum-Wah Creek; turn left (west) and follow the creek.

9.0   Cross the Kil-So-Quah Campground road.

10.0   Cross the boat ramp road.

11.0   Arrive back at the trailhead.

19 Salamonie Reservoir: Bloodroot Trail

A loop hike through meadows, over ravines, and along bluffs overlooking Salamonie Reservoir.

Location: South of Huntington, Huntington County
Distance: 13.0 miles of interconnecting loops
Elevation change: Minimal
Approximate hiking time: 4 to 5 hours
Difficulty: Easy to moderate
Jurisdiction: Indiana Department of Natural Resources, Division of State Parks & Reservoirs
Fees and permits: Seasonal entry fee at Lost Bridge West State Recreation Area; season passes available

Maps: USGS Andrews and Mount Etna; Salamonie Reservoir brochures
Special attractions: Bluffs at Salamonie Reservoir
Camping: Lost Bridge West State Recreation Area—246 modern campsites, 38 primitive campsites, a 51-site horseman's camp, and a youth group area that will accommodate 200
Trailhead facilities: Restrooms and water fountains available at both ends of the loop; most conveniences available at the Lost Bridge West interpretive center

Finding the trailhead: Go 9 miles south on IN 9 from its intersection with US 24 near Huntington. Turn right (west) onto IN 124 and go 2.5 miles to IN 105. Turn right (north) onto IN 105 and go 1.8 miles to Huntington CR 400 South. Turn left (west) and go about 100 yards to the main entry to Lost Bridge West State Recreation Area, just past the property office. Turn right (northwest) and go 0.6 mile, passing the main gatehouse and taking the first right turn (north) to reach the Salamonie Interpretive Center parking lots. Go to the lot on the left, farthest from the interpretive center, and locate the trailhead in the southwest corner of the lot.

An alternate trailhead is at Mount Etna State Recreation Area. From its intersection with IN 9, go west on IN 124 for about 0.4 mile and turn right (north) onto Huntington CR 700 West. Go 0.4 mile to a crossroad and turn left (west) into a small parking lot. The trailhead sign is off the west side of the parking lot.

The Hike

The Bloodroot Trail was developed in 2007 as an extension of the former Lakeview and Boundary Trails. The multiuse trail is open to mountain bikes and in winter is part of the 40.0-mile Salamonie Snowmobile Trail along the south side of the reservoir, a flood-control impoundment of the U.S. Army Corps of Engineers. The reservoir extends 17 miles during summer months, and the surrounding land is managed by the Indiana Department of Natural Resources (DNR) for a variety of recreational pursuits.

The Bloodroot Trail gets its name from bloodroot, a plant once used by Native Americans to make a yellow paint. Bloodroot was a common plant along the banks of the Salamonie, a named derived from the Native American word *O-sah-mo-nee*, which means "yellow paint."

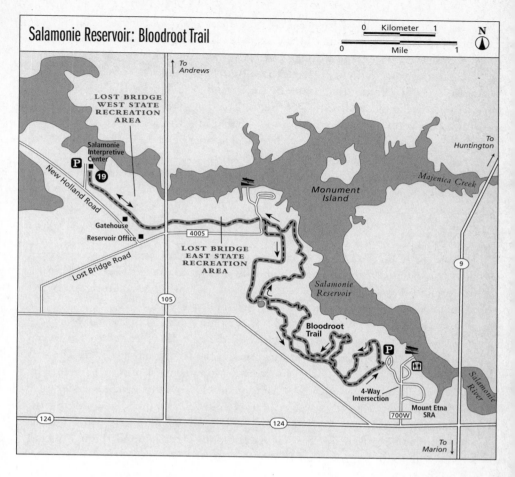

Salamonie Reservoir: Bloodroot Trail

The trail is easy to follow and easy to hike. It is well marked with frequent directional arrows and other signage. The early half of the trail is over relatively flat terrain along wide, well-groomed pathways through meadows and sparse woodland.

The trail begins at a wooden trailhead sign in the southwest corner of the Salamonie Interpretive Center parking lot. Go south along a mowed path that parallels the access road from the main road. When the trail reaches the main road, turn left (southeast) to cross the access road.

Continue southeast, passing the first of two junctures with the Kin-To-Onki Mountain Bike Trail before reaching the second juncture at 0.5 mile. Go left (northeast) and slightly downhill to enter a meadow that passes behind the Salamonie property office to the right (south) as the trail curls to the east and reaches IN 105 at 1.1 miles.

Cross the highway and reach a trail juncture at 1.2 miles that begins a stretch of one-way traffic control. To the right is the outbound leg. To the left, marked by a wrong way sign, is the inbound leg.

Go right (east). The trail parallels Lost Bridge East Road, weaving along in a zigzag fashion before coming to the first of two old paved access roads. The second, at 1.6 miles, is the former entrance to Lost Bridge East Recreation Area, which is now closed.

Continue east, crossing Lost Bridge East Road at 2.0 miles to connect with what was the starting point for the former Boundary and Lakeview Trails.

After crossing the road, turn right (south). The trail skirts the edge of a patchwork of meadows and farm fields, occasionally slipping into the woods. At 3.6 miles the two trails link for a short distance while passing a large pond. As the trail splits again, go right (south) at the twin yellow and white arrows.

Zigzag along meadow boundaries for another 0.5 mile before crossing a gully. At 4.5 miles cross another gully; at 4.8 miles reach the second spot where the two trails join. Continue straight, dipping into another gully, before reaching the trail turnaround at 6.0 miles. The spot is marked by a sign matching the one at the west end of the trail.

(*Note:* To reach the Mount Etna State Recreation Area facilities—water supply, restrooms, primitive campground—follow the paved road to the right [south] for 0.2 mile to a four-way intersection and turn left [north]. Go 0.1 mile and turn right [east] to reach the facilities. Backtrack to the eastern trailhead.)

From the eastern trailhead you will find the return portion of the trail more scenic as it scallops the edge of several gullies over the next 4.0 miles and crosses several footbridges while offering occasional glimpses of the lake from high bluffs. The best views come near the 10.5-mile mark, where Monument Island can be seen. The island marks the previous location of Monument City, most of which is underwater now. A monument to twenty-seven men from Polk Township who died in the Civil War and the town cemetery were moved 1 mile north when the reservoir was built.

Go another 0.5 mile before crossing the last footbridge. Go uphill through a stand of younger trees to return to Lost Bridge East Road. Cross over the road again and pick up the right trail option.

The inbound trail pretty much parallels the outbound leg and comes to IN 105 at just short of 12.0 miles. After crossing the highway and going uphill, the trail splits one last time.

Take the right (northwest) leg and come to a trail juncture on the right. Continue straight (west) through the largest meadow portion of the entire trail for another 0.3 mile.

At 12.5 miles reconnect to the outbound leg for the last time. Go uphill and turn right (northwest) to return to the parking lot.

Miles and Directions

0.0 Begin at the trailhead.

0.2 Turn left (south) to cross the access road.

1.1	Cross IN 105.
1.2	Trail juncture; go right (east).
1.6	Arrive at access road to former Lost Bridge East Recreation Area; go straight (east).
2.0	Cross Lost Bridge East Road to trail juncture; turn right (south).
3.6	Trails link and pass a large pond.
4.5	Cross a gully.
4.8	Trails join again.
6.0	Reach the east trailhead at Mount Etna State Recreation Area.
10.5	Arrive at the Monument Island vista.
11.0	Return to Lost Bridge East Road; cross the road and continue straight (west).
12.0	Cross IN 105; bear right (northwest) at trail split, then keep straight at next juncture.
12.5	Reconnect to outbound leg; go uphill and turn right (northwest) to return to parking lot.
13.0	Arrive back at the trailhead.

20 Salamonie Reservoir: Switchgrass Marsh and Tree Trails

A double-loop trail traverses first through a marsh meadow, then a forest, and then back to the marsh meadow.

Location: Salamonie Reservoir, southwest of Huntington
Distance: 2.5-mile double loop
Elevation change: Mostly level, except for 40-foot ravine on the Tree Trail
Approximate hiking time: 1 hour
Difficulty: Easy to moderate
Jurisdiction: Indiana Department of Natural Resources, Division of State Parks & Reservoirs
Fees and permits: No fees or permits required if parking at the visitor center; park entry fee to the Lost Bridge West State Recreation Area, higher for out-of-state vehicles; season passes available
Maps: USGS Lagro; Salamonie Reservoir trail pamphlet

Special attractions: Viewing area at Switchgrass Marsh; identifying markers for about 50 native Indiana trees
Camping: Lost Bridge West State Recreation Area—246 modern campsites, 38 primitive campsites, a 51-site horseman's camp, and a youth group area that will accommodate 200 campers
Trailhead facilities: Restrooms and water fountains at Lost Bridge West State Recreation Area Visitor Center (open 8:00 a.m. to 4:00 p.m. daily from Easter weekend through the weekend before Thanksgiving and weekdays through winter); additional water sources in the campground area

Finding the trailhead: Go south on IN 9 from its intersection with US 24 southwest of Huntington. Take Indiana 9 for about 5.5 miles to Huntington CR 200 South and turn right (west). Follow CR 200 South for 1 mile, where the county road merges into IN 105. Follow IN 105 3.2 miles west and south before turning right (west) at the sign pointing to Lost Bridge State Recreation Area. Go 0.1 mile to the visitor center parking lot. The trailhead, which also marks the beginning of a cross-country ski trail, can be accessed without entering the state recreation area. It is west of the parking lot and across the main road to the state recreation area.

The Hike

In 1961 construction began on Salamonie Reservoir, part of a three-stage U.S. Army Corps of Engineers flood-control project in the Upper Wabash Valley. Salamonie is situated between Roush Lake to the northeast and Mississinewa Reservoir to the southwest. The $17 million earth-fill dam at Salamonie became operational in 1966 and created a lake that at its summer pool is 17 miles long.

The lake is surrounded by almost 12,000 acres of state-managed recreational land open to hiking, camping, cross-country skiing, horseback riding, hunting, and snowmobiling. There are two longer hikes at Salamonie—the 40.0-mile Snowmobile Trail and the 13.0-mile Bloodroot Trail.

The Switchgrass Marsh and Tree Trails are separate but can be linked together for a 2.5-mile hike through vastly different environments. Switchgrass Marsh Trail is lightly used in spring, summer, and fall; the Tree Trail gets slightly more traffic. Number markers make the Tree Trail easy to follow. The Switchgrass Marsh Trail is equally

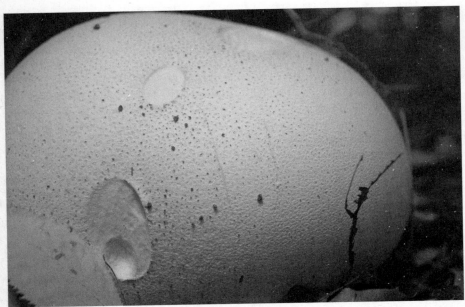

Giant puffball mushrooms can be found along trails from late summer to mid-autumn.

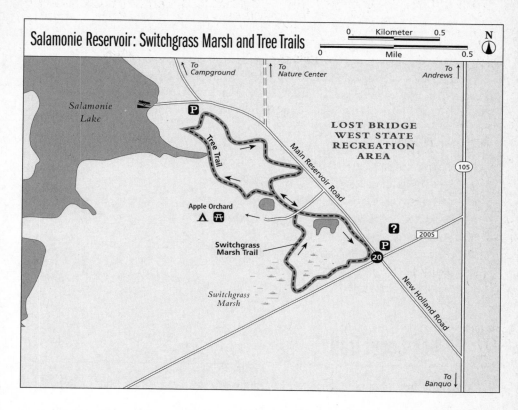

Salamonie Reservoir: Switchgrass Marsh and Tree Trails

0   Kilometer   0.5

0   Mile   0.5

N

To Campground

To Nature Center

To Andrews

Salamonie Lake

Tree Trail

Main Reservoir Road

LOST BRIDGE WEST STATE RECREATION AREA

105

Apple Orchard

Switchgrass Marsh Trail

2005

20

Switchgrass Marsh

New Holland Road

To Banquo

easy to follow because of mowed paths surrounding the marshes.

From the visitor center parking lot, head west across a paved road and walk through a stand of pine trees to a sign marking the trailhead. Continue west along a row of pine trees on the mowed path for 0.3 mile to reach the first marsh pond. Follow the path as it turns right to slip between the pond and a larger pond on the left. A bench for viewing marsh wildlife, including birds, is at 0.4 mile. As the trail circles clockwise to the north side of the first marsh pond, turn left to pass through the Apple Orchard primitive campground. Cross the paved road at 0.6 mile and go northwest on the link path that will connect to the Tree Trail near a small pond at 0.8 mile.

The Tree Trail is easy to follow because of its numbered markers, beginning with post 6 by the pond. Go left (northwest) to walk the Tree Trail in a clockwise direction. Along the way, about fifty trees native to Indiana are identified with small signs. How many can you name without looking at the signs? Can you find shagbark hickory or pignut hickory, flowering dogwood, American hornbeam, slippery elm, honey locust, black walnut, white or bur oak, hackberry, sweetgum, sweet cherry, or Osage orange?

Walk about 0.25 mile and drop into a ravine. Cross a short metal footbridge and climb up the other side of the ravine, after which the remainder of the hike is on pretty level terrain.

Upon reaching the parking lot for the picnic area, veer right (northeast) to the marked trailhead for the Tree Trail. Follow the path north as it enters the woods and pass white ash, white pine, and Virginia pine trees. A water tower is on the left.

Cross four footbridges before coming back to the small pond at post 6 (2.0 miles). Turn left (southeast) and go 0.2 mile back to the Switchgrass Marsh Trail. Turn left (southeast) and proceed the remaining 0.3 mile to the trail's end.

Miles and Directions

0.0 Begin at the trailhead and go left.

0.3 Reach Switchgrass Marsh.

0.4 Come to a bench for viewing wildlife.

0.6 Cross road and go northwest to link to the Tree Trail.

0.8 Reach the Tree Trail; bear left (northwest).

2.0 Return to the link to Switchgrass Marsh Trail.

2.2 Reach the Switchgrass Marsh Trail; bear left.

2.5 Arrive back at the trailhead.

21 Boy Scout Trail

A loop trail through ravines and over logging roads, with its closing stretch along the Mississinewa River.

Location: Southeast of Peru
Distance: 5.0-mile loop
Elevation change: Several 100-foot climbs
Approximate hiking time: 3 hours
Difficulty: Moderate
Jurisdiction: Indiana Department of Natural Resources, Division of State Parks & Reservoirs
Fees and permits: No fees or permits required
Maps: USGS Peoria; Pokagon-Kekionga Trails, Inc., brochure
Special attractions: Deep ravines, pine forest, Mississinewa River

Camping: 375 sites at two campgrounds—the Frances Slocum State Recreation Area on the north side of the reservoir and the Miami State Recreation Area
Trailhead facilities: Large paved parking lot; pit toilets; and the Peoria public fishing site at trailhead; no water supply at the fishing site; water available nearby at the Observation Pavilion overlooking the dam

Finding the trailhead: From the courthouse square in downtown Peru, go 0.2 mile south on IN 19 cross a bridge over the Wabash River, and turn left (east) onto IN 124. Go about 6 miles to where IN 124 makes a 90-degree right turn and then a left turn. Go another 0.5 mile on IN 124 to Miami CR 675 East and turn right (south). Go 1 mile to the turnoff for the Peoria Fishing Site. Turn right (southwest) and go downhill about 0.5 mile before turning right (east) into a parking area. Disregard the trailhead sign and hike in a counterclockwise direction.

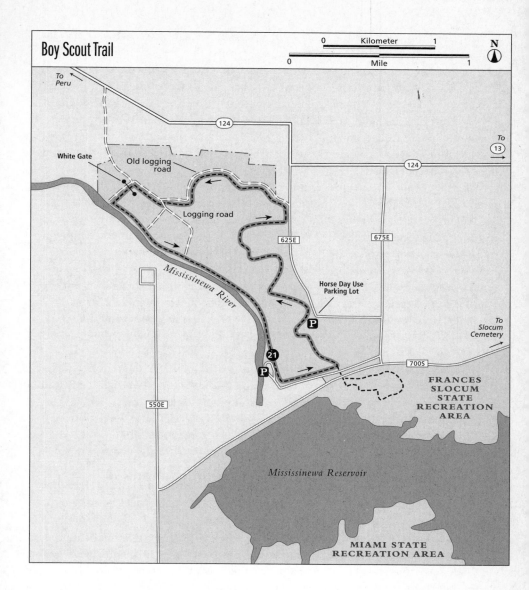

Boy Scout Trail

The Hike

It might seem that the name Frances Slocum is on everything around here—a bank, a cemetery, a road, a state recreation area, and the state forest in which this hike is located.

Frances Slocum was five years old when she was kidnapped by Delaware Indians from her Quaker home in Pennsylvania in 1778. The Delaware named her Weleta-wash and raised her to adulthood, later changing her name to Maconaquah, meaning Little Bear Woman. She married the war chief Shepconnah and lived among the

Indians until she was found in 1837 by her brother, Isaac, who was able to identify her by a scar on her left hand. Once it was revealed that she was a white woman, Frances Slocum lost her claim to government payments to Indians proscribed in the Treaty of 1826, but John Quincy Adams took her case to Congress. Slocum and her family were allowed to remain in Indiana, and two daughters were granted almost 650 acres of land, including the original homesite. A memorial marks the homesite, which is adjacent to the Slocum cemetery, 4.3 miles east of the Boy Scout trailhead on Mississinewa Road. Frances Slocum died in 1847 and is buried about 8 miles from the Mississinewa Dam.

The Boy Scout Trail that passes through Frances Slocum State Forest is no longer maintained by the DNR, but it is still a good hike. About one-third of the hike is on old logging roads and another third is along the Mississinewa River. Local Boy Scouts of America have marked the trail with yellow blazes, so it easy to follow. Although some stretches are marked for foot traffic only, horseback riders make regular use of other sections, so the path is relatively clear of debris. Still, the trail is scenic and remote from beginning to end. The trail can be hiked in either direction from the park lot, but the yellow blazes are placed only for the counterclockwise circuit.

Begin at the parking lot below the dam. Hike back up the paved road for 0.4 mile to a Boy Scout trail sign on the left (north) side of the road. Although yellow markers indicate the trail continues east, turn left (north) at the trail sign to enter the woods.

The next 2.0 miles are the most rugged part of the hike, as the trail negotiates waves of ravines and ridges. Parts of this section of the trail lead through hardwood forest; other parts weave through thick stands of pine. Complete the second ravine-ridge combination at a day-use parking lot for horseback riders at 0.9 mile. Turn left (northwest) to exit the lot and cross a flat plateau before descending into the third ravine. The trail turns right (northeast) at the bottom of the ravine and works uphill before cutting left (west) to parallel private property.

After dropping into and climbing out of one more ravine, hike along the north side of a field while heading east to the edge of a county road. Turn left (north) at the road and go 0.1 mile to link with the old logging road at 2.2 miles. Follow the road west and downhill for almost 1.0 mile to a metal gate and the intersection of another gravel road at 3.1 miles. Turn right (northwest) and go 0.2 mile to a white metal gate on the left (southwest) side of the road at 3.3 miles. Turn left (southwest) and follow the gravel road 0.2 mile to reach the banks of the Mississinewa River at 3.5 miles. Turn left (southeast) for a leisurely finish that passes beneath steep bluffs and deep ravines before reaching the parking lot.

Miles and Directions

0.0 Begin at the trailhead and go right.

0.4 Turn left at the Boy Scout Trail marker.

0.9	Reach the horse day-use parking lot; turn left (northwest) out of the lot.
2.1	Turn left (north) at county road.
2.2	Arrive at the old logging road.
3.1	Turn right at the gravel crossroad.
3.3	Turn left at the white gate.
3.5	Reach the Mississinewa River; turn left (southeast) to return to parking lot.
5.0	Arrive back at the trailhead.

22 Kokiwanee Nature Preserve

This trail meanders through woodlands and along a creek, takes a side trip past several scenic waterfalls, and loops through forests and meadows.

Location: Southwest of Huntington
Distance: 2.5-mile loop with side spur
Elevation change: 60 feet
Approximate hiking time: 1.5 hours
Difficulty: Moderate to strenuous
Jurisdiction: ACRES Land Trust
Maps: USGS Lagro; ACRES Land Trust map

Fees and permits: No fees or permits required
Special attractions: Waterfalls and other rock formations
Camping: No camping permitted
Trailhead facilities: Small parking lot; no drinkable water or restrooms at trailhead; a couple of old latrines along the trail

Finding the trailhead: From the intersection of IN 9 and US 24 near Huntington, go south on IN 9 for 3.5 miles to Division Road. Turn right (west) and go 7.5 miles to Wabash CR 600 East. Turn left (south) and go 0.4 mile to Wabash CR 50 South. Turn right (west) and go 0.2 mile to the trailhead parking lot on the left (south).

The Hike

Because of presettlement influences, Native American place names—Salamonie, Mississinewa, etc.—are common in this area of the state.

Kokiwanee has a similar ring, but it actually is a spin on the Kiwanis Club of Kokomo, which donated the land for a Girl Scout camp in 1945. The camp closed in 1996 and was acquired in 2003 by ACRES Land Trust, a land conservation group that has preserved more than sixty unique natural areas in northeast Indiana and northwest Ohio totaling nearly 4,500 acres. The Kokiwanee site contains a forested upland, small creeks, and an array of small waterfalls spilling off a bluff overlooking the north bank of the Salamonie Reservoir.

The Girl Scout era at Kokiwanee left an abundance of trails and other vestiges, but the natural settings are relatively undisturbed. Because of the old trail system, it is advised to pick up a trail map at the sign-in post near the parking lot.

The hike described here is a combination of the Little Fox, Waterfall, River, Riding Ring, Main, and Fawn Lake Trails. It begins at the Little Fox/outer trail sign about 70 yards south of the parking lot on the left (east) side of the gravel road that once served as the main road into the Girl Scout camp.

Pass through the woods and across a meadow to a stand of pine trees. After passing the first of several footbridges, turn left (east) along the side of a hill. The trail turns right (south) and descends into a gully.

Follow a similar course into and out of gullies and across footbridges until you reach the Farmhouse Trail juncture at 0.5 mile. Go left (south) and continue for about 0.25 mile to cross over the smooth rock that forms the top of Kissing Falls. Only a small amount of water trickles over the 20-foot-high falls most of the year.

Little Fox Trail ends on the other side at a T intersection with the Waterfall Trail. Turn left (southwest) and descend wooden steps to the base of the bluff. Proceed northwest along the trail, passing the Stairwell Crevice, Riding Ring Crevice, Daisy Low Falls, Broken Falls, and Skunk Cabbage Falls.

At Skunk Cabbage Falls turn left (southwest) toward the river and a T intersection with the River Trail. Turn right (northwest) and go through Skunk Cabbage Marsh, past Sponge Rock and Sleepy Hollow Bluff to reach Frog Falls at 1.1 miles.

Backtrack along the River Trail to connect with the outbound Waterfall Trail. Climb back up the wooden steps and turn left (northwest) at the top of the bluff.

Follow the well-mowed path to reach a T intersection with the Riding Ring Trail at 1.6 miles. Turn right (north) and go 0.1 mile to connect with the Main Trail. Look to the left of the trail for the stone foundation of the camp's former riding stable.

Turn left (northwest) and continue past a series of trail junctures (Hillcrest Trail from the right; Daisy Low and Sleepy Hollow as crossroads) on the wide, gravel Main Trail as it passes through deep woods.

At 1.9 miles the trail turns sharply right (northeast) and uphill to pass the Star Lodge Activity Center, one of the few remaining buildings on the site, on the left side of the road. Just ahead and on the right is the Tribal House Activity Center; just past it on the right is the Fawn Lake Trail.

Turn right (south) and go 0.1 miles to Fawn Lake, a one-acre pond. A bench provides a good resting spot to sit quietly and wait for wildlife to show up.

From the west edge of the lake, go north about 0.1 mile to reconnect with the main gravel road. Turn right (north) and return to the parking lot.

Miles and Directions

0.0   Begin at the trailhead; turn left onto Little Fox Trail.

0.5   Trail juncture with Farmhouse Trail; go left (south).

0.7   Cross over creek above Kissing Falls; turn left (west) at trail juncture.

0.8   Trail juncture at Waterfall Trail; turn left (southwest) and go downhill.

0.9   Arrive at Daisy Low Falls.

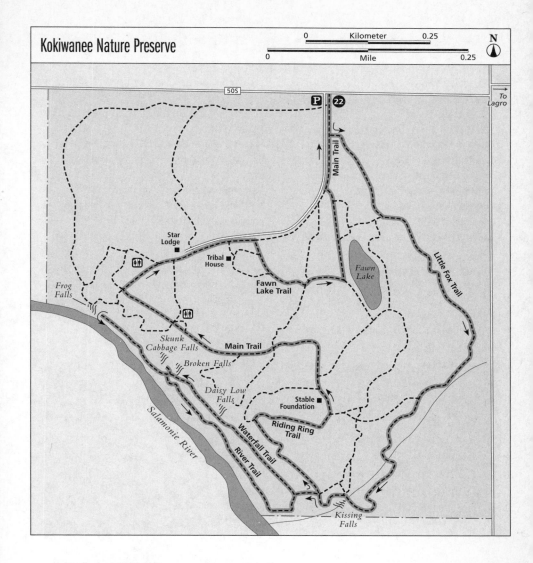

Kokiwanee Nature Preserve

1.1 Come to Frog Falls.

1.4 Complete Waterfall Trail loop; go uphill.

1.5 Trail juncture; turn left (northwest).

1.6 Reach the Riding Ring Trail juncture; turn right (north).

1.7 Arrive at the Main Trail; turn left (northwest).

1.9 Pass Star Lodge Activity Center.

2.1 Trail juncture to Fawn Lake; turn right (southeast).

2.3 Reconnect to Main Trail; turn right (north).

2.5 Arrive back at the trailhead.

23 Hathaway Nature Preserve at Ross Run

This trail skirts a high bluff over a tributary of the Wabash River and passes through woods and meadows.

Location: Southwest of Huntington
Distance: 1.7-mile loop
Elevation change: Minimal; mostly level
Approximate hiking time: 1 hour
Difficulty: Easy to moderate
Jurisdiction: ACRES Land Trust.
Fees and permits: No fees or permits required

Maps: USGS Wabash; ACRES Land Trust map
Special attractions: Trail rim views of Ross Run
Camping: No camping permitted
Trailhead facilities: Parking at the trailhead; no drinking water or restrooms

Finding the trailhead: From the intersection of IN 9 and US 24 near Huntington, go west 14 miles on US 24 to Wabash CR 300 East, also listed as Lagro Road. Turn left (south) onto CR 300 East and go 0.8 mile to the intersection with IN 524. Go straight to pick up IN 524; pass through Lagro Road and continue south approximately 1.3 miles to Baumbauer Road. Turn right (west) and go 2.2 miles to the trailhead on the right (north).

Ross Run trickles across layered rock at Hathaway Nature Preserve in Wabash County.

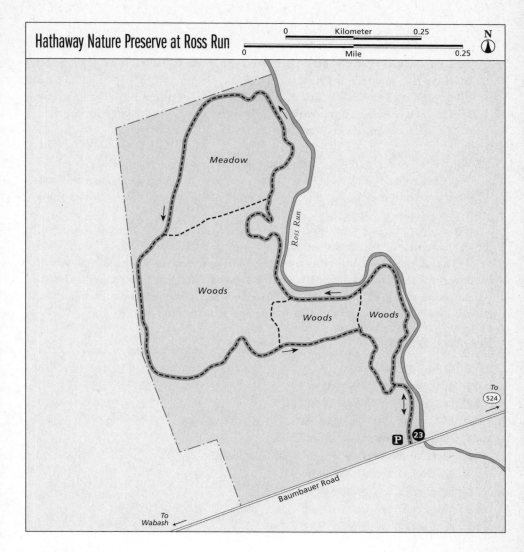

Meadow

Ross Run

Woods

Woods

Woods

To
524

To
Wabash

Baumbauer Road

The Hike

ACRES Land Trust has been acquiring and preserving unique natural areas for nearly fifty years, and Hathaway Preserve at Ross Run is one of the newest. Added to the ACRES roster in 2007, the preserve is named for Dr. Harvey Hathaway Jr. The eastern boundary of the seventy-two-acre property is Ross Run, a tributary of the Wabash River.

Though small, Ross Run performed its magic on the area by carving an impressive gorge with 75-foot cliffs and exposing the stream's bedrock. Because the trail skirts the rim of the gorge, much of the geologic artistry is hidden from view except for an occasional glimpse.

The trail begins at the northeast corner of the parking lot near a stone marker. Go 0.1 mile to a trail juncture and turn right (north).

The gorge is to the right, and it deepens as the trail progresses over relatively flat terrain. Two connecting trails intersect the main trail from the left over the next 0.5 mile. Continue on the main trail to reach the southeast corner of a meadow at 0.6 mile.

The trail slips into and out of the woods before making a counterclockwise loop along the edge of the meadow. At the northern edge of the property, the trail cuts diagonally across the meadow and uphill to reach the northwest corner of the property's main woods at 1.0 mile.

Continue south along the edge of a farm field (right) to the southwest corner of the main woods and turn left (east) through another meadow.

Pass a trail juncture connecting from the left before reentering the woods, which features some massive oak trees. Reach another trail juncture at 1.5 miles and turn right (south), skirting the edge of the woods and a farm field before coming to a juncture with the outbound trail. Turn right and return to the parking lot.

Miles and Directions

0.0 Begin at the trailhead.

0.1 Trail juncture; turn right (north).

0.3 Trail juncture; continue straight (west).

0.4 Trail juncture; turn right (northwest).

0.6 Arrive at the meadow; go straight (north).

1.0 Finish meadow loop at woods; go straight (southwest).

1.4 Trail juncture; turn right (east).

1.5 Trail juncture; turn right (southeast).

1.6 Trail juncture; turn right (east) and return to parking lot.

1.7 Arrive back at the trailhead.

24 Delphi Canal Trails

A loop trail, with two short spurs at the beginning and end of the hike.

Location: On the outskirts of Delphi, west-central Indiana
Distance: 2.0-mile loop with spurs
Elevation change: Minimal
Approximate hiking time: 1 hour
Difficulty: Easy
Jurisdiction: Carroll County Wabash & Erie Canal Association

Maps: USGS Delphi; Wabash & Erie Canal Association brochure
Fees and permits: No fees or permits required
Special attractions: Access to a remnant section of the historic Wabash & Erie Canal
Camping: No camping permitted
Trailhead facilities: Restrooms, a water pump, and a small shelter house

Finding the trailhead: Go 1.4 miles southwest from downtown Delphi on IN 25 to Trailhead Park on the right side of the road.

The Hike

These interconnecting trails provide a glimpse of a bygone era, when farm products and other goods were transported over the Wabash & Erie Canal. The canal was a system of locks built between 1832 and 1863 to link Lake Erie to Evansville. The 468-mile stretch from Fort Wayne to Evansville was the largest man-made structure in the country at the time, and its construction and operation plunged the state into bankruptcy.

The area near Delphi is the only accessible location where water still flows through the historic canal, which went out of business in the 1870s as railroad transportation expanded. These are well-marked and well-maintained trails over pea gravel. Traffic is generally light most of the year.

The hike begins in Trailhead Park at a footbridge across Deer Creek. After crossing the bridge, turn left (west) for a short walk to Sunset Point, an overlook where Deer Creek and the canal spill into the Wabash River. Canal builders constructed a dam here to create a pool of water deep enough for barges to cross Deer Creek. The towpath at the confluence collapsed in 1874, sweeping the mules and driver into the river, where they drowned.

From Sunset Point retrace your steps to the junction with the VanScoy Towpath, which horses and mules once used while towing barges through the canal. At 0.4 mile turn left (northwest) off the VanScoy Towpath to follow the Obear Millrace Towpath northeast along a millrace that once fed water to two paper mills on the outskirts of Delphi. The Obear path reconnects to the VanScoy path at 0.9 mile.

The trail network goes another 0.75 mile to Canal Park in Delphi, but turn right (south) instead and follow the VanScoy Towpath back along the Wabash & Erie Canal to the footbridge. Turn left (northeast) at the footbridge at 1.5 miles and follow the Robbins Towpath 0.25 mile along Deer Creek. Pass under IN 25 before turning left and climbing a slight incline to the Lawrence Van Der Volgen Overlook at 1.8 miles. Return down the same path to the trailhead.

Option

The hike described above is only a portion of the Delphi Historic Trails complex featuring ten named trails ranging in length from 0.3 mile to 1.5 miles and totaling 8.6 miles. Several of the trails are through historic areas of downtown Delphi.

A wintery stroll along the towpath at Delphi Canals, site of a section of the Wabash and Erie Canal.

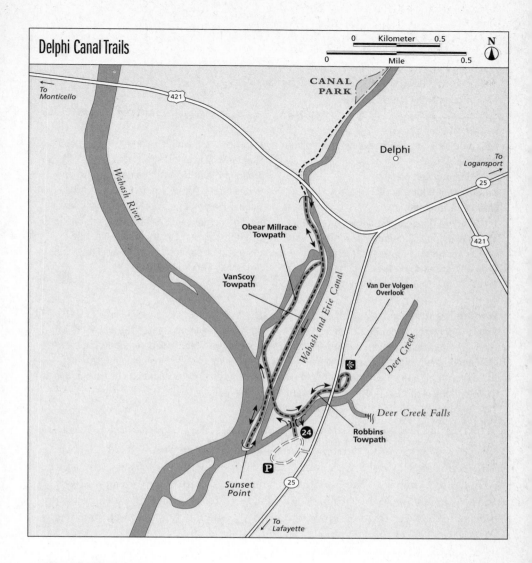

Delphi Canal Trails

Miles and Directions

0.0 Begin at the trailhead and go left.

0.2 Reach Sunset Point; retrace your steps.

0.3 Arrive at the VanScoy Towpath junction.

0.4 Reach the Obear Millrace Towpath junction; turn left (northwest).

0.9 Take the VanScoy Towpath return leg.

1.5 Cross the footbridge at the Robbins Towpath junction; turn left (northeast).

1.8 Arrive at the Lawrence Van Der Volgen Overlook. Return down same path to trailhead.

2.0 Arrive back at the trailhead.

25 Wabash Heritage Trail

A linear trail along the Wabash River that is full of historic locations, from Battle Ground to Tapawingo Park.

Location: Near Lafayette, west-central Indiana
Distance: 9.5-mile shuttle
Elevation change: Minimal
Approximate hiking time: 5 hours
Difficulty: Moderate
Jurisdiction: Tippecanoe County Historical Association; parks departments for Tippecanoe County, Lafayette, and West Lafayette
Fees and permits: No fees or permits required
Maps: USGS Brookston, Lafayette East, and Lafayette West; Wabash Heritage Trail brochure
Camping: No camping permitted
Trailhead facilities: The battlefield museum is open from 10:00 a.m. to 5:00 p.m. Mon through Sat; noon to 5:00 p.m. Sun. Admission fee. The nature center is open seasonally. There is a drinking fountain at the museum but no other sources of potable water available until Tapawingo Park in West Lafayette.

Finding the trailhead: Go 3 miles northeast on US 25 from the I-65 interchange to IN 225. Turn left (northwest) onto IN 225 and go over the one-lane bridge that crosses the Wabash River. The highway passes between the two sections of Prophetstown State Park before reaching the village of Battle Ground. Cross the railroad tracks at the center of town; take an immediate left (southwest) turn and go 0.4 mile farther to the Tippecanoe Battlefield Memorial. The trailhead is at the Wah-bah-shik-a Nature Center at the north end of the parking lot.

The Hike

In 1811 Shawnee leader Tecumseh attempted to establish a confederacy of Native American tribes to resist the advancement of white settlers. Fourteen tribes gathered at a site known as Prophet's Town, named for Tecumseh's brother, the Prophet. Military forces directed by General William Henry Harrison were attacked by the Indians at Prophet's Town on November 7, 1811, and quickly crushed the uprising to effectively end Tecumseh's ambition. Harrison was elected U.S. president in 1839 but died after only thirty days in office.

Two landmarks commemorate the famous battle—Prophetstown State Park and a local historic park at the battlefield site on the west edge of Battle Ground. Thirteen miles downstream from the battlefield is Fort Ouiatenon, the first military outpost in Indiana. It was established in 1717 by the French to counter British expansion.

The hike begins at the Battle Ground historic park. Explore the 104-acre battlefield and military graveyard or visit the museum or nature center.

The linear nature and distance of this trail will require you to arrange a vehicle shuttle or be willing to backtrack. There are additional trailheads along the route—at Davis Ferry Park, Lafayette Municipal Golf Course, and Tapawingo Park. Spring rains can flood out some sections of the trail, but rerouting has taken care of most problems.

Trail conditions sometimes are posted at the nature center. The busiest segments are at the battlefield and paved areas in downtown Lafayette.

To start the hike, walk down a concrete stairway near the nature center to a footbridge over Burnett Creek, named for William Burnett, a French trader and early settler. Just short of 0.1 mile arrive at a marked juncture of the Wabash Heritage and Prophet's Rock Trails. An optional side trip, Prophet's Rock Trail leads 0.2 mile to the rock. Popular legend relates that the Prophet chanted encouragement and instructions to the Indian warriors during the 1811 battle. Native American historians dispute this tale.

From the juncture with Prophet's Rock Trail, turn left (southwest) at the Wabash Heritage Trail marker and follow a path that hugs the north bank of Burnett's Creek as it cuts a southwesterly path toward its confluence with the Wabash River. Interpretive signposts help mark the way on what is an easy walk, with only three minor inclines over the entire stretch to Fort Ouiatenon.

Two short footbridges cross drainage ditches that feed Burnett's Creek before the path passes under I-65 at 1.4 miles. Go 0.1 mile to another footbridge, followed by a climb of 30 feet up a steep bank. Drop back down to the creekbed and at 1.8 miles pass under a bridge at Burnett's Creek Road.

The trail crosses Burnett's Creek on round concrete stepping-stones and then continues along the southeast bank of the creek for another 1.8 miles to Davis Ferry Bridge (3.6 miles). Pass behind private homes and along a farm field to a paved road, following trail markers that point to the iron suspension bridge built over the Wabash

The trailhead of Wabash Heritage Trail at Burnett Creek, its northern terminus.

in 1912. John Davis, who married William Burnett's daughter, operated a ferry at this location until the bridge was built. Davis charged 6 cents per person and 12½ cents per car or horse. Today the bridge is restricted to pedestrian use. Cross the bridge and turn right (west) as the path proceeds along the southeast bank of the Wabash. At 4.1 miles pass Heron Island, a twelve-acre wildlife refuge in the Wabash that is accessible only by boat. Continue along the banks of the Wabash for about 1.7 miles to another footbridge before passing under the US 52 bridge at 5.8 miles.

Concrete pilings provide the stepping stones to cross Burnett Creek on the Wabash Heritage Trail.

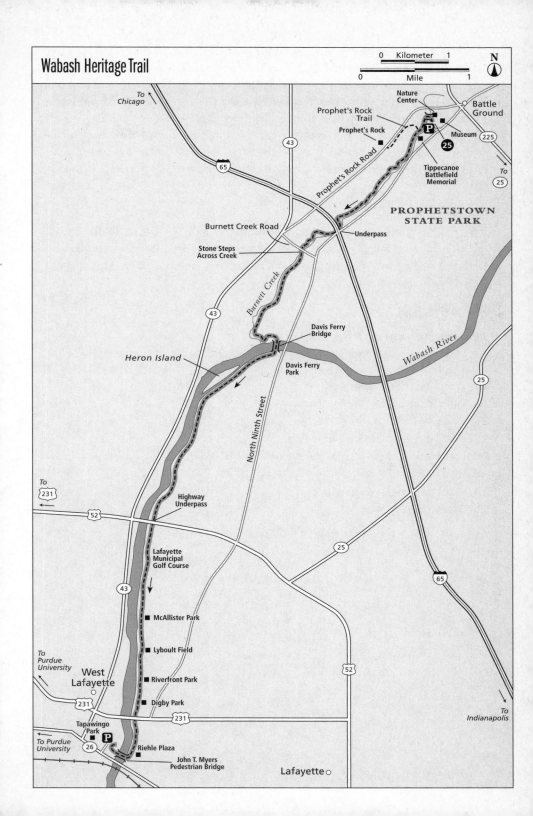

Wabash Heritage Trail

Kilometer
0 — 1
0 — 1
Mile

N

To Chicago

Nature Center

Prophet's Rock Trail

Prophet's Rock

P

25 Museum

225

Tippecanoe Battlefield Memorial

Battle Ground

To **25**

43

65

Prophet's Rock Road

PROPHETSTOWN STATE PARK

Burnett Creek Road

Underpass

Stone Steps Across Creek

Burnett Creek

43

Davis Ferry Bridge

Davis Ferry Park

Heron Island

Wabash River

25

North Ninth Street

To **231**

Highway Underpass

52

Lafayette Municipal Golf Course

25

43

65

McAllister Park

Lyboult Field

52

To Purdue University

West Lafayette

Riverfront Park

Digby Park

231

231

To Indianapolis

Tapawingo Park

P

26

To Purdue University

Riehle Plaza

John T. Myers Pedestrian Bridge

Lafayette

From here the trail is unmarked but follows a service road that parallels the river, Lafayette Municipal Golf Course, and an open field that is home to a local model airplane club. At 6.5 miles you will come to McAllister Park and a paved section of trail that is also open to bicycles. Walk past several ball fields on the left (east) and under another bridge to reach the final leg into downtown Lafayette.

At 9.3 miles reach the Big Four Depot, a restored train stop at the foot of the John T. Myers pedestrian bridge, which crosses the Wabash River into West Lafayette, home of Purdue University. After crossing the bridge, turn right into Tapawingo Park at 9.5 miles.

Option

It is possible to continue another 3.5 miles south along the west bank of the Wabash to Fort Ouiatenon, but the trail may be washed out in some locations and the last 0.25 mile is along busy South River Road. Efforts are underway to upgrade the trail between Tapawingo and the fort.

Miles and Directions

0.0 Begin at the trailhead and go straight.

0.1 Reach the Prophet's Rock Trail juncture; turn left. (**Option:** Take the 0.4-mile round-trip to Prophet's Rock.)

1.4 Reach the I-65 underpass.

1.8 Arrive at the Burnett's Road underpass.

3.6 Cross the Davis Ferry Bridge.

4.1 Pass the Heron Island Wildlife Preserve.

5.8 Take the US 52 underpass to Lafayette Municipal Golf Course.

6.5 Reach McAllister Park.

9.3 Cross the John T. Myers Bridge.

9.5 Reach Tapawingo Park.

26 Portland Arch Nature Preserve

A short loop trail with several creek crossings.

Location: Southwest of Lafayette near Attica, west-central Indiana
Distance: 0.8-mile loop
Elevation change: Less than 50 feet
Approximate hiking time: 30 minutes
Difficulty: Moderate
Jurisdiction: Indiana Department of Natural Resources, Division of Nature Preserves

Fees and permits: No fees or permits required
Maps: USGS Stone Bluff; Portland Arch Nature Preserve brochure
Special attractions: Portland Arch, Bear Creek Ravine
Camping: No camping permitted
Trailhead facilities: Small gravel parking lot; no drinking water available

Finding the trailhead: Go south from Attica on US 41 for 4 miles to the intersection of US 41, IN 55, and IN 28. Continue south for 5 miles to Fountain CR 650 North and turn right (west). Go about 5 miles on CR 650 North to Walnut Street, which is on the west edge of Fountain. Turn left (southwest) and go 1 block to Scout Camp Road. Turn left (southeast) onto a gravel road and go 0.4 mile to a parking lot on the right (west) side of the road. The trailhead is on the west side of the parking lot.

The Hike

Legend has it that following the defeat of his Indian confederacy at the Battle of Tippecanoe in 1811, Shawnee chief Tecumseh sought refuge at this site. If true, it was a good hiding place. Bear Creek already had carved a deep but narrow channel through layers of rock when a small adjoining stream—Spring Creek—punched a hole in the sandstone to create a natural bridge.

The archway that Spring Creek formed is the focal point of the hike, but it's not the only attractive feature of the state-protected nature preserve, which is listed as a National Natural Landmark by the U.S. Department of the Interior. Plant life is abundant in the moist ravine environment, where steep slopes host a mix of oak, hickory, and native white pine trees. Berry bushes, lichens, and mosses grow in the thin soil, and a variety of other plants cling to small crevices in the surrounding cliffs. This is the only place in the state where Canada blueberry grows.

The trail alternates between being rugged, muddy, steep, and level. It is designed as an interpretive nature trail, but several markers are missing.

Begin the hike by passing through the fence opening at the west end of the parking lot to pick up an interpretive brochure at the registration box. Turn right (north)

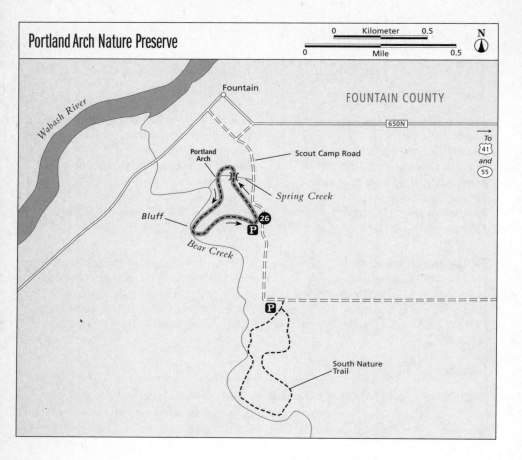

and begin a short walk toward the ravine before making a sharp descent at 0.1 mile. Cross a footbridge and continue downhill to Spring Creek at 0.2 mile. The trail turns left (west) beside a cliff, with Spring Creek on the right (north). Walk over two footbridges to reach the sometimes–muddy passageway beneath the arch.

Once through the archway, turn left (south) and follow the pathway beside the sandstone ridge to begin a fairly straight walk alongside Bear Creek. At about 0.6 mile turn left and climb uphill to a ledge along the east side of the ravine, eventually turning toward the east to return to the parking lot.

Option:

The 0.9-mile South Nature Trail is also available in the preserve. Access the trail by turning right (south) from the Portland Arch parking lot and going 0.3 mile to its parking area.

Miles and Directions

0.0 Begin at the trailhead and go right.

0.2 Reach Spring Creek; turn left (west).

0.3 Reach Portland Arch.

0.6 Climb the rocky ledge on Bear Creek.

0.8 Arrive back at the trailhead.

Central Plain

Among the various geographic regions in Indiana, this is the largest. It also gives the impression of being the most featureless area of the state. Nothing could be further from the truth.

Three unique properties in Indiana are located here—Shades and Turkey Run State Parks and Pine Hills Nature Preserve. Each is marked by deep ravines, canyons, flowing water, and lush vegetation. Even the state capital, Indianapolis, has its share of scenic locations, including those along Fall Creek at Fort Benjamin Harrison State Park and at Eagle Creek Park on the northwest side.

The area is bounded on the north by the Wabash River and on the south by a jagged line just below midstate that marks the farthest advance of the last glacier thousands of years ago. Rolling plains and flat farmland typify most of the Central Plain, but the Shades and Turkey Run parks, on the western edge of the region, are notable exceptions.

Sandy sediment was dumped here, at the mouth of the ancient Michigan River, and it solidified like cement. Later the exposed sandstone was carved and gouged by glacial meltwaters to create a maze of canyons and ravines.

Nearby Pine Hills further exemplifies the erosive power of water. Two small, winding creeks—Clifty and Indian—have sliced through the bedrock to create four narrow backbone ridges. The formations are 100 feet high and as much as 1,000 feet long. Devil's Backbone is a scant 6 feet wide at one spot.

The splendor and abundance of the scenery of Shades, Turkey Run, and Pine Hills is unmatched in the state.

The trails in this section are presented in a clockwise sweep, heading south from Mounds State Park near Anderson to Indianapolis and west from Indianapolis toward Crawfordsville.

27 Mounds State Park

A loop trail past prehistoric earthworks and burial mounds.

Location: Near Anderson
Distance: 1.5-mile loop
Elevation change: About 70 feet from White River to the Great Mound
Approximate hiking time: 1 hour
Difficulty: Easy to moderate
Jurisdiction: Indiana Department of Natural Resources, Division of State Parks & Reservoirs
Fees and permits: Park entry fee, higher for out-of-state vehicles; season passes available

Maps: USGS Anderson South and Middletown; Mounds State Park brochure
Special attractions: The Great Mound and several smaller earthworks
Camping: 75 modern campsites in the park; youth camp area
Trailhead facilities: Large parking lot near the pavilion; water and restrooms located throughout the park

Finding the trailhead: From I-69 drive 1.1 miles north on IN 9. Turn right onto IN 232 and go about 0.75 mile to the Mounds State Park entrance on the left (northwest). Past the gatehouse, follow the main park road less than 0.1 mile to the pavilion parking lot on the left.

The Hike

As state parks go in Indiana, Mounds is a tiny one. At just over 280 acres, it is about one-tenth the average size of Indiana parks. It is one of the busiest, though, with an annual

The entrance sign at Mounds State Park.

average of more than 400,000 visitors, which usually ranks in the top 10.

Despite its size, the park has several attractions—picnic areas, a newly renovated swimming pool and splashpad—plus the extensive earthworks and ceremonial mounds for which the park is named. These mounds are circular, fiddle-shaped, or rectangular and were constructed from about 160 B.C. to A.D. 50 by Adena and Hopewell peoples. The largest is the Great Mound, more than 1,200 feet around, 9 feet high, and 60 feet wide at the base. An archaeological excavation of the mound in the late 1960s uncovered bone awls, a ceremonial stone pipe, pottery shards, projectile points, and a long tomb.

These trails get heavy use. Crowds normally can be avoided by visiting the park on weekdays or in late fall and winter. People are not alone in swarming this small park. Mosquitoes can be a problem too, especially along the river portion of the trail.

Trail 2, which leads down to White River, begins across a grassy area behind the pavilion. Go down the wooden staircase and across a small creek to reach the White River. At 0.2 mile Trail 2 joins Trail 5, which circles the perimeter of the park. Turn left (south) and go 0.3 mile along the riverbank to where Trail 1 turns left (southeast); a uniquely shaped tubular bench sits at this juncture. Trail 1 goes uphill to a plateau where the mounds complex is located. Here you will find the Great Mound and the Fiddleback, Woodland, and Fomalhault Mounds.

Between Fiddleback Mound and the Great Mound, at 0.7 mile, bear left (north) on Trail 1 for a winding walk along bluffs and around the high side of a ravine. Circle back to the intersection with Trail 2 (1.2 miles) near the northeast side of the Great Mound.

Turn left (east) at Trail 2 and cross a multitiered boardwalk and staircase above a moist ravine through which a small creek flows. At the end of the boardwalk at 1.5 miles, enter the grassy area near the pavilion.

The Great Mound is 1,200 feet around and 9 feet high.

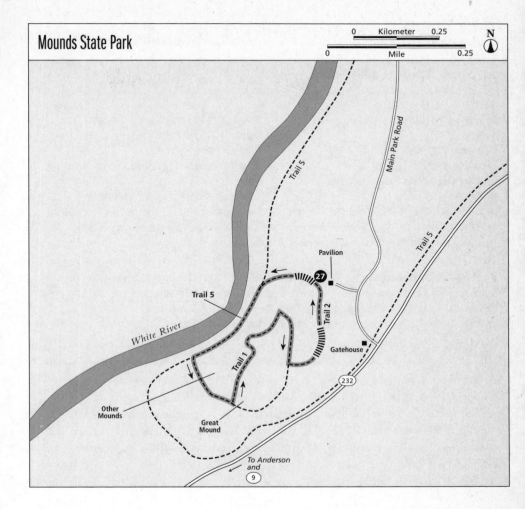

0   Kilometer   0.25

N

0   Mile   0.25

Trail 5

Main Park Road

Pavilion

Trail 5

27

Trail 5

Trail 2

White River

Trail 1

Gatehouse

232

Other
Mounds

Great
Mound

To Anderson
and

9

Option

The park has six trails. Trail 5, the longest, is a 2.5-mile lap around the outer edges of the park and past Circle Mound.

Miles and Directions

0.0   Begin at the trailhead and go right.

0.2   At the junction of the boardwalk path (Trail 2) and Trail 5, turn left onto Trail 5.

0.5   At the trail juncture turn left and go uphill on Trail 1.

0.7   Trail 1 continues behind Fiddleback Mound.

1.2   Trails 1 and 2 meet; turn right onto Trail 2 (boardwalk).

1.5   Reach the pavilion and the trailhead.

28 Fort Harrison State Park: Fall Creek Trail

A loop trail along the banks of Fall Creek.

Location: The east side of Indianapolis, central Indiana

Distance: 2.2-mile lollipop

Elevation change: 75 feet

Approximate hiking time: 1.5 hours

Difficulty: Moderate

Jurisdiction: Indiana Department of Natural Resources, Division of State Parks & Reservoirs

Fees and permits: Park entry fee, higher for out-of-state vehicles; season passes available

Maps: USGS Fishers and Indianapolis; Fort Harrison State Park brochure

Special attraction: Secluded woodland along Camp Creek

Camping: No camping permitted in park

Trailhead facilities: Large parking lot; modern restrooms nearby equipped with drinking fountains

Finding the trailhead: From I-465 take exit 40 and go 2 miles on 56th Street east to Post Road. Turn left (north) and drive 0.5 mile to a three-way stop at the main park road. Turn left (northwest) and go to the park gatehouse. From the gate travel 0.7 mile to a T intersection. Turn right (east) and go 0.2 mile to the Delaware Lake Picnic Area parking lot.

The Hike

Fort Benjamin Harrison, or "Fort Ben," is one of Indiana's newer state parks, established in 1996 after the Indiana Department of Natural Resources acquired about two-thirds of the former military post from the U.S. government. Fort Ben was dedicated in 1906 by President Theodore Roosevelt and was used by the military until its closure in 1991. It is named for Benjamin Harrison, the only U.S. president elected from Indiana.

The 1,700-acre state park contains several large tracts of hardwood forest, three small lakes, Fall and Lawrence Creeks, and a championship golf course. Low spots along Fall Creek can be muddy in wet weather. A popular new urban park, Fort Ben draws lots of visitors (about 400,000 annually), and the trails get considerable use.

Leave the northeast corner of the main parking lot at Delaware Lake Picnic Area and walk 0.25 mile on the crushed stone path to the junction with the loop trail. Take the left (northeast) path, sticking to the south bank of Fall Creek.

At 0.7 mile the connector trail from the paved Harrison Trace Bike Trail joins on the right (southeast) side. Continue straight (northeast) ahead for 0.1 mile to where the trail bends right (south). Climb an extensive wooden staircase system to reach a flat ridgetop and the highest point on the trail—about 75 feet above Fall Creek. Along the trail, look for signs of the former military post, including a sandbag bunker and concrete markers.

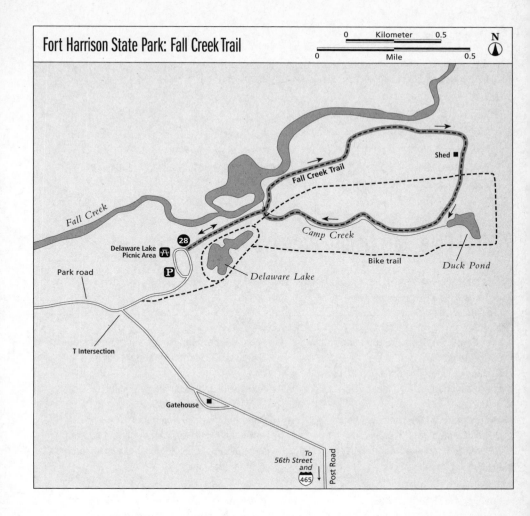

Fort Harrison State Park: Fall Creek Trail

0   Kilometer   0.5

0   Mile   0.5

N

Shed

Fall Creek Trail

Fall Creek

Camp Creek

Delaware Lake
Picnic Area

28

P

Bike trail

Duck Pond

Park road

Delaware Lake

T Intersection

Gatehouse

To
56th Street
and
465

Post Road

At 1.2 miles reach a gravel road that crosses the paved Harrison Trace Bike Trail at 1.4 miles. Walk through a series of small forest openings to Duck Pond and cross a small footbridge at 1.5 miles; reenter the woods on a gravel lane.

At 1.8 miles begin a downhill walk on the winding gravel lane to a quiet ravine containing Camp Creek. The area is home to some of the largest trees—oak, hickory, and maple—in the park plus a variety of wildflowers.

Cross the bike path one more time at 2.0 miles and turn left (southwest) at the connecting leg of the Fall Creek Trail to return to the parking lot.

Miles and Directions

0.0   Begin at the trailhead.

0.7   Reach the trail intersection and go straight (northeast).

1.2   Reach gravel road.

1.4   Cross the Harrison Trace Bike Trail.

1.5   Pass Duck Pond and cross a footbridge to reenter woods.

1.8   Reach the gravel road; follow Camp Creek west.

2.0   Cross bike trail again and turn left (southwest) onto connecting leg of Fall Creek Trail.

2.2   Arrive back at the trailhead.

29 Pine Hills Nature Preserve

A passage over two narrow backbone ridges above a deep gorge in the state's first dedicated nature preserve.

Location: Near Shades State Park, southwest of Crawfordsville

Distance: 1.8-miles of lollipop loops

Elevation change: 100 feet to Devil's Backbone

Approximate hiking time: 1.5 hours

Difficulty: Moderate to strenuous

Jurisdiction: Indiana Department of Natural Resources, Division of State Parks & Reservoirs

Fees and permits: No fees or permits required

Maps: USGS Alamo; state park nature preserve brochure

Special attractions: Turkey Backbone, Devil's Backbone, and Honeycomb Rock

Camping: No camping permitted

Trailhead facilities: Water fountain and pit toilet in the parking lot located across the road from the trailhead

Finding the trailhead: Go 7.5 miles southwest from Crawfordsville on IN 47 to IN 234 and turn right (west). Drive 6 miles to a gravel parking lot on the left (west) side of the road. Cross the road and climb over a stile to access the trailhead.

The Hike

Don't be fooled by the easy pace with which this trail begins. The deep gorge the entry trail leads to may be the most spectacular piece of natural landscape in Indiana.

Dedicated in 1971 as the first state nature preserve, Pine Hills presents perhaps the finest examples of "incised meanders" in the eastern United States. Glacial meltwater formed two meandering streams—Clifty Creek and Indian Creek—that carved two deep gorges through the bedrock, leaving four narrow ridges, or backbones, that rise 70 to 100 feet. The pathway over Devil's Backbone is a mere 6 feet wide, with a sheer drop-off on both sides. Caution should be used in this area.

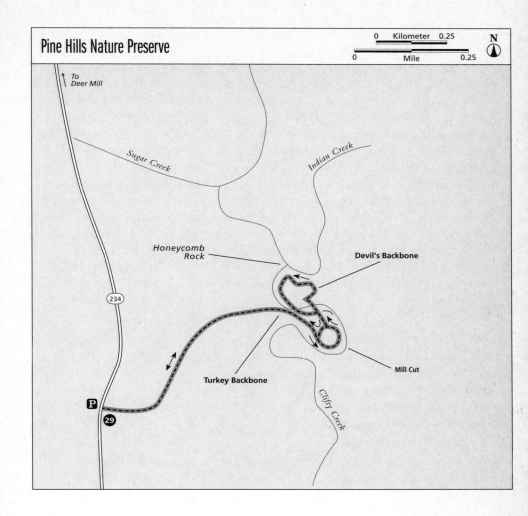

Two other geologic features are The Slide, a smooth patch on Clifty Creek created by constant rockslides, and Honeycomb Rock, a wall of sandstone where the two creeks meet.

There is more to the preserve than rocks, however. When the last glacier receded thousands of years ago, Indiana had a Canada-like environment in which white pine, hemlock, and Canada yew prospered. They remain as prominent features of the preserve.

Despite its uniqueness, the area did not avoid human intervention. Timber interests removed many large hardwoods in the 1850s, and in 1868 the Pine Hill Woolen Company dammed Clifty Creek and cut a notch in one of the backbones through which water flowed to power the mill. The business pulled out five years later, and the area has been mostly undisturbed since then.

Part of Shades State Park, the site covers 480 acres. Portions of the trail are steep and hazardous, so proceed with caution.

An entrance trail begins at the stile and proceeds along a gravel road for 0.4 mile to the Turkey Backbone. At the east end of the backbone, descend a set of wooden steps to the floor of the gorge at 0.6 mile. Turn right (southeast) to make a loop along the banks of Clifty Creek past the old woolen mill site, the mill cut, and The Slide. At 0.8 mile the loop intersects the trail leading to Devil's Backbone. Bear right (north) at another trail fork at 0.9 mile. Take the right (northeast) fork and scramble up the steep slope to the east end of Devil's Backbone at 1.0 mile.

Use extreme caution in crossing the narrow ridge to a hemlock grove. Descend the western slope of the ridge to Honeycomb Rock, where the two creeks merge and flow north to Sugar Creek. Turn left and follow the path a short ways along Clifty Creek before crossing the creek to link up with the main trail near the base of Turkey Backbone. Climb the staircase to begin backtracking to the trailhead parking lot.

Note: Pine Hills Nature Preserve also can be accessed via a 1.5-mile trail (Trail 10) that begins at the Dell Shelter in Shades State Park.

Miles and Directions

0.0 Begin at the trailhead.

0.4 Reach the Turkey Backbone.

0.6 Arrive at the base of gorge; turn right (southeast).

0.8 Turn right (northeast) at the trail fork.

0.9 Bear right (north) at the trail fork.

1.0 Reach the Devil's Backbone.

1.1 Arrive at Honeycomb Rock.

1.3 Reach the Turkey Backbone staircase. Climb the staircase and backtrack to the trailhead.

1.8 Arrive back at the trailhead.

30 Shades State Park: Ravine Trails

A combination of loop trails that follow the streambeds of rocky ravines.

Location: Southwest of Crawfordsville
Distance: 3.5 miles of lollipop loops
Elevation change: A drop of 150 feet from the trailhead to Sugar Creek
Approximate hiking time: 2 hours
Difficulty: Strenuous
Jurisdiction: Indiana Department of Natural Resources, Division of State Parks & Reservoirs
Fees and permits: Park entry fee, higher for out-of-state vehicles; season passes available
Maps: Alamo USGS; Shades State Park brochure
Special attractions: Kintz, Frisz, and Kickapoo Ravines; Inspiration Point; Silver Cascade Falls; Devil's Punch Bowl
Camping: 104 campsites in the park; youth camp area
Trailhead facilities: Water spigot at trailhead parking lot, plus a pit toilet nearby; water supply and restroom facilities located elsewhere in the park

Finding the trailhead: From Crawfordsville go 7.5 miles southwest on IN 47 to IN 234 near Waveland. Turn right (north) and go 5 miles to where IN 234 curves to the right. Turn left (west) onto Montgomery CR 800 South, passing a SHADES STATE PARK sign. Go 0.8 mile to the entrance road to the park. From the gatehouse take the first paved road to the right (north) and go 0.4 mile to a parking lot northwest of Dell Shelter at the end of the road. The trail begins at a metal gate.

The author's wife, Jessie, climbs one of the ladders in the Kintz Ravine at Shades State Park.

The Hike

Long before it became a state park in 1947, the dark, shadowy forest along the banks of Sugar Creek was called "Shades of Death." Stories vary on origins of the name, but the eerie legends it evoked led to it being simplified to "The Shades."

Hikers work their way along the canyon from Devil's Punch Bowl at Shades State Park.

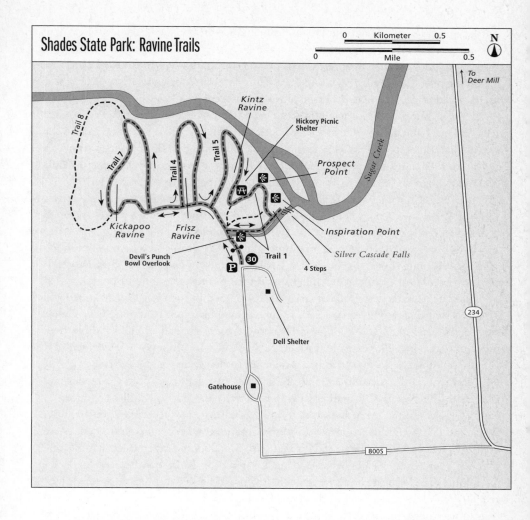

Shades State Park: Ravine Trails

In 1887 a forty-room inn was built as part of a health resort on a hill just south of the Devil's Punch Bowl. The inn later closed due to fire damage, but Joseph W. Frisz gained financial control of the association that owned the surrounding property. Frisz protected the natural features while adding more land.

Acquired by the state in 1947, the park now covers nearly 3,100 acres and includes the adjacent Pine Hills Nature Preserve. The remote location of Shades and the popularity of nearby Turkey Run State Park make Shades an overlooked jewel in the state park system. Although fifth in size among Indiana parks, Shades is one of the least visited with slightly more than 15 percent of the attendance at Turkey Run.

Perhaps another reason for the park's relative lack of visitors is that hiking the trails here is a challenge, particularly along the ravine streambeds. However, Shades is popular with hard-core hikers, although the rugged ravines are a limiting factor.

Most visitors congregate at the Devil's Punch Bowl and Silver Cascade Falls, where the multitiered wooden staircases reduce the difficulty of the steep climbs. Trail sections that follow ravine streambeds can be wet and hazardous after heavy rain. The following hike links Trails 1, 4, 5, and 7, traveling through four ravines and passing two scenic overlooks more than 200 feet above Sugar Creek.

Begin at the parking lot just north of Dell Shelter, site of the old inn. Pass a metal gate on Trail 1 and go 0.1 mile to a wood deck above the Devil's Punch Bowl. From the deck hike left (west) over two gullies on a pair of footbridges. Climb a set of stairs to a gravel road that circles Hickory Shelter. Turn left (west) onto the gravel road at 0.2 mile and follow markers leading to Trail 7, passing the starting points of Trails 5 and 4.

Turn right (north) at the Trail 7 juncture at 0.4 mile to make a counterclockwise loop of Kickapoo Ravine. The narrow dirt path descends to Sugar Creek through a dense forest. Stairs aid the downhill walk in a couple places, including one set of eighty-five steps. Two sets of steps go uphill; take the left set to continue uphill through Kickapoo Ravine (the right set leads to Shawnee Canyon and Trail 8). Stay left (east) when the trail joins Trail 8 at 1.3 miles, and return to the starting point of Trail 7.

Backtrack to the first Trail 4 marker at 1.4 miles and turn left (north) onto Trail 4, which begins as a wide gravel path leading downhill. Upon reaching Sugar Creek, turn right (east, then south) to Frisz Ravine, a more rugged uphill scramble than Kickapoo Ravine. The narrow passage of Frisz Ravine follows a streambed and requires climbing a staircase and two ladders in some of the roughest spots.

After exiting the top of the ravine at 2.0 miles, turn left (east) onto the feeder trail and go to the first Trail 5 marker. Turn left (north) and go downhill once more to Sugar Creek. Several sets of steps lead to the creek. Turn right (east, then south) at the creek and begin another scramble through Kintz Ravine. Frisz and Kintz ravines are similar in that they are narrow and littered with boulders and fallen trees that must be climbed over. A set of stairs bypasses a small waterfall in Kintz Ravine.

Climb a ladder near the top end of the ravine and enter an open area near Hickory Shelter at 2.9 miles. Rejoin the feeder trail at a Trail 5 marker on the right (west) side of the shelter restroom and turn left (southeast) to backtrack to Trail 1. Follow Trail 1 uphill to the east side of the Hickory Shelter area and take the left fork of Trail 1 (northeast) to Prospect Point, the first of two overlooks high above Sugar Creek.

After passing the second overlook—Inspiration Point—at 3.0 miles, turn left and climb down the stairs to get a view of Silver Cascade Falls at 3.1 miles. At the base of the stairs, turn left (northeast) and take a spur trail about 30 yards to get a full view of the falls. Backtrack on the spur trail to the main trail and follow the creek through a sandstone canyon to get a ground-level view of Devil's Punch Bowl at 3.4 miles. A set of stairs leads up from the canyon to the wood deck. Backtrack from here to the parking lot.

Miles and Directions

0.0 Begin at the trailhead.

0.1 Reach the Devil's Punch Bowl overlook.

0.2 Turn left (west) on the trail to Trail 7.

0.4 Turn right (north) at the Trail 7 juncture.

1.3 Stay left at the Trail 8 juncture.

1.4 Turn left (north) at the Trail 4 juncture.

2.0 Turn left at the trail juncture.

2.1 Turn left at the Trail 5 juncture.

2.9 Reach the Hickory Picnic Shelter.

3.0 Visit Prospect and Inspiration Points.

3.1 Go down the stairs to Silver Cascade Falls.

3.4 Reach the Devil's Punch Bowl. Climb the stairs up from the canyon and backtrack from the wood deck to the parking lot.

3.5 Arrive back at the trailhead.

31 Shades State Park: Pearl Ravine

A loop trail through a rugged ravine, with a spur trail to the scenic Lover's Leap overlook.

Location: Southwest of Crawfordsville

Distance: 1.3-mile loop

Elevation change: A drop of 150 feet from the trailhead to Sugar Creek

Approximate hiking time: 1 hour

Difficulty: Strenuous

Jurisdiction: Indiana Department of Natural Resources, Division of State Parks & Reservoirs

Fees and permits: Park entry fee, higher for out-of-state vehicles; season passes available

Maps: USGS Alamo; Shades State Park brochure

Special attractions: Lover's Leap, Pearl Ravine, and Maidenhair Falls

Camping: 104 campsites in the park; youth camp area

Trailhead facilities: Parking lot with water and pit toilets, about 100 yards north of Dell Shelter

Finding the trailhead: From Crawfordsville go 7.5 miles southwest on IN 47 to IN 234. Turn right (north) and go 5 miles to where IN 234 curves to the right. Turn left (west) onto Montgomery CR Road 800 South, passing a SHADES STATE PARK sign. Travel 0.8 mile to the entrance road to the park. From the gatehouse take the first paved road to the right (north) and go 0.4 mile to a parking lot below Dell Shelter. The trail begins east of the shelter house.

Maidenhair Falls is 6 feet wide and about 6 feet high. The falls are situated on the Pearl Ravine Trail in Shades State Park.

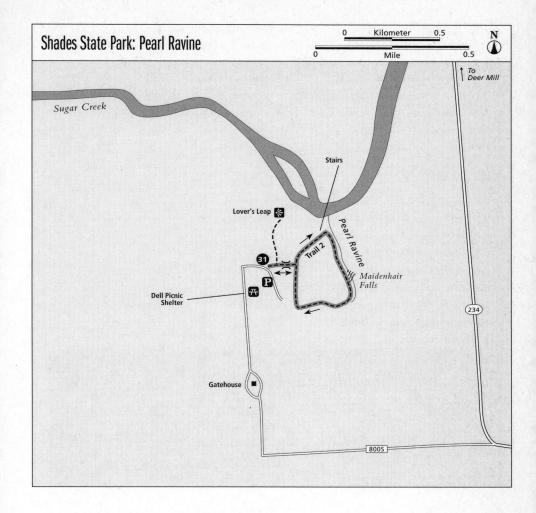

Shades State Park: Pearl Ravine

0 — Kilometer — 0.5
0 — Mile — 0.5

N

To Deer Mill

Sugar Creek

Stairs

Lover's Leap

Pearl Ravine

Trail 2

31

P

Maidenhair Falls

Dell Picnic Shelter

Gatehouse

234

800S

The Hike

Trail 2 at Shades State Park provides a hike up Pearl Ravine. Most visitors congregate at the Lover's Leap overlook or return from Pearl Ravine via the stairs. The trail section following the ravine streambed can be wet and hazardous after heavy rain.

Begin by heading northeast from the Dell Picnic Shelter parking area to locate a TRAIL 2 sign. At 0.1 mile a spur trail leads to Lover's Leap, a superb overlook 200 feet above Sugar Creek. Backtrack to the main trail and turn left (east). Go 0.2 mile to a staircase, then cross a footbridge over a ravine to a trail juncture. Turn left (northeast) and proceed to a long staircase at 0.3 mile. There are 180 steps to the bottom of the ravine; the last couple of sections are very steep.

Turn right (south) at the bottom and work up Pearl Ravine. Take notice along the way of the layered bedrock of sandstone, limestone, and siltstone that has been exposed over time by the eroding forces of water.

At 0.6 mile reach Maidenhair Falls, a fitting name for the delicate waterfall that is only 6 feet wide and 6 feet high. A stairway bypasses the falls, and at about 0.7 mile you take another set of steps out of the ravine. The trail loops west and then north to rejoin the entry trail that leads back to the footbridge and stairway leading to the parking lot.

Miles and Directions

0.0 Begin at the trailhead.

0.1 Turn right at trail split. (**Option:** Left fork leads to Lover's Leap.)

0.3 Follow stairs down to Pearl Ravine.

0.4 Turn right in Pearl Ravine.

0.6 Reach Maidenhair Falls.

0.7 Climb the stairway out of Pearl Ravine.

1.1 At the trail juncture, turn left to parking lot.

1.3 Arrive back at the trailhead.

The author steps over a pile of rocks and logs that clog the way on one of the ravines in Shades State Park.

32 Turkey Run State Park

A combination of park trails looping through canyons and along scenic Sugar Creek.

Location: Southwest of Crawfordsville
Distance: 3.0-mile loop
Elevation change: About 150 feet from the north bank of Sugar Creek to the ridgetops above the various canyons
Approximate hiking time: 2.5 hours
Difficulty: Strenuous
Jurisdiction: Indiana Department of Natural Resources, Division of State Parks & Reservoirs
Fees and permits: Park entry fee, higher for out-of-state vehicles; season passes available
Maps: USGS Wallace; Turkey Run State Park brochure

Special attractions: Ice Box, Falls Canyon, Boulder Canyon, 140 Steps, Punch Bowl, Rocky Hollow, and Wedge Rock
Camping: 213 modern campsites in the park; youth camp area; campground entrance located about 0.5 mile west of the main park entrance on IN 47
Trailhead facilities: Parking lot accommodates cars and buses. Water is available at the nature center and at other locations throughout the park. Restrooms also are located around the park, although there is no water supply or restrooms on the north side of Sugar Creek.

Finding the trailhead: From Crawfordsville go 23 miles west on IN 47 to the Turkey Run State Park entrance on the right (north) side of the highway. Go about 0.25 mile from the gatehouse to the main parking lot near the nature center. The trailhead is on the north side of the nature center and leads to a suspension bridge that crosses to the north bank of Sugar Creek.

The Hike

The sandstone cliffs of Turkey Run State Park had their origins 320 million years ago when the ancient Michigan River left behind sandy deposits as it spilled into a great inland sea. A few thousand years ago, postglacial streams carved the canyons that are distinguishing characteristics of the park. The retreating glacier also left two other notable features—boulders carried here from Canada and the eastern hemlock. A native species in colder regions of North America, this tree makes one of its rare Indiana appearances here.

Turkey Run was set aside as a state park in 1916. Pioneers are responsible for the name. Wild turkeys were abundant and known to congregate in the warmer canyon bottoms, or runs, during winter. Legend has it that the pioneers took advantage of the situation by herding the turkeys together for an easy hunt.

Turkeys still roam the park, as do white-tailed deer. Pileated woodpeckers are common. Warblers pass through during their spring and fall migrations, and turkey vultures have used the park as a winter roost since the late 1800s. The park contains sycamore, walnut, oak, and hemlock trees that are several hundred years old. Wildflowers are abundant, and more than half the varieties of mosses and lichens in the state can be found here. The park is bisected by scenic Sugar Creek, considered one of the cleanest streams in Indiana. The fish population of the creek is quite diverse, including seven different species of darters, further evidence of a clean, cool aquatic environment.

There are eleven trails in the park, and elements of three are included in the following hike. The spectacular nature of the sandstone canyons and their accessibility are major factors in the popularity of Turkey Run State Park. Although smaller than neighboring Shades State Park, Turkey Run draws six times as many annual visitors and usually ranks second in visitation only to Brown County State Park in southern Indiana. Trails can be jam-packed on weekends, especially at features in the vicinity of the suspension bridge. At the busiest times, waiting lines form to pass through some areas.

To begin, follow the path from the north side of the nature center and cross the suspension footbridge at Sugar Creek to a Trail 3 marker on the north bank. Turn left (west); climb over a large rock formation and then over a boardwalk. A gravel path leads uphill to a platform overlook above Sugar Creek. The trail descends from here across a footbridge and downhill over stone steps to the Icebox, an eroded opening in the cliff at 0.2 mile.

Continue west along Sugar Creek, walking over a couple of footbridges and through virgin forest featuring gigantic beech and walnut trees. Where Trails 3 and 5 intersect at 0.6 mile, continue straight (west) on Trail 5. Hike along the creek through pine and hemlock stands to where Trails 5 and 9 intersect in a hemlock grove. Go straight (west and north) on Trail 9 to the first of two ravines at 0.9 mile. Falls Canyon, a moss- and fern-covered ravine, follows the creekbed uphill to wooden steps that lead to a ridgetop. At 1.2 miles head downhill on wooden steps to Boulder Canyon. Passing through this canyon requires climbing over large boulders and exposed tree roots.

Stone steps lead out of the canyon to an upland forest. Head right (east) from the canyon across a broad ridge to a wooden staircase with sixty-four steps. At the junction with Trail 5, which comes in from the right (south), stay left (east) and go about 0.1 mile to "140 Steps" at 1.8 miles. This stone staircase descends to the end of Trail 5 at its junction with Trail 3 and a set of ladders at the north end of Bear Hollow. Skip the ladders and stay left (northeast) on Trail 3, passing through a canyon and streambed before climbing over a ridge to the first of two junctions with Trail 10.

Go straight (north and then east) on Trail 3 and cross several footbridges and stairways to the second Trail 10 junction on the left (north). Go straight (east) on Trail 3 to the wooden steps leading into Rocky Hollow Canyon at 2.4 miles and the junction with Trail 4, which breaks off to the left (north). Go right (south) on Trail 3 and proceed through Rocky Hollow, passing the Punch Bowl—a pothole scoured by glacial boulders—on the left (east) side of the trail.

Slip through narrow passages in which you can either walk through the stream or along a sometimes-slippery ledge of sandstone. The canyon becomes wider and the walls steeper. Pass Wedge Rock on the left (east) side of the canyon before you arrive at the end of Trail 3 near the suspension bridge over Sugar Creek at 2.8 miles.

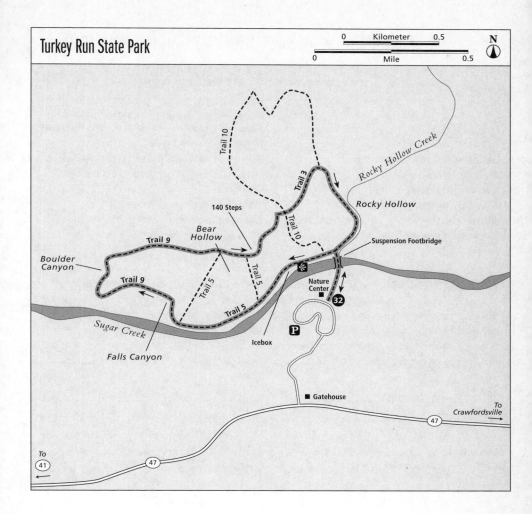

Turkey Run State Park

Kilometer 0.5
Mile 0.5
N

Trail 10
Rocky Hollow Creek
Trail 3
Rocky Hollow
140 Steps
Trail 10
Bear Hollow
Suspension Footbridge
Trail 9
Boulder Canyon
Nature Center
32
Trail 9
Trail 5
Trail 5
Trail 5
Icebox
P
Sugar Creek
Falls Canyon
Gatehouse
To Crawfordsville
47
To 41
47

Miles and Directions

0.0 Begin at the trailhead.

0.1 Cross the suspension bridge and turn left (west) at the Trail 3 marker.

0.2 Reach the Icebox.

0.6 At junction of Trails 3 and 5, continue straight (west) on Trail 5.

0.9 Walk through Falls Canyon.

1.2 Arrive at Boulder Canyon.

1.8 Descend "140 Steps."

2.4 Reach Rocky Hollow Canyon.

2.8 Return to the suspension bridge.

3.0 Arrive back at the trailhead.

33 Big Walnut Creek Nature Preserve: Tall Timbers Trail

This trail skirts a bluff before looping through a broad, deep ravine.

Location: Near Bainbridge, west-central Indiana

Distance: 1.7-mile loop with spur

Elevation change: 90 feet

Approximate hiking time: 1 hour

Difficulty: Moderate

Jurisdiction: The Nature Conservancy; Indiana Department of Natural Resources, Division of Nature Preserves

Fees and permits: No fees or permits required

Maps: USGS Roachdale

Special attractions: Rolling hills, deep ravines, large trees, and a bluff overlooking Big Walnut Creek

Camping: No camping permitted

Trailhead facilities: Gravel parking lot; no drinking water or restrooms

Finding the trailhead: From its intersection with I-465 on the west side of Indianapolis, go west on US 36 for 21 miles to a stoplight in Bainbridge. Turn right (north) and go 1 mile to where the road curves right (east) and becomes Putnam CR 800 North. Go 0.5 mile to where the road curves left (north) and becomes Putnam CR 250 East. Go 1.5 miles, passing North Putnam High School, and turn right (east) at the first gravel road, Putnam CR 950 North. Continue for 1.4 miles, making several left and right turns to reach the trailhead parking lot on the right side of the road.

The Hike

If not for the perseverance of a few folks who recognized the unique qualities of this area, this would be a large reservoir managed by the U.S. Army Corps of Engineers. Instead the few hundred acres that encompass the Tall Timbers Trail form a small part of the larger Big Walnut Nature Preserve, which stretches along this valley dug by the flowing waters of Big Walnut Creek.

The Corps of Engineers had plans to dam up the creek, creating a 1,000-acre impoundment, but conservation and environmental groups fought the idea and gained critical support when the National Park Service designated the valley a National Natural Landmark in 1968.

The designation was granted for a variety of reasons. The area was formed by glacial melt and postglacial water erosion, producing an environment where plant species flourish that are otherwise rare in Indiana—most notably eastern hemlock and Canada yew trees. Some of the largest hemlock trees in the state can be found on north-facing slopes; and large beech, walnut, and oak trees are sprinkled throughout the preserve. Wildflowers are abundant as well, and the area is considered a treasure trove for bird watchers.

Piece by piece, the Nature Conservancy and the IDNR Division of Nature Preserves have worked with private landowners to assemble a 3,000-acre tract known as the Big Walnut Creek Natural Area.

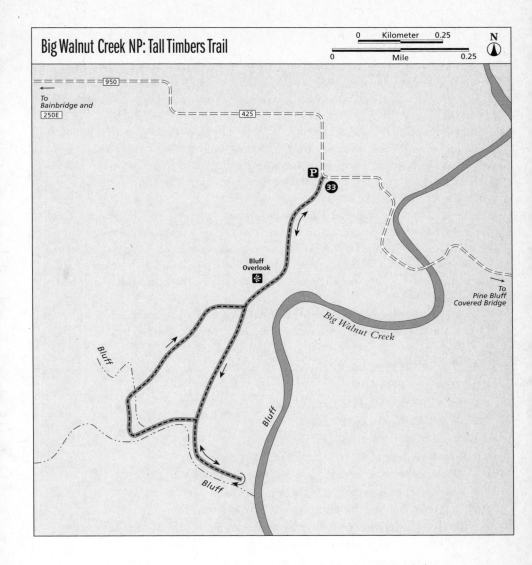

Big Walnut Creek NP: Tall Timbers Trail

0   Kilometer   0.25

0   Mile   0.25

N

950

To
Bainbridge and
250E

425

P

33

Bluff
Overlook

To
Pine Bluff
Covered Bridge

Big Walnut Creek

Bluff

Bluff

Bluff

Bluff

Begin the hike on the south side of the parking lot near a registration box. The trail splits a wide buffer zone between a farm field to the right (west) and the gravel road to the left (east) before reaching a wooden trail post. Turn left (southeast), hike in a short clockwise sweep, and come to a wooden bridge at 0.1 mile. After going over the bridge, turn left (south); cross a utility corridor, reenter the woods, and continue straight (southeast).

At 0.3 mile reach a bluff that provides a dramatic view from 100 feet above Big Walnut Creek. Pause for a moment to soak up the scenery before continuing the hike as the trail curves right (southwest) before coming to a trail juncture with the inbound loop. Go straight (southwest) and come to a sign marking the entrance to Big Walnut Natural Area.

The 120-acre area was preserved for years by Eileen and Ralph Hultz (the log cabin where he was born in 1837 is still on the property) and later given in perpetuity to The Nature Conservancy by Jane H. and William L. Fortune on their 55th wedding anniversary.

Turn left (southeast) and descend to the point of a ridge leading to an overlook of Big Walnut Creek. Turn right (southwest) and continue downhill into a valley seemingly boxed in by bluffs on all sides. Cross a footbridge and two short boardwalks to reach a trail juncture at 0.7 mile. Turn left (southeast) for a short out-and-back spur trail to Big Walnut Creek.

After returning to the trail juncture, go straight (northwest) to a shallow creek whose branches must be crossed three times in the next 0.25 mile. Pick your way across this first creek crossing and turn right (northwest) before bending to the southwest and the second crossing. Descend a staircase at 1.1 miles; cross the creek one last time and climb the forty-five-step wooden staircase on the other side to return to high ground.

Back on the ridgetops, turn left (north) and continue back to the trail juncture with the outbound loop. Turn left (north) and return to the parking lot.

Miles and Directions

0.0 Begin at the trailhead.

0.1 Cross a wooden bridge and turn left (south).

0.3 Reach a bluff overlooking Big Walnut Creek.

0.4 At a trail juncture go straight (southwest).

0.5 Enter the Big Walnut Natural Area and turn left (southeast).

0.7 Reach a trail juncture; turn left (southeast) onto a spur loop to Big Walnut Creek.

0.8 Return to the trail juncture; go straight (northwest) to continue the loop trail.

0.9 Make the first of three creek crossings and turn right (northwest).

1.1 Descend wooden steps; cross the creek and turn left (north) to reach a wooden staircase.

1.3 Return to the first trail juncture; turn left (north).

1.7 Arrive at the parking lot and the trailhead.

Southeast

Diversity is the calling card of this region of the state. Whether it is the rugged hills of Clark State Forest, the marshes and meadows of Muscatatuck National Wildlife Refuge, the waterfalls and deep canyon of Clifty Falls State Park, or the rivers and bluffs of Harrison-Crawford State Forest and O'Bannon Woods State Park, southeast Indiana has a bit of everything.

Much of this area escaped the influences of the last glacial advance, which accounts for the variety in landscape. The most recognizable feature is the Knobstone Escarpment, a steep slope that runs from the Ohio River at a northwest angle for more than 100 miles. The ridge separates two land features—the Norman Upland to the west and the Scottsburg Lowland to the east. The southeast region chapter of this book encompasses both areas.

This chapter includes hikes in several of Indiana's state forests, which were established in the early 1900s to rebuild what had been ravaged during pioneer settlement. The initial intention of the Indiana legislature, which created a State Forestry Board in 1901, seemed to be directed toward ensuring Indiana's place in the timber industry. The goals were twofold—to preserve remnants of Indiana's once-great forests and to explore methods of reforestation. Purdue University in West Lafayette began offering courses in forestry management in 1905, and Charles C. Deam was named the state's first forester in 1909.

Clark State Forest, located southwest of Scottsburg, was established in 1903. It initially covered 2,000 acres but now exceeds 25,000 acres. Harrison-Crawford State Forest, located west of Corydon, was established in 1926 and has 24,000 acres within its boundaries, including O'Bannon Woods. Both forests, along with Jackson-Washington State Forest to the north, are primarily of hardwoods with occasional stands of white pine.

The Indiana Department of Natural Resources Division of Forestry still operates with its original primary mission of managing sustainable forests, but it also has embraced many recreation opportunities, including hiking, camping, hunting, fishing, and horseback riding.

Clifty Falls, outside Madison, was dedicated as a state park in 1920. Five waterfalls splash over the cliffs of the 3-mile-long canyon. The four primary falls—Big Clifty, Little Clifty, Hoffman, and Tunnel Falls—range from 60 to 83 feet high. The exposed limestone and shale through the canyon is among the oldest bedrock in the state—425 million years old.

John Brough, a local railroad company owner, tried to take advantage of the canyon and its access to the Ohio River during the 1850s. Brough attempted to build two tunnels through the canyon for a rail system. It was a financial failure that became known as Brough's Folly.

Muscatatuck National Wildlife Refuge may lack the geographic splendor of Clifty Falls, but it certainly makes up for it in other ways. A variety of wildlife species make the refuge a year-round home, while hundreds of migratory bird species pass through during spring and fall migrations. Whooping cranes have been high-profile visitors in recent years as part of an effort to reintroduce an eastern population of the giant bird that migrates seasonally between nesting sites in Wisconsin and wintering grounds in Florida.

Hikes in this section are presented heading south in a clockwise sweep from Muscatatuck National Wildlife Refuge near Seymour toward the Ohio River.

34 Muscatatuck National Wildlife Refuge

A double loop trail through meadows and along river bottoms.

Location: Near Seymour in Jackson County
Distance: East River Trail, 2.8-mile loop; West River Trail, 3.9-mile loop; hike as described, 5.5-mile double loop
Elevation change: Minimal
Approximate hiking time: 2.5 hours
Difficulty: Easy
Jurisdiction: Muscatatuck National Wildlife Refuge; U.S. Fish & Wildlife Service

Maps: USGS Chestnut Hill; refuge brochure and trail information sheet
Fees and permits: No fees or permits required
Special attractions: Muscatatuck River and Myers Cemetery
Camping: No camping permitted
Trailhead facilities: Small parking lot at the trailhead with restrooms but no drinking water; water available at the visitor center

Finding the trailhead: From I-65 near Seymour, go 2 miles east on US 50 to the Muscatatuck National Wildlife Refuge entrance on the right (south) side of the road. Go 0.5 mile on the main refuge road to the visitor center. From the center go 3 miles south on the main refuge road, passing Richart and Stanfield Lakes, to a gravel parking lot on the right (west) at a T intersection. From the parking lot go south to the T intersection and begin the trail at the gated entrance on an old farm lane.

A nest of young rabbits snuggling together. How many can you count?

The Hike

Muscatatuck is the first national wildlife refuge established in Indiana and one of more than 500 across the country whose purchase were funded by revenue from the sale of federal duck stamps.

Land acquisition at Muscatatuck began in 1966 and encompasses more than 7,800 acres of varied habitat providing sanctuary for an abundance of wildlife. Birds are particularly noteworthy inhabitants, with more than 250 species observed at the refuge, including birds uncommon in Indiana, such as the least bittern and yellow-crowned night heron.

Muscatatuck also has been a stopover for whooping cranes that are part of an effort to restore an eastern migratory flock of the majestic bird. Young "whoopers" have been raised at a national wildlife refuge in Wisconsin and led by ultralight plane through Indiana to another refuge in Florida.

Spring and fall bring other migrating waterfowl to Muscatatuck by the thousands. Sandhill cranes, ospreys, and bald eagles can be seen during the fall. Deer, wild turkeys, rabbits, beavers, muskrats, quail, and raccoons are common; and Muscatatuck was the launch site in recent years of restoration efforts for river otters and trumpeter swans. Another common inhabitant of the refuge is the nonpoisonous copperbelly water snake, so rare nationwide that it has been considered for threatened status by the U.S. Fish & Wildlife Service.

There are eight maintained hiking trails at the refuge, but most are less than 1.0 mile long. The two river trails are the longest and together make a substantial hike through meadows and along the river. Distance and location make both loops the least-traveled trails in the refuge. Both trails can be closed during periods of high water on the Muscatatuck, usually in spring. There are very few markers along either trail.

Start at the gated entrance and follow an old farm lane south for 0.5 mile to the beginning of the East River Trail. It is a wooded pathway at the outset but soon opens into rolling meadows.

At 1.2 miles the trail curls to the south and meanders through a meadow before intersecting with an optional spur to Half-Moon Lake at 1.5 miles. At 1.6 miles pass Myers Cemetery, a small graveyard of the family the settled in this river bottom in the early 1800s. The Myers cabin and barn are located 0.25 mile west of the gated entrance to the river trails.

From the cemetery continue west, crossing a couple of shallow gullies and intermittent streams. The trail parallels the streams at times before coming back to the old farm road at 2.4 miles. Turn left (south) and go 0.1 mile to the start of a clockwise loop of the West River Trail. Unlike the East River Trail, the West River Trail more closely hugs the Muscatatuck River, winding along its banks for a little more than 1.5 miles before turning north to a service road. Turn right on a straight, eastbound stretch that borders the south side of the waterfowl sanctuary for almost 1.0 mile before reaching the old farm road. Turn left (north) and return to the trailhead.

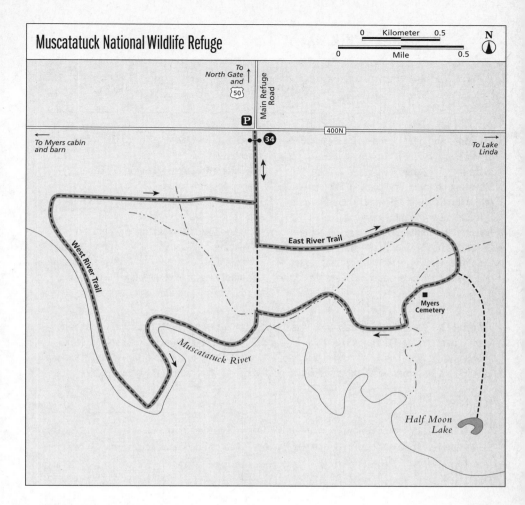

Miles and Directions

0.0   Begin at the trailhead.

0.5   Go left (east) at the East River Trail intersection.

1.5   Reach the optional spur to Half-Moon Lake.

1.6   Pass Myers Cemetery.

2.4   Go left (south) at the old farm road.

2.5   Reach the West River Trail intersection and go right (west).

4.0   Turn right (north) onto service road.

5.0   Reach the old farm road; turn left (north).

5.5   Arrive at the trailhead.

35 Versailles State Park

A loop trail circling upland woods, ravines, and sinkholes along the eastern bluff of Laughery Valley.

Location: Southeast Indiana, 24 miles north of Madison
Distance: 2.25-mile loop
Elevation change: One climb of 80 feet
Approximate hiking time: 1.5 hours
Difficulty: Easy to moderate
Jurisdiction: Indiana Department of Natural Resources, Division of State Parks & Reservoirs
Fees and permits: Park entry fee, higher for out-of-state vehicles; season passes available

Maps: USGS Milan; Versailles State Park brochure
Special attractions: Overlook of Laughery Valley and sinkholes
Camping: Versailles State Park—220 modern campsites; youth tent area
Trailhead facilities: Ample parking and restrooms are available at Oak Grove Shelter, but there is no potable water. Water is available at other locations in the park, including the campgrounds, nature center, and camp store.

Finding the trailhead: Go east from Versailles for 0.8 mile on US 50/IN 129 to the entrance road to the state park. Turn left (north) and drive 0.7 mile to the gatehouse. Go straight for 0.4 mile and turn right (east) toward the campgrounds. Go 0.6 mile to the Oak Grove Shelter parking lot and turn left (northwest). The trailhead is located on the west side of the shelter house.

The Hike

Much of present-day Versailles State Park was marginal farmland when the National Park Service acquired it in the 1930s. The NPS teamed with the Civilian Conservation Corps (CCC) to develop the 5,900-acre property into the Versailles Recreation Demonstration Area before turning it all over to the state of Indiana in 1943.

The second-largest state park, Versailles is largely undeveloped, with much of the facilities centralized around Versailles Lake. Six state nature preserves lie within the park boundaries, but none are easily accessible.

There are three hiking trails in the park, including Trail 1, which is described here. Because there are so few hiking trails in Versailles (which, by the way, Hoosiers pronounce Ver-SALES), they get plenty of use. There is less traffic on this trail because the other two are closer to the restrooms. Day hiking also is permitted on 24 miles of bridle trails and more than 10 miles of mountain bike trails.

Begin the hike by walking west from the parking area toward the Oak Grove Shelter, one of the original contributions constructed by the CCC. Locate the trail marker off the southwest corner of the building near an out-of-service stone drinking fountain. Descend the hill to the south and cross a footbridge, then the park road. On the opposite side of the road, walk up the ravine and then turn east to cross another footbridge.

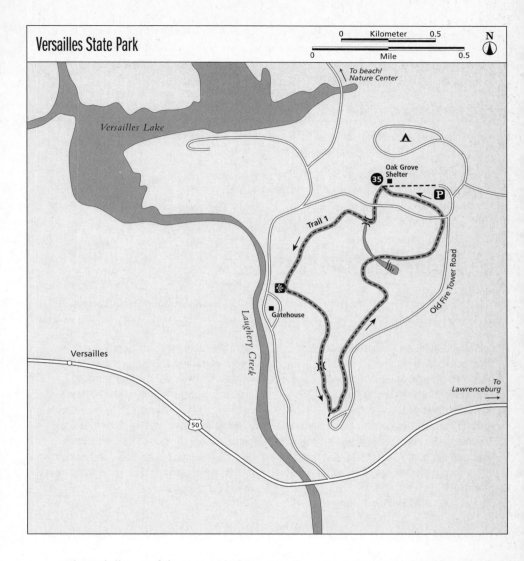

Versailles State Park

To beach/Nature Center

Versailles Lake

Oak Grove Shelter
35

Trail 1

Gatehouse

Laughery Creek

Old Fire Tower Road

Versailles

To Lawrenceburg

50

Hike uphill out of the ravine and turn south again. It is about an 80-foot climb. Once on top of the ridge, begin looking along the left (east) side of the trail for some of the numerous sinkholes that are sprinkled throughout the woods, or look right and soak up the view of Laughery Valley. Laughery, also the name of the creek below and to the west, is a misprint that has endured. The creek actually was named for Col. Archibald Lochry, who was killed with half his Pennsylvania volunteer army during a confrontation with Native Americans in 1781.

Cross over another bridge and head uphill. Reach the southern tip of the trail at 1.2 miles near an access path that leads to a parking area at the end of Old Fire Tower Road. The trail turns north at this point and follows a level course for nearly 0.5 mile before dropping down into a ravine that features a picturesque little water fall. Hike up the other side of the ravine onto a flat area before dropping down once more as the trail intersects the park road. Cross the road, turn left (west) on the trail and follow it for 0.25 mile parallel to the park road to the Oak Grove Shelter.

Miles and Directions

0.0 Begin at the trailhead and go right.

0.7 Reach the Laughery Creek overlook.

1.2 The trail turns north.

2.2 Go straight at the road crossing, and then turn left.

2.25 Arrive back at the trailhead.

36 Clifty Falls State Park

A combination of park trails forming a loop hike through Clifty Falls Canyon.

Location: Southeast Indiana near Madison
Distance: 10.5-mile loop
Elevation change: About 300 feet
Approximate hiking time: 5 hours
Difficulty: Strenuous
Jurisdiction: Indiana Department of Natural Resources, Division of State Parks & Reservoirs
Fees and permits: Park entry fee per vehicle, higher for out-of-state vehicles; season passes available
Maps: USGS Clifty Falls and Madison West;

Clifty Falls State Park brochure
Special attractions: Ohio River overlook; Hoffman, Clifty, Little Clifty, and Tunnel Falls
Camping: Clifty Falls State Park—104 modern campsites, 59 primitive sites; youth tent area
Trailhead facilities: Parking lot and nature center (open 9:00 a.m. to 4:00 p.m. Wednesday through Sunday); restrooms and drinkable water sources available throughout the park at picnic shelter locations

Finding the trailhead: Clifty Falls State Park has gatehouses at the north and south ends. From US 421 in downtown Madison, go 2 miles west on IN 56 to reach the south entrance. From the south gatehouse go 1.1 miles and turn left into the nature center parking lot. To reach the north entrance from US 421 in Madison, go 3.8 miles west on IN 62. From the north gate go 4.2 miles on the main park road and turn right to the nature center parking lot. Trail 1 begins at the south end of the parking lot.

The Hike

Most highlights of Clifty Falls State Park can be seen by combining elements of eight of the park's ten trails. In doing so, you will pass five waterfalls, walk a rock-strewn portion of Clifty Creek, and see the sheer-walled canyon from both above and below.

The canyon is over 300 feet deep and so narrow in places that it is said sunlight can only reach the canyon floor at noon. Because the Trail 2 portion of this hike is along the streambed of Big Clifty Creek, it is a very rugged hike with difficult footing and some steep climbs. Traffic is heaviest around Hoffman, Big Clifty, and Little Clifty Falls, but it is noticeably lighter on Trail 8 along the west rim of the canyon.

Trail access has changed considerably in recent years, partly due to safety factors and partly due to ecological considerations. A staircase at Big Clifty Falls that once was an exit and entry point for Trail 2 no longer exists. But it is still possible to loop through and around the canyon.

Begin hiking at the nature center on Trail 1. Head south toward the Ohio River, coming to an observation tower after at 0.2 mile. The tower provides a spectacular view of the Ohio and the nearby river town of Madison.

From the tower head north on Trail 1 as the trail enters the canyon, hugging a ledge about midway between the top of the canyon and Big Clifty Creek below. The trail narrows and crosses a couple of footbridges over areas wet with water

Big Clifty Creek.

seeping from the shale and limestone that, at 425 million years old, is among the oldest exposed bedrock in the state.

At 0.5 mile Trail 1 joins Trails 2 and 3 at a three-way fork. Take Trail 3, the middle fork, and continue along the ledge toward Hoffman Falls—at 78 feet the third highest of the park's waterfalls. At 0.9 mile an unmarked trail breaks off to the left. Stay right, climbing up a steep grade over stone steps toward the canyon lip. Go east along the ledge for another 0.25 mile and cross a footbridge over Hoffman Branch to connect with Trail 4. The trail turns left (west) along the north side of Hoffman Branch and leads to a wooden walkway and platform that extends over the canyon to provide a clear view of Hoffman Falls.

Continue away from the falls on Trail 4 with the canyon to the left of the trail. At 1.5 miles Trail 4 cuts right (north), but go left (south) on a downhill path marked to Trail 2. This link is steep—a 150-foot drop to the canyon floor in the span of about 0.1 mile.

At the bottom of the canyon, turn right (north) to begin a rugged 1.5-mile stretch over loose rocks and running water in Clifty Creek to reach the base of Big Clifty Falls. About two-thirds of the way there, you will first pass Trail 5's entry point and then Dean's Branch, both on the right (east) side of Clifty Creek.

The best sign that the falls are getting closer is the size of the rocks in the stream. They are much bigger; some are as big as a compact car. Just before you reach Big Clifty, a branch of Little Clifty Creek breaks off to the right (east). Stay left to get a look at Big Clifty Falls from below.

Backtrack along Clifty Creek for 0.5 mile to the Trail 5 juncture. Turn left (east) and follow the switchback uphill toward Oak Grove Shelter. Turn left (northeast) before reaching the shelter and continue on Trail 5 to an overlook of Tunnel Falls, the tallest falls in the park at 83 feet. From there turn left to reach the main park road. Turn left (northeast) and walk the roadway in a counterclockwise sweep for 0.75 mile to the Hickory Grove parking area and the start of Trail 6.

At 5.3 miles connect with Trail 7. Go left for a spectacular overlook of Little Clifty and Big Clifty Falls before taking a 100-yard jaunt to the Clifty Shelter Picnic Area. The shelter house is the last water source before heading out on the return leg to the nature center.

Turn left on the paved road and follow it north toward the gatehouse to pick up Trail 8, which is in a clearing west of the gatehouse at 6.0 miles. Cross Big Clifty Creek below a bridge on IN 62 and turn southward as the trail hugs the west rim of the canyon for the next 4.5 miles.

Before reaching Big Clifty Falls, look across to the east side of the creek to see an abandoned stone building. This pumphouse, built by the Civilian Conservation Corps (CCC) nearly seventy years ago, created a reservoir for a water supply for the CCC during their work to develop the park. The building thus has historical significance but cannot be restored, since it now rests in a state nature preserve that encompasses the area north of the falls.

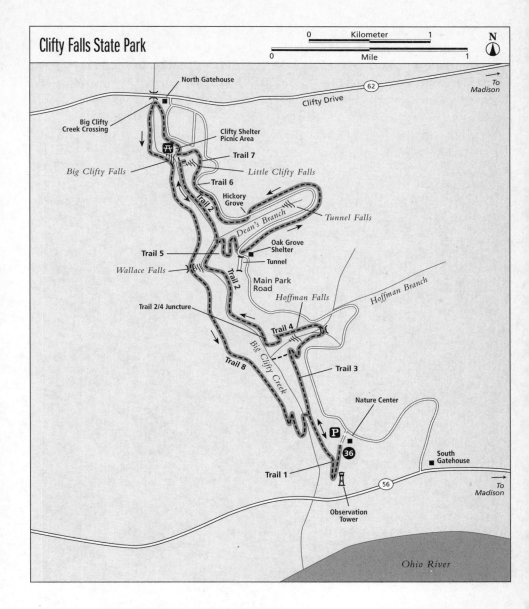

0   Kilometer   1

0   Mile   1

N

North Gatehouse

62

To
Madison

Clifty Drive

Big Clifty
Creek Crossing

Clifty Shelter
Picnic Area

Trail 7

Big Clifty Falls

Little Clifty Falls

Trail 6

Hickory
Grove

Trail 2

Dean's Branch

Tunnel Falls

Oak Grove
Shelter

Trail 5

Tunnel

Wallace Falls

Trail 2

Main Park
Road

Hoffman Falls

Hoffman Branch

Trail 2/4 Juncture

Trail 4

Trail 8

Big Clifty Creek

Trail 3

Nature Center

P

36

South
Gatehouse

Trail 1

56

To
Madison

Observation
Tower

Ohio River

The west-rim hike begins on a relatively flat grade but is punctuated by occasional cuts for small streams that spill and tumble down the canyon walls. Signs stating NO HIKERS BEYOND THIS POINT bear witness to the dangers of getting too close to the edge. Continue to ridge-hop to an intersecting trail at 7.0 miles that goes left (east) and down to the canyon floor. Stay straight (south), hugging the west rim, crossing a footbridge, and continuing south over humps and ridges of the canyon rim.

The trail begins to slide easily down from the rim and reaches a switchback at 9.5 miles that leads down to Big Clifty Creek. At 9.9 miles look for a sign hung across the creek by wire pointing to Trails 1, 2, and 8. Follow Trail 2 and begin the climb on the east side of the canyon. When Trail 2 joins Trail 1 at 10.0 miles, turn right (south) and continue uphill past the observation tower to the nature center parking lot.

Hikers under the Big Clifty Falls at Clifty Falls State Park. Big Clifty is one of five major falls in the park.

Miles and Directions

0.0 Begin at the trailhead.

0.2 Reach the Ohio River observation tower.

0.5 At the intersection of Trails 1, 2, and 3, take Trail 3 (the middle fork).

0.9 An unmarked trail goes left; turn right.

1.4 Reach the Hoffman Falls overlook.

1.5 Turn left at the to Trail 2 marker.

3.0 Arrive at Big Clifty Falls; backtrack on Trail 2.

3.5 Reach the juncture with Trail 5; turn left (east).

4.0 Arrive at the Tunnel Falls overlook; go to the park road and turn left (northeast).

4.8 Reach the Hickory Grove parking area and Trail 6 trailhead.

5.3 Join Trail 7 to reach overlooks for Big Clifty and Little Clifty Falls; go north toward park's north gatehouse to join Trail 8.

6.0 Trail 8 begins west of the park's north gatehouse.

7.0 An unmarked trail goes left; stay straight (south).

9.5 Make a switchback descent to Big Clifty Creek.

9.9 Reach a marker for Trails 1, 2, and 8 over the creek; follow Trail 2.

10.0 Trail 2 joins Trails 1 and 3; turn right onto Trail 1.

10.5 Arrive back at the trailhead.

37 Charlestown State Park

A loop trail through dense floodplain forest along exposed rock outcroppings above Fourteenmile Creek.

Location: Southeast Indiana on the Ohio River

Distance: 2.2-mile loop

Elevation change: Several elevation changes but never more than about 100 feet from the trail's beginning elevation

Approximate hiking time: 1.5 hours

Difficulty: Moderate to strenuous

Jurisdiction: Indiana Department of Natural Resources, Division of State Parks & Reservoirs

Fees and permits: Park entry fee, higher for out-of-state vehicles; season passes available

Maps: USGS Charlestown; Charlestown State Park brochure

Special attractions: Fourteenmile Creek

Camping: Charlestown State Park—192 campsites, from full hookups to modern

Trailhead facilities: Water pumps located near the picnic shelters

Finding the trailhead: From the Henryville exit on I-65, go east 9.5 miles on IN 160 to intersection with IN 403. Turn right (southeast) and go 0.8 mile to IN 62. Turn left (northeast) and go 1.1 miles to the Charlestown State Park entrance on the right (south). From the park gatehouse go 0.1 mile to a T intersection. Turn left (northeast) and go 1.1 miles to the Trail 1 parking lot.

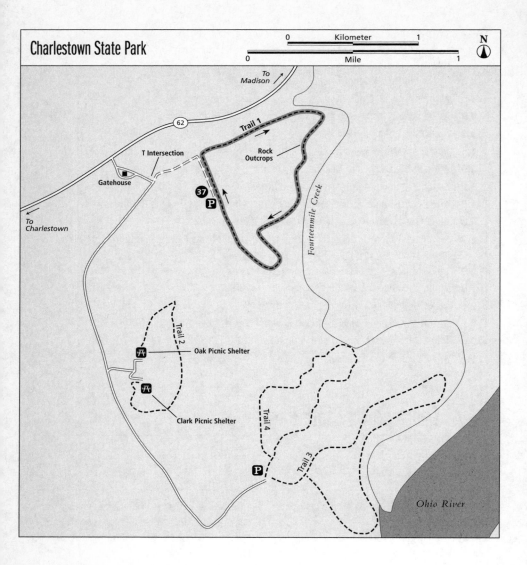

0   Kilometer   1

0   Mile   1

N

To Madison

62

Trail 1

Rock Outcrops

T Intersection

Gatehouse

37

To Charlestown

Fourteenmile Creek

Trail 2

Oak Picnic Shelter

Clark Picnic Shelter

Trail 4

Trail 3

Ohio River

The Hike

Established in 1996, this park has begun to catch on in popularity with the recent addition of modern campgrounds (including full RV hookups at sixty sites) and an award-winning boat ramp that provides access to the Ohio River.

The 5,100-acre park was carved from the larger Indiana Army Ammunition Plant (15,000 acres) that operated here from 1940 until closing in 1995. The area was farmed extensively prior to ownership by the Army, which reforested the hills and valleys during its occupancy.

The beginning leg of this trail is less than impressive—a 0.25-mile jaunt back along the gravel entry road to the parking lot, followed by a slightly longer walk on an old service road as it descends toward Fourteenmile Creek. Depending on water levels in the creek, you are apt to catch sight of it before the trail takes a slow turn to the right (south). The creek winds through an unglaciated valley to the Ohio River. Locks and dams that control the Ohio River affect Fourteenmile Creek, giving it the appearance of a narrow lake rather than a flowing stream.

Once the turn is made at 0.9 mile, it is easy to see why the trail builders came this direction. The trail climbs along a narrower path, crosses a footbridge, and meanders through the high ground past moss-covered rock abutments. As you work your way up and down the east-facing slope of Fourteenmile Creek's valley, you'll pass several rock slabs that have sheared off the cliff and tumbled toward the creek. This can be the trickiest part of the trail during wet weather, which can transform the rich soil into slippery muck.

The trail curves southwest away from the creek, crossing another creek via a footbridge near the 1.5-mile mark in the midst of a cedar thicket. Follow the trail as it swings back to the southeast below the ridgetop to a point overlooking Fourteenmile Creek. Here the trail curves back to the northwest on a 100-foot uphill climb over the next 0.25 mile.

The trail levels off at the 1.8-mile mark as it connects with the old service road. Look for the scattered concrete pilings that are remnants of the Army era. It is a little more than 0.25 mile along a level grade to the Trail 1 parking lot.

Options

There are three other trails in the park. The most noteworthy is Trail 3, which features a steep, 250-foot descent on a gravel service road to Fourteenmile Creek. The road once led to a footbridge that provided access to Rose Island, where an amusement park operated until a flood destroyed it and the bridge in 1937. A small waterfall, rock outcroppings, and views of Fourteenmile Creek highlight the middle section of this trail before concluding with a gradual ascent to the parking lot.

Miles and Directions

0.0 Begin at the trailhead and go left.

0.2 Make a right turn from gravel road onto old service road.

0.9 Leave the service road.

1.3 Pass rock outcrops.

1.5 Cross a footbridge over the creek.

1.8 Reconnect to the service road; go straight.

2.2 Arrive back at the trailhead.

38 Adventure Hiking Trail

A long-distance loop trail along forested river bluffs, ravines, sinkholes, and caves.

Location: O'Bannon Woods State Park, southeast Indiana between Corydon and Leavenworth

Distance: 23.0-mile loop

Elevation change: Eight elevation increases of more than 200 feet, including two of 300 feet or more

Approximate hiking time: Three days

Difficulty: Strenuous

Jurisdiction: Indiana Department of Natural Resources, Division of State Parks & Reservoirs and Division of Outdoor Recreation

Fees and permits: Park entry fee, higher for out-of-state vehicles; season passes available

Maps: USGS Leavenworth and Corydon West; Indiana State Forest brochure

Special attractions: Bluffs overlooking Ohio River, Blue River, and Indian Creek; four overnight shelters

Camping: O'Bannon Woods State Park—386 campsites, ranging from primitive to modern; youth tent area. Backpackers can camp along the trail, which has four overnight shelters.

Trailhead facilities: The Adventure Hiking Trail can be accessed at several spots, but the preferred starting location is the large parking lot at the Ohio River Picnic Area. There is no water supply at the picnic area, but there are pit toilets. Water is available in the O'Bannon Woods campgrounds and at other locations. It can be scarce along the trail, though.

Finding the trailhead: Go west 6.8 miles on IN 62 from the IN 135 intersection in Corydon. Turn left (south) onto Indiana 462 and follow it south for 3 miles to gatehouse. Go another 0.5 mile to the second paved road; turn left (southwest) and follow the main road past the nature center, group camp, and Potato Run Church. Go 0.9 mile past the church to the Pioneer Cabin picnic shelter on the left (east) side of the road. Post 1 for the Adventure Hiking Trail is located here. Additional parking is available at the Ohio River and Blue River Picnic Areas farther down the road to the southwest.

The Hike

The Adventure Hiking Trail, or AHT, keeps getting shorter, but it remains one of the premier long–distance trails in the state. Some sources still list it at 40 miles long, others at 27 to 30 miles, but the AHT now measures just over 23 miles and is still under revision. Check with the property office, nature center, or gatehouse for updates.

The AHT has been shortened to eliminate dangerous crossovers of IN 62, and the entire trail now lies south of the highway in the 24,000-acre complex of Harrison-Crawford State Forest and O'Bannon Woods State Park. The terrain consists of narrow ridgetops alternating with deep ravines, coupled with breathtaking views from bluffs 300 to 400 feet above the Ohio River and two of its tributaries—Blue River and Indian Creek.

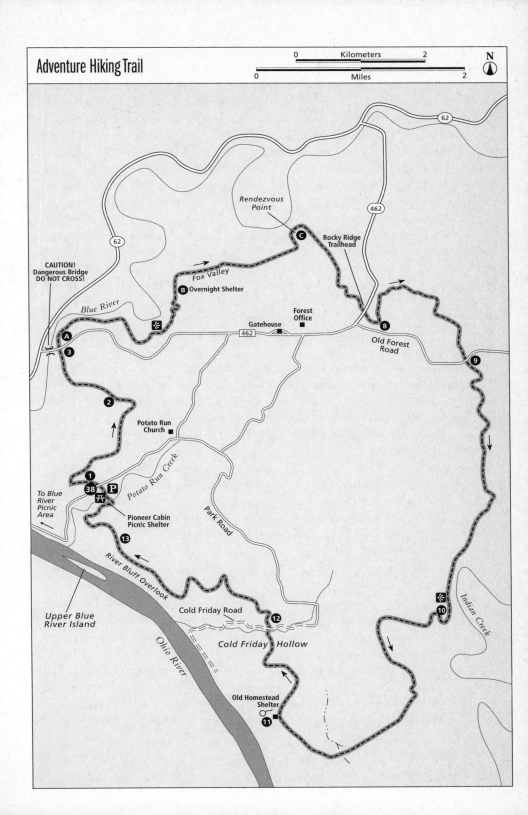

The AHT also features several overnight shelter houses along the way plus the option of primitive camping along the trail, as long as camp is made on public land, is at least 1 mile from all roads and recreation areas, and cannot be seen from the trail.

With twelve climbs between 150 and 300 feet, the AHT typically takes three days to complete. It is marked with posts painted green and white and with numbers and letters designating specific locations along the trail. The trail is definitely rugged, with numerous steep climbs. Once poorly marked and confusing to follow, the AHT has benefited from trail maintenance in recent years. Traffic is usually highest around the Pioneer Cabin and the O'Bannon Woods campground, but overall the AHT gets a modest amount of use.

The trail begins at the Pioneer Cabin, about 0.5 mile northeast of the Ohio River Picnic Area. Locate post 1 near the cabin and turn left (northwest) to begin the first uphill challenge—a 250-foot climb to a knob. Atop the knob, turn right (northeast) and follow the saddles that connect it to two more knobs.

At post 2—1.6 miles from post 1—turn right to reach the O'Bannon Woods campground or continue on a northwest course down a ravine to connect with an old road that leads to post 3. Previously this is where the AHT crossed the Blue River via an iron bridge. The bridge fell into disrepair, providing another reason for closing off the north section of the trail.

Instead the AHT continues for about 0.75 mile along the east bank of the Blue River through a state wildlife management area. Head right (southeast) into a ravine and go uphill to follow a bluff overlooking a bend in the Blue River. Descend from the bluff on a steep grade to cross a creek and reach an old barn that now serves as an overnight shelter option. At only 4.8 miles from the starting point, it is an unlikely place to stop on the first day.

Continue through Fox Valley, aptly named for its abundant red fox population. The valley once was a thriving farm. At post C, 7.4 miles into the trail, the AHT reaches the Rendezvous Point—a spot where hikers used to be able to turn left (north) and hike about 8.0 miles to Wyandotte Caves. All but 2.0 miles of that leg, however, are north of IN 62 and currently closed to hikers.

Turn right (south) at post C and follow a ridgeline for 1.2 miles to a gravel parking lot at IN 462 (8.6 miles). A sign marks the spot as the Rocky Ridge trailhead. Cross the highway to post 8.

There are two ravine crossings in the 1.6 miles between posts 8 and 9. The first is a drop of more than 200 feet, followed by a climb of about 250 feet, then a drop of 180 feet and a climb of 160 feet. Cross an old forest road just before reaching post 9 at 10.2 miles.

The next 3.2 miles to post 10 travel through a wildlife management area. The manipulated clearings and small ponds attract white-tailed deer, ruffed grouse, and wild turkeys. To improve chances of seeing wildlife, approach these areas quietly. The last 1.5 miles before post 10 traverse a ridgetop that leads to a sheer bluff overlooking

Indian Creek. The 300-foot drop is a good place to see turkey vultures and hawks as they soar near the cliff.

A trailside shelter is located at post 10 (13.4 miles). From there the trail descends gradually before skirting the high side of a ravine and passing several sinkholes. From a high knob descend a wide ravine on a southeast course and cross a creek before embarking on a climb of nearly 300 feet to post 11 and the Old Homestead Shelter. The shelter is located on a broad plateau at 17.8 miles and is built on the foundation of an 1860s–era log cabin, complete with the original chimney. Water usually can be obtained from a nearby spring.

Go northeast from post 11 for almost 0.5 mile before turning northwest to descend a broad ridge point into Cold Friday Hollow. Cross a creek and old Cold Friday Road in the hollow to reach a demanding stretch of the trail—three ridge and two ravine crossings in the span of just over 1.5 miles. The last climb curls southwest around a ridge point and leads to the most scenic stretch of the AHT along a steep bluff overlooking the Ohio River.

The last overnight shelter is located here at post 13 (22.2 miles) and is the place to be in springtime when bald eagles frequent Upper Blue River Island, almost 400 feet below. From post 13 go downhill 0.8 miles to the Pioneer Cabin, which is beyond the Potato Run Creek crossing.

Miles and Directions

0.0   Begin at the trailhead; turn left at post 1.

1.6   Reach post 2 and go straight to continue the trail; turn right to reach O'Bannon Woods State Park campground.

2.8   Go right at post 3. *Do not cross the bridge.*

4.8   Reach an overnight shelter at post B.

7.4   Turn right at post C.

8.6   Reach post 8 and the junction with IN 462.

10.2   Arrive at post 9 and the junction with an old forest road.

13.4   Reach post 10 and the Indian Creek overlook shelter.

17.8   The Old Homestead Shelter is at post 11.

19.1   Go straight at post 12 and the junction with Cold Friday Road.

22.2   The Ohio River Shelter is at post 13.

23.0   Reach post 1 and the Pioneer Cabin Picnic Shelter at the trailhead end.

39 Shaw Lake Loop

A trail over rugged, hilly terrain of Clark State Forest.

Location: Near Henryville in southeast Indiana
Distance: 5.5-mile loop, with optional 3.3-mile wildlife spur
Elevation change: Two steep climbs over 250 feet
Approximate hiking time: 4 hours
Difficulty: Strenuous
Jurisdiction: Indiana Department of Natural Resources, Division of Forestry

Maps: USGS Henryville; Clark State Forest brochure
Fees and permits: No fees or permits required
Special attractions: High knob vistas
Camping: No camping permitted on the trail; 45 primitive campsites near the Clark State Forest office
Trailhead facilities: Parking lot only at trailhead; no restrooms or drinking water available

Finding the trailhead: From the Clark State Forest main entrance on US 31 on the north side of Henryville, go 0.5 mile to Brownstown Road and turn left (west). Go 3.4 miles, passing under I-65, to the Shaw Lake parking lot on the right (north) side of the road. The trail begins in the northwest corner of the parking lot at a red metal gate.

The Hike

Established in 1903, Clark State Forest is the oldest in the Indiana system. Portions of the original forest are on land granted to General George Rogers Clark and his soldiers for their service during the Revolutionary War. Originally encompassing a mere 2,000 acres, Clark State Forest now covers more than 25,000 acres and is Indiana's largest state forest. The property was used as an experimental forest in its early years.

The forest has nine trails designated for horseback riding, but hikers are welcome to use them too. Shaw Lake is typical of the trail system, with scenic vistas, narrow backbones, and steep hills. This is an easy trail to follow, but because it is shared with equestrians, the footing can be loose on steep slopes and muddy in low areas. It is definitely not a hike to take in wet conditions.

To begin the hike, pass the gate and follow a path of crushed stone less than 0.1 mile to a trail juncture that forms the beginning and end points of the loop. Take the left (north) fork, which leads over a ridgetop and downhill to another juncture at 0.2 mile. Here the left fork is marked with a green sign that directs horse traffic around the dam that forms Shaw Lake. Take the right fork down to the lake and cross over the dam to the northwest corner of the lake at 0.5 mile.

Reenter the forest and hike up and over a series of ridges as the trail turns northeast. In addition to green markers that help point the way, look for occasional green paint blazes on trees. At 1.2 miles come to another split in the trail. Go right (northeast), following the green markers as the trail descends into and out of two

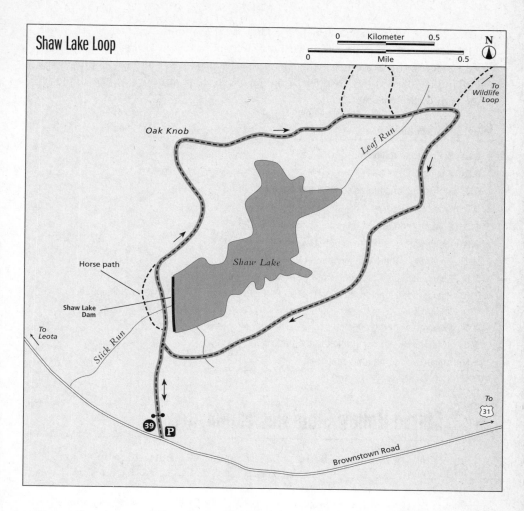

deep gullies, both of which can be wet and muddy. From here the hiking really gets tough, beginning with a steep climb to a narrow ridge. The trail stays suspended along the ridgetop, with sharp slopes dropping off on either side. Remember to follow the green trail markers or green blazes on trees.

After climbing to Oak Knob at 1.6 miles, the trail splits once more at 2.2 miles. The left fork leads through an optional 3.3-mile wildlife management unit. Stay to the right (south) and hike down a steep incline to where the trail crosses Leaf Run at 2.5 miles. Head uphill at a steep angle to another high knob. At 3.0 miles the main trail veers to the south; the optional 3.3-mile Wildlife Loop branches off to the left (northeast).

Stay on the main trail, walking south along a narrow ridgetop that dips and rises for another mile or so. At 4.5 miles begin an extremely sharp descent where the footing can be loose dirt and stone, depending on the amount of recent horse traffic. At the bottom of the hill, cross a rocky stretch and a stream before climbing over a small ridge and picking up a wider path that leads back to the intersection at the beginning leg of the loop. Turn left at the intersection at 5.3 miles; return along the stone path to the parking lot.

Miles and Directions

0.0 Begin at the trailhead.

0.1 Bear left at the trail fork.

0.2 At the trail juncture go straight over the dam.

0.5 Cross dam.

1.2 Go right (northeast) at the trail juncture.

1.6 Reach Oak Knob; turn right (east) and go downhill.

2.2 Go straight at the trail juncture at the knob.

2.5 Reach the Leaf Run creek crossing and go straight.

3.0 Reach a trail juncture at a knob and veer right. (**Option:** The 3.3-mile wildlife spur is to the left.)

4.5 Descend from the ridgetop.

5.3 At the trail juncture, turn left to the parking lot.

5.5 Arrive back at the trailhead.

40 Starve Hollow State Recreation Area

A combination of three short trails, including rugged section to ridgetop vistas.

Location: South of Brownstown in Jackson County

Distance: 4.6 miles of interconnecting loops

Elevation change: 315-foot difference from Starve Hollow Lake to the top of the Vista Trail

Approximate hiking time: 3 hours

Difficulty: Moderate to strenuous

Jurisdiction: Indiana Department of Natural Resources, Division of Forestry

Fees and permits: Entry fee, higher for out-of-state vehicles; season passes available

Maps: USGS Vallonia; Starve Hollow State Recreation Area brochure

Special attractions: Interpretive nature trail, Starve Hollow vistas

Camping: Starve Hollow State Recreation Area—168 individual campsites, from nonelectric to full RV hookups

Trailhead facilities: Restrooms and water located near the campground gatehouse and between the campgrounds near the trailhead kiosk

Finding the trailhead: From its intersection with US 50 on the west side of Brownstown, go 2.9 miles south on IN 135. Turn left onto Jackson CR 300 West (also known as Lake Road) and go south 2.3 miles to the Starve Hollow State Recreation Area entrance on the left (east). Enter through the first gatehouse and go to the campground gatehouse (second gatehouse). Noncampers must park in the lot next to this gatehouse and walk from there to the trailhead.

The Hike

Starve Hollow State Recreation Area is carved out of Jackson-Washington State Forest, an 18,000-acre property noted for its "knobby" ridges. Two other DNR operations—Driftwood Fish Hatchery and Vallonia Nursery—are located in the valley below the high ridges of the Knobstone Escarpment. This hike features one of the knobs typical of this natural feature.

The first leg of this route, which is an interpretive nature trail, gets most of the traffic. The Lakeshore Loop (marked by yellow blazes) can be muddy and wet at times, but the gravel fire lane provides an alternate route. The Vista Trail is the least traveled of the three but is clearly marked with blue blazes.

The hike has a slow start due to the location of the trailhead in the campground. From the parking lot trek east through the electric campground to a boat ramp for Starve Hollow Lake, a 145-acre reservoir constructed in 1938. Turn left (north) at the

A scenic overlook on the Vista Trail offers an almost unobstructed view of Starve Hollow Lake.

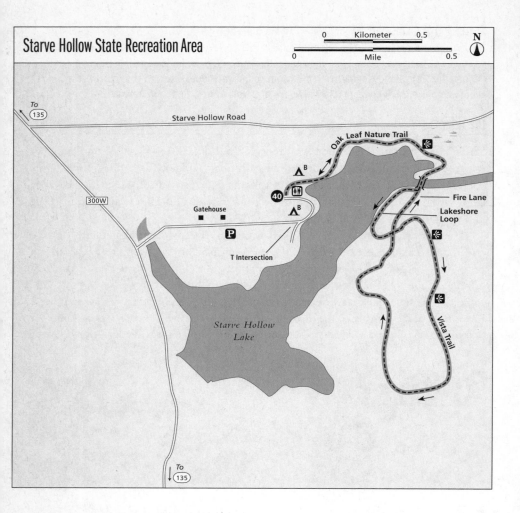

Kilometer

Mile

Starve Hollow Road

Oak Leaf Nature Trail

Fire Lane

Lakeshore
Loop

Gatehouse

T Intersection

*Starve Hollow
Lake*

Vista Trail

To 135

To 135

300W

40

B

B

T intersection and follow the paved road as it goes north and then curves west to a brick restroom building (Comfort Station No. 2). Turn right (north) at the building and follow the paved road to the nonelectric campground, where the trailhead kiosk is located adjacent to a lake dock near Campsites 301 and 303. All hiking options begin here.

What follows is a description of the three trails—Oak Leaf Nature Trail, Lakeshore Loop, and Vista Trail—combined to create one hike. The Oak Leaf segment is an interpretive trail with a brochure that identifies numbered markers for plants or trees such as sumac, big-tooth aspen, club moss, red pine, persimmon, bald cypress, horsetail (or scouring rush), red cedar, sycamore, tulip poplar, and beech. Just past the second footbridge is a viewing platform for a woodland marsh, which previously was used to raise northern pike for the lake. A third footbridge at 0.7 mile crosses one of the creeks that feed the lake. Link with the Lakeshore Loop at this point.

The loop has two possible routes, both marked by yellow blazes. Follow the right (southwest) fork, which hugs the lakeshore while passing up and over several finger-like ridges until turning uphill to meet a fire lane. Cross the lane to a long wooden bench and turn left (north) to follow the blue-marked Vista Trail through a mature hardwood forest. A very steep climb covers the 315-foot elevation difference from the lakeshore to the top of the ridge at 1.7 miles and one of two vistas or overlooks. The trail bends south from here and follows a ridgeline that offers occasional glimpses of Starve Hollow Lake before coming to a nearly unobstructed view near the south tip at 2.0 miles. The trail makes a sharp descent from here into a ravine where streams run intermittently, depending on rainfall. Hike through this area, which features a continual series of small fingerlike ridges and occasional stream crossings to return to the end of the Vista Trail at the wooden bench at 3.2 miles.

Either retrace your steps along the lakeshore or turn right (north) and follow the fire lane downhill to the footbridge and the end of the Lakeshore Loop at 3.9 miles. Walk back over the Oak Leaf Trail to the trailhead at 4.6 miles.

Miles and Directions

0.0 Begin at the trailhead.

0.7 Cross the third footbridge; bear right onto the Lakeshore Loop.

1.4 Reach the intersection of Lakeshore Loop and Vista Trail; cross road and turn left.

1.7 Turn right (south) on the Vista Trail ridgetop.

2.0 At the south vista go downhill.

3.2 The Vista Trail ends; rejoin Lakeshore Loop.

3.9 Lakeshore Loop ends; rejoin Oak Leaf Trail.

4.6 Arrive back at the campground gatehouse and the trailhead.

41 Knob Lake Trail

A loop hike, with a linear spur near the finish, that includes climbs up some of the highest hills in the Jackson-Washington State Forest.

Location: East of Brownstown, south-central Indiana

Distance: 4.3-mile loop with spur

Elevation change: Difference of 345 feet between trail's low and high spots

Approximate hiking time: 3 hours

Difficulty: Strenuous

Jurisdiction: Indiana Department of Natural Resources, Division of Forestry

Maps: USGS Tampico, Vallonia, and Seymour; Jackson-Washington State Forest brochure

Fees and permits: No fees or permits required

Special attractions: High Point Knob, Old Tower Site, Pinnacle Peak

Camping: Knob Lake Campground—54 primitive sites

Trailhead facilities: Pit toilets and drinking water available in the Knob Lake Campground

Finding the trailhead: From its intersection with US 50 in Brownstown, go 2 miles east on IN 250 to the Knob Lake turnoff. Turn left (northeast) off IN 250 and follow the paved road. Pass the forest office and Knob Lake and continue past the Museum Shelterhouse (sitting on a hill above the lake) to a parking lot below the CCC playground and Oven Shelter. Park in the lot and walk up the stone steps to the Oven Shelter. Walk to the south end of the playground to begin the trail.

The Hike

This hike begins at a rather casual pace, but the last 3.0 miles are as challenging as it gets, with a string of high, round hills—or knobs—connected together like a backbone. The Trail 1 portion gets more traffic than Trails 2 and 3, largely because of the attraction of Pinnacle Peak. All trails are well maintained, well marked, and easy to follow.

Begin at the Oven Shelter in the CCC playground and picnic area built by the Civilian Conservation Corps and placed on the National Register of Historic Places in 1997. Go to the southeast corner of the picnic area and continue along a wide gravel path until you reach the first trail marker—a brown plastic post. Cross a stone bridge at the north end of Knob Lake and turn right at the Trail 3 marker. The trail curves to the right and begins to climb nearly 100 feet to a ridge that runs southwest, gradually descending to a youth camp area.

At the camp take a left turn onto the gravel road and follow it around to a service area at 1.0 mile before turning left at a Trail 2 marker. This is a transition point from the end of Trail 3 and the south terminus of Trail 2. Walk a short distance to the first Trail 2 marker and head northeast up a ravine along a meandering stream. Crisscross from one side of the stream to the other several times before turning away from the stream at 1.5 miles to begin the toughest part of the hike.

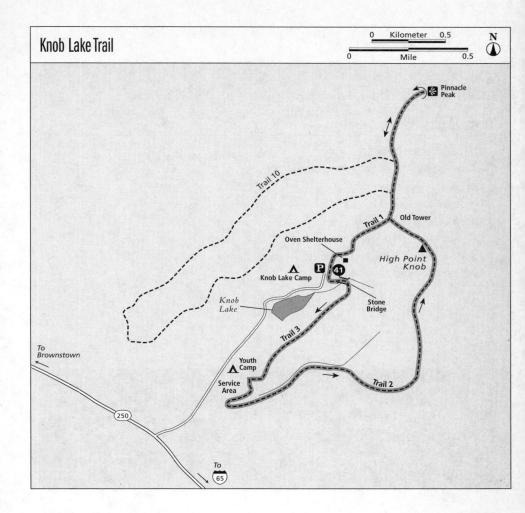

Knob Lake Trail

0   Kilometer   0.5

0   Mile   0.5

N

Pinnacle Peak

Trail 10

Trail 1

Old Tower

Oven Shelterhouse

High Point Knob

Knob Lake Camp

41

Knob Lake

Stone Bridge

Trail 3

To Brownstown

Youth Camp

Service Area

Trail 2

250

To 65

What starts as a gradual climb turns into a demanding scramble that rises more than 250 feet over the next 0.5 mile to a knob that is not the highest on the hike but is a pretty good warm-up. Over the next mile, hike a series of six knobs, the second one, appropriately name High Point, at 2.5 miles. It is followed by the Old Tower Site at 2.7 miles, which is marked by the concrete footings of an old fire tower that was torn down years ago.

Turn right (north) from the Old Tower Site and proceed north, now on Trail 1, passing two points that intersect another trail (Trail 10). After the second intersection, skirt the east side of a knob and walk along a ledge that leads to Pinnacle Peak, an exposed face of loose rock that provides a spectacular scenic view to the south and east. From Pinnacle Peak (3.3 miles) backtrack to Old Tower Site and turn right (southwest), descending a steep grade that eventually levels off before returning to the CCC playground and picnic area.

Options

Additional trails, including interpretive trails, are available in the area.

Miles and Directions

0.0 Begin at the trailhead.

0.7 Pass youth camp; turn left onto gravel road.

1.0 Reach the service area.

1.5 Leave stream and begin to climb.

2.5 Reach High Point Knob.

2.7 Arrive at Old Tower Knob.

3.3 Reach Pinnacle Peak; backtrack to Old Tower Site and turn right (southwest).

4.3 Arrive back at the trailhead.

Trees frame High Point, the highest of several knob-like hills that are climbed on the rugged Knob Lake Trail.

Hill Country

Time has not stood still in the picturesque Hill Country of south-central Indiana, but in many ways the region and its residents have not completely outgrown the pioneer lifestyle. Instead they have capitalized on it.

The sleepy Brown County town of Nashville has been a tourist mecca since the 1930s because of its craft shops and artist galleries. An estimated four million visitors clog its streets each year in search of antiques, collectables, or something that simply looks old or handmade.

The area's greatest ambassador was a cartoon character—Abe Martin. The creation of Indianapolis newspaperman and humorist Kin Hubbard, Martin spun folksy wisdom about life in fictional "Bloom Center" and its odd assortment of residents. "It ain't a bad plan to keep still occasionally, even when you know what you're talking about," is one of the 16,000 sayings attributed to Abe Martin. The lodge at nearby Brown County State Park is named for the popular cartoon character.

The park is the crown jewel of the state system. At approximately 16,000 acres it is Indiana's largest state park and annually draws 1.5 million visitors, many who come to enjoy the autumn colors of the hardwood forest. The park and the neighboring town of Nashville are often favorably compared to the Great Smoky Mountains National Park and Gatlinburg, Tennessee. Authentic log cabin homes are a common sight, and colorful place names are plentiful—Graveyard Hollow, Deadman Hollow, Gnaw Bone, Weed Patch Hill, Hesitation Point, Scarce O'Fat Ridge, and Greasy Creek, to name a few.

Spared the forces of the last great glacier, the region is noted as much for its deep valleys and ravines as it is for rolling hills. Stripped of native timber more than a century ago, the land became an affordable dream for those hoping to carve out an existence on small farms. The thin, rocky soil, coupled with the highly erodible terrain, proved unsuitable for agriculture, however, and most of the pioneer farms failed during the Great Depression.

The state acquired approximately 40,000 acres of abandoned farmland in 1929 and with it established Brown County State Park and Morgan-Monroe State Forest. Yellowwood State Forest was added to the picture in 1947 when federal land was deeded to the state.

The northern boundary of the Hoosier National Forest abuts the three state properties, creating a massive block of public land available for outdoor recreation opportunities. Farther south is Spring Mill State Park, noted for its karst cave topography. The area is riddled with sinkholes and caves.

Hikes in this section are presented in a clockwise sweep, heading north from Bloomington.

42 Morgan-Monroe State Forest: Low Gap Trail

A loop trail covering steep, forested ridges, ravines, creeks, and the Backcountry Area of Morgan–Monroe State Forest.

Location: Midway between Bloomington and Martinsville in south-central Indiana
Distance: 10.0-mile loop; optional 1.0-mile round-trip spur to Draper Cabin
Elevation change: Several changes of 200 to 270 feet from ridgetops to ravines and back
Approximate hiking time: 7 hours or overnight backpack
Difficulty: Strenuous
Jurisdiction: Indiana Department of Natural Resources, Division of Forestry
Fees and permits: No fees or permits required
Maps: USGS Hindustan; Morgan-Monroe State Forest pamphlet

Special attractions: Draper Cabin; rock cliffs in Sweedy Hollow
Camping: 35 primitive campsites at Morgan-Monroe State Forest—21 at Mason Ridge and 11 at Oak Ridge; additional sites located in the Scout Ridge youth tent area. The campgrounds are located on the main forest road north of the trailhead. Camping also is permitted in the Backcountry Area in the eastern section of Low Gap Trail.
Trailhead facilities: Small gravel parking lot at the trailhead; water, restrooms, and picnic shelters available at several locations along the main forest road

Finding the trailhead: Go 13 miles north on IN 37 from Bloomington and turn right (northeast) at the MORGAN-MONROE STATE FOREST signs. Go 0.6 mile to Old SR 37 and turn right. Go 1.7 miles to the main forest road and turn left (northeast) to enter Morgan-Monroe State Forest. Go 4.5 miles to a parking area on the right (south) side of the main road. The trailhead is about 10 yards off the road.

The Hike

It is almost impossible to imagine this area devoid of trees, but it was treeless after the original settlers cleared it in a vain attempt to establish farms. The rocky soil proved unsuitable, and the land was abandoned. The state stepped in during the Great Depression to purchase 24,000 acres of the eroding hillsides and established Morgan-Monroe State Forest.

The intervening years have allowed the lush forest to be reestablished, including 2,700 acres designated as the Backcountry Area in 1981. Low Gap Trail passes through this area and is one of two 10-mile hikes in Morgan-Monroe State Forest. The trail is well marked with white blazes on trees, plus blue paint markings at mile intervals. Although a good part of the trail follows abandoned roads and service roads, the rugged segments through Sweedy Hollow and along Gorley and Shipman Ridges discourage all but avid hikers.

The trail begins at a small gravel parking lot just off the main forest road. Head west for 0.1 mile to connect with an old road and turn left (south), following the roadway and trail south along Tincher Ridge. At 1.0 mile turn left off the trail and make the steep descent via a series of switchbacks over a fern-carpeted slope into Sweedy Hollow, a state-designated nature preserve. At the bottom of the ravine, follow the creek, which the trail crosses several times, for almost another mile before passing below stone cliffs that overhang the west side of the ravine. Continuing on

Rock overhangs are a rugged component of Sweedy Hollow, which is on the Low Gap Trail in Morgan-Monroe State Forest.

the trail, make the steep climb out of Sweedy Hollow to reach the 2.0-mile mark on a ridgetop.

At 2.4 miles link up with Landram Ridge Road, a gravel service road. A sign marks the spot, pointing left (northwest) for the 3.0-mile Rock Shelter Loop and right (southeast) for the continuation of the Low Gap Trail. Go right, crossing the high end of a ravine while keeping to a southeast course. The service road soon breaks to the right (south), but the trail continues left (east) and downhill along a power line corridor.

Pass a pond after another 0.5 mile, and then leave the power line corridor to enter the woods. Continue downhill to the first crossover of Low Gap Road at 4.0 miles. A gravel parking lot marks the entry to the Backcountry Area. Cross a pair of footbridges over the North Fork and East Fork of Honey Creek before making a steep uphill march to the top of Gorley Ridge, which is about the midway point of the hike. Part of the climb is over an old roadbed, but the trail eventually leaves the roadbed to drop into a ravine to the East Fork of Honey Creek. Cross the creek a couple of times, passing through a pine plantation that is a popular backcountry camping site.

The last challenging portion of the trail begins with a climb to a narrow ridgetop that leads to Shipman Ridge and the linkup with Orcutt Road, a service road. At the intersection at 6.7 miles, turn left (northwest) and follow Orcutt Road as it winds gradually downhill to the second crossover of Low Gap Road. A small parking lot at 7.8 miles marks the spot, with the trail continuing uphill to the northwest along the gravel Orcutt Road, which leads to private residences.

Stay on the road, splitting off to the right at a cable barricade at the 8.2-mile mark. The trail follows the service road past a radio tower and continues toward the main forest road.

Low Gap Trail turns left (west) off the service road about 50 yards before reaching the main forest road at 8.8 miles. Hike parallel to the main road, reaching a gravel road at the 9.7-mile mark. The gravel road leads south for 0.5 mile to the Draper Cabin, a rustic log home on the banks of the North Fork of Honey Creek. The cabin, which has stone floors and no plumbing, can be rented for overnight stays between April and Thanksgiving and during the winter, depending on weather conditions.

Visit the cabin, then backtrack uphill to the Low Gap Trail and turn left (south), following a path parallel to the main forest road for less than 0.5 mile to reach the trailhead parking lot.

Miles and Directions

0.0   Begin at the trailhead.
0.1   Go left (south) on Tincher Ridge.
1.0   Go left (east) to Sweedy Hollow.

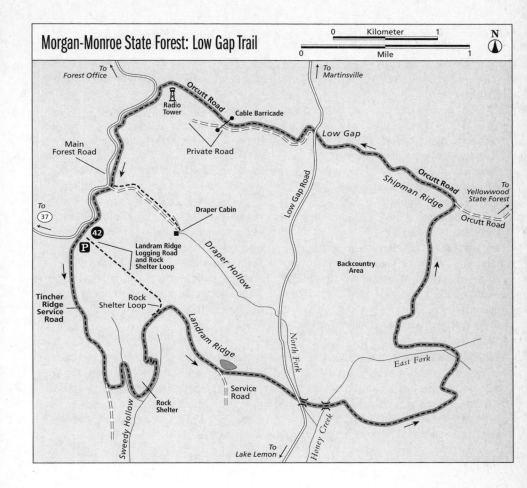

2.4 Link up with Landram Ridge Road; turn right (southeast).

2.8 At the trail juncture, go right on the Landram Ridge logging road.

4.0 Cross over Low Gap Road to the parking lot and footbridge.

6.7 At the trail juncture, turn left onto Orcutt Road.

7.8 Cross Low Gap Road and follow the gravel Orcutt Road uphill.

8.2 Go right on logging road past the cable barricade.

8.7 Pass the radio tower on left.

8.8 At the trail juncture go left (west).

9.7 At the gravel road go straight to complete trail. (**Option:** Go left [south] for a 1.0-mile round-trip to Draper Cabin.)

10.0 Reach the trailhead parking lot.

43 Morgan-Monroe State Forest: Three Lakes Loop

This trail visits the steep, forested ridges, ravines, creeks, and lakes of Morgan–Monroe State Forest.

Location: Midway between Bloomington and Martinsville, south-central Indiana
Distance: 10.0-mile loop
Elevation change: Five descents of 140 to 250 feet; four climbs of 140 to 200 feet
Approximate hiking time: 6 hours
Difficulty: Strenuous
Jurisdiction: Indiana Department of Natural Resources, Division of Forestry
Fees and permits: No fees or permits required
Maps: USGS Hindustan; Morgan-Monroe State Forest brochure
Special attractions: Lush woodland valleys,

Bryant Creek Lake, creekbanks, and a pioneer cemetery
Camping: 32 primitive campsites at Morgan-Monroe State Forest—21 at Mason Ridge and 11 at Oak Ridge; additional sites located in the Scout Ridge youth area. The campgrounds are located on the main forest road north of the trailhead.
Trailhead facilities: Small parking lot at the trailhead; water and restrooms located nearby at the Cherry Lake picnic shelter and at other locations in the state forest

Finding the trailhead: Go 13 miles north from Bloomington on IN 37 and turn right (northeast) at the MORGAN-MONROE STATE FOREST signs. Go 0.6 mile to Old SR 37 and turn right (southeast). Go 1.7 miles to the main forest road and turn left (northeast) to enter Morgan-Monroe State Forest. Go 4.8 miles to the first paved road. Turn left (north) and go 0.2 mile to a small paved parking lot on the right (northwest) overlooking Cherry Lake. The trail begins 0.1 mile farther down the road on the left (south) side at a metal gate blocking a forest service road.

The Hike

The name for this trail is no longer accurate because it actually only goes to two lakes—Bryant Creek and Cherry. The third lake on the original triangular-shaped trail, Beanblossom Lake, dried up after its dam failed in 1993. Regardless of name accuracy, the Three Lakes Loop is every bit as demanding as the Low Gap Trail, the other long-distance hike in Morgan-Monroe State Forest. The trail stretches along narrow ridgetops and through creekbeds in deep ravines and requires a lot of up-and-down climbing. The seclusion of the hardwood forests, the abundance of wildflowers, and the opportunity to encounter wildlife make the Three Lakes Loop a quality hiking opportunity.

Except for some areas in the valleys where vegetation grows thick, the trail is well marked with white blazes and brown plastic markers. Direction changes are clearly marked with double blazes. Most traffic revolves around the shelter houses at Cherry and Bryant Lakes, but the trail receives only modest use.

Morgan-Monroe State Forest: Three Lakes Loop

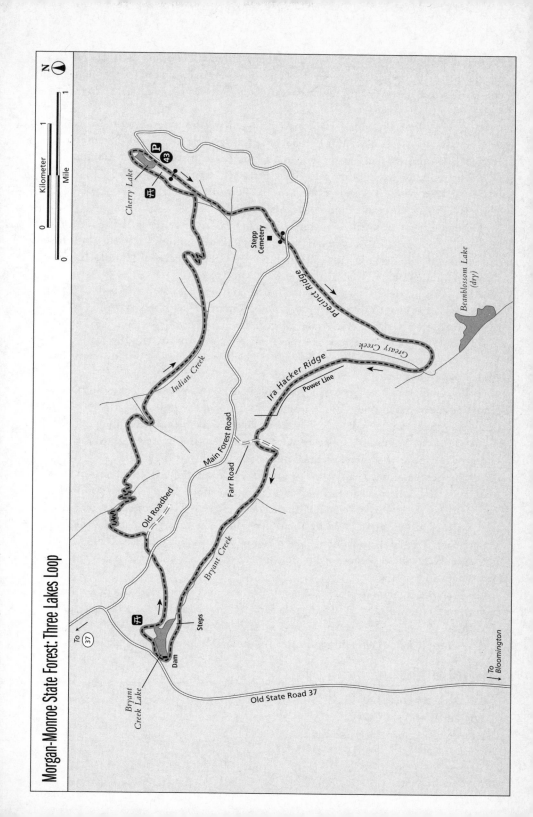

Begin the hike on an old roadbed that starts downhill after about 100 yards and reaches the first of what will be several creek crossings over the next 10.0 miles. The creeks are small, however, and flow intermittently with seasonal rainfall, so they normally present little trouble.

Continue along the creek, breaking to the left (south) after about 0.75 mile to head up a ravine—again on an old roadbed. After leveling off, pass the Stepp Cemetery at 1.0 mile. Markers in the graveyard include at least three that memorialize Civil War veterans, and another is for Isaac Hartsock, a private in the Virginia Militia during the War of 1812. An inscription on the headstone for Jay Alberto Coffa reads "The quiet man who is dreaming a clear labrynth."

Head southeast from the cemetery on the gravel road to reach the main forest road at 1.1 miles. Cross over, picking up the trail as it continues southeast over Precinct Ridge before dropping into a ravine to cross Greasy Creek at 2.3 miles. You are about 0.25 mile north of the former Beanblossom Lake.

After crossing the creek, turn right (north) and begin a steep climb of 200 feet up Ira Hacker Ridge to follow a power line easement. When the power line takes a right (north) turn, the trail goes straight (northwest). At 3.5 miles the trail crosses Farr Road. Look for trail makers on the trees directly across from where the road bends. Weave through a stand of young trees before heading downhill to join up with Bryant Creek at 4.0 miles.

Follow the creek for almost 1.0 mile through heavy vegetation, climbing over a long, straight hump at one point before reaching a stand of pines near Bryant Creek Lake. At 5.0 miles reach and circle the lake in a clockwise direction, climbing wooden steps around the high south shoreline. Cross the dam at the west end of the lake and continue northeast to a picnic shelter in the woods north of the lake.

From the shelter head east over a broad ridge to reach the main road near the 6.0-mile mark. Cross the road and zigzag across an old roadbed to a double-blaze marker. Turn left and walk along a ridge before descending a switchback to cross a branch of Indian Creek at 6.5 miles. Head up the other side of the ravine and cross a ridgetop. Descend once more to Indian Creek and follow its banks for almost 1.0 mile, crossing several side creeks before turning left (northeast) at 8.5 miles and heading uphill on a steep ridge point.

Beyond the ridgetop, slip across a ravine to another ridgetop and follow a winding path through the woods to Indian Creek. Turn left (northeast) at the creek and follow it to the Cherry Lake Picnic Shelter at 9.6 miles. Go to the north side of the shelter and proceed in a clockwise direction around the lake to the trailhead parking lot.

Miles and Directions

0.0 Begin at the trailhead.

1.0 Reach the Stepp Cemetery.

1.1 Go straight to the main road crossing.

2.3   Cross Greasy Creek.

3.5   Cross Farr Road.

4.0   Meet and follow Bryant Creek.

5.0   Reach Bryant Creek Lake; circle the lake clockwise.

6.0   Go straight at the main road crossing.

6.5   Cross Indian Creek.

8.5   Turn left (northeast) and go uphill.

9.6   Return to the Cherry Lake Picnic Shelter. Go clockwise around the lake.

10.0   Arrive back at the trailhead.

44 Scarce O'Fat Trail

A loop trail along a ridgetop, through a deep ravine, and over a steep hill featuring a north-facing vista overlooking Yellowwood Lake.

Location: Between Bloomington and Nashville in Yellowwood State Forest

Distance: 4.5-mile-loop

Elevation change: About 290 feet from the trailhead to highest point, just north of Caldwell Hollow

Approximate hiking time: 3 hours

Difficulty: Strenuous

Jurisdiction: Indiana Department of Natural Resources, Division of Forestry

Fees and permits: No fees or permits required

Maps: USGS Belmont; Yellowwood State Forest brochure

Special attractions: Caldwell Hollow and High King Hill

Camping: Yellowwood State Forest—horsemen's campground with 80 modern sites

Trailhead facilities: Small parking lot but no water supply or restrooms; water and restrooms available at the forest office on Yellowwood Lake Road

Finding the trailhead: Go east from Bloomington for 10 miles on IN 46 toward Nashville. Turn left (north) on Duncan Road at the brown signs for Yellowwood State Forest. Follow Duncan Road 1.3 miles until it crosses a bridge and dead-ends at a T intersection with Dubois Ridge Road. Turn left (south) and travel 0.9 mile to a Y intersection—the right (north) fork is Yellowwood Lake Road; the left (west) fork is Jackson Creek Road. Take Jackson Creek Road 0.5 mile to signs pointing right to Scarce O'Fat Trail. Turn right (north) onto a gravel road; drive through a creekbed and go 0.2 mile to the parking lot near the trailhead.

The Hike

Scarce O'Fat Ridge is the name pioneer settlers gave to this site because of the difficulty they faced scratching out anything more than a meager living on the rocky ground. While Scarce O'Fat lends its name to the trail, the trail's best features are actually the segments through Caldwell Hollow and the finishing climb up and down High King Hill. Although High King makes for a clever play on words (High King/hiking), it is so named because it is the highest point on the property once owned by a man named King.

Also worth noting is the forest's name—Yellowwood. The yellowwood tree is a close cousin of the black locust and is common in the mid-South, but it is so rare this far north that it is on the Indiana endangered species list. The forest covers 23,300 acres, of which only 200 are suitable yellowwood habitat.

What the first two-thirds of this trail lacks in scenic splendor, it more than makes up for in hiking ease. Also, the first section sets the stage for the best features of Scarce O'Fat Trail—the solitude of Caldwell Hollow and the accomplishment of conquering High King Hill for a clear view of Yellowwood Lake.

The first two-thirds of the trail follows service roads through the forest (the Indiana DNR Division of Forestry has plans to reroute the trail off these service roads). Brown plastic posts and wooden signs mark the early segments of the trail. White blazes on trees and boot outlines on wood posts direct the way through Caldwell Hollow and over High King Hill. The entire trail gets limited use, with most visitors preferring only to climb High King Hill to enjoy the view before returning to the parking area.

The trail begins at the base of the Yellowwood Lake dam. From the small parking lot it is easy to locate the marked trailhead at a gate that blocks a forest service road. The road is the trail for about the first 3.0 miles. It begins with a gradual climb of 140 feet to Bill Jack Ridge and winds through a forest of oak, beech, poplar, and shagbark hickory trees. If you schedule a hike for midsummer, you will find wild raspberries in plentiful supply along the edge of the road.

Once atop Bill Jack Ridge, the trail levels off for the next 2.0 miles. The trail is clearly marked along this portion with brown plastic signs. At 1.7 miles turn left (south) as the trail connects with Scarce O'Fat Ridge. The turnoff is marked by a wooden sign with two white blazes. Be alert for occasional spurs that veer to the right off the main service road; stay to the left (south). It is through this stretch that the trail reaches its highest point, but the elevation change is so slight it is hard to notice.

At 2.8 miles another double-blaze marker and brown plastic markers indicate a left (east) turn into the forest. This begins the descent into Caldwell Hollow. The trail follows a switchback that drops almost 220 feet in elevation in the span of 0.5 mile. Trail markers through Caldwell Hollow consist of white blaze markings on trees and wood posts sporting the outline of a boot. Once at the bottom of the hollow, the trail crosses a creekbed several times as it meanders through a corridor of other ravines that converge with Caldwell Hollow.

At 3.8 miles turn left (northeast) and begin the climb up High King Hill. The steepest part is over the next 0.25 mile as the elevation changes almost 150 feet. The remaining climb is much more gradual.

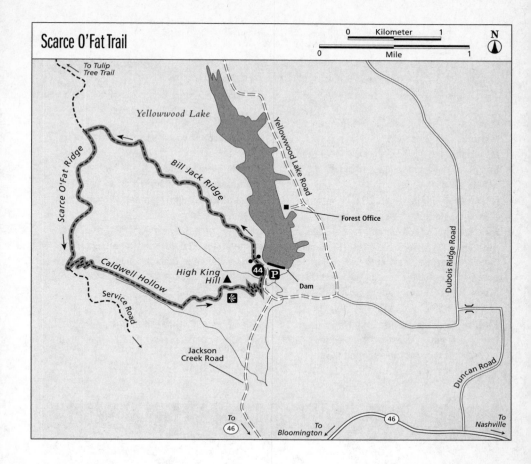

Scarce O'Fat Trail

Technically Scarce O' Fat Trail ends atop High King Hill, where it joins High King Trail for the final 0.25 mile. A series of switchbacks drops almost 200 feet to an intermittent streambed. Cross through the creekbed to the road; turn left (north) and walk a few hundred feet back to the parking lot.

Miles and Directions

- **0.0** Begin at the trailhead.
- **1.7** Turn left (south) onto Scarce O'Fat Ridge.
- **2.8** Turn left (east) to enter Caldwell Hollow.
- **3.8** Turn left (northeast) to climb High King Hill.
- **4.3** Reach the High King Hill vista.
- **4.5** Arrive back at the trailhead.

45 Brown County State Park: Trail 8

A trail through remote ravines of Brown County State Park.

Location: Outside Nashville in Brown County
Distance: 3.5-mile loop
Elevation change: More than 300 feet from Hesitation Point to the low end of Upper Schooner Creek Valley
Approximate hiking time: 2 hours
Difficulty: Moderate to strenuous
Jurisdiction: Indiana Department of Natural Resources, Division of State Parks & Reservoirs
Fees and permits: Park entry fee, higher for out-of-state vehicles; season passes available
Maps: USGS Belmont and Nashville; Brown County State Park brochure
Special attractions: Hesitation Point vista, Upper Schooner Creek valley
Camping: Brown County State Park—404 individual campsites, from modern to primitive; rally and youth camping area; 204 sites in the horsemen's camp
Trailhead facilities: Large parking area at the trailhead but no drinking water or restrooms; water available at other locations in the park, including the picnic area near Ogle Lake

Finding the trailhead: From Nashville go 2.5 miles south on IN 46 to Brown County State Park's west gatehouse. Go 1.2 miles to the West Lookout Tower parking lot. The trail begins on the east side of the stockade-shaped tower.

Dutchman's breeches.

Brown County State Park: Trail 8

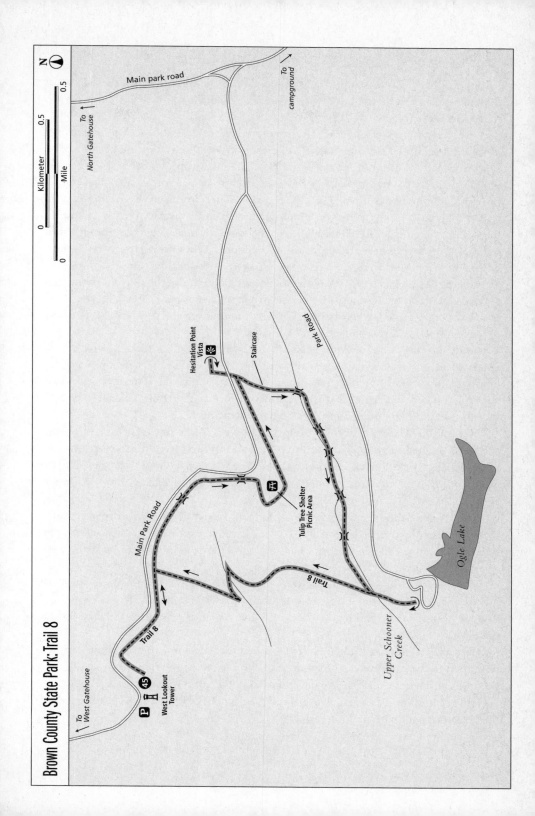

The Hike

Although Brown County is the largest state park in the Indiana system, it has a very limited supply of designated hiking trails—ten trails totaling just over 17 miles. At 3.5 miles, this is the longest.

Visited by thousands of people in the fall because of the brilliant displays as leaves change color, Brown County State Park is just as colorful in the spring because of its abundance of wildflowers, including toothwort, Dutchman's breeches, Jack-in-the-pulpit, spring larkspur, bluets, large-flowered trillium, wood sorrel, celandine poppy, fire pink, and prairie trillium. The entire park suffered from severe grazing damage inflicted by an overpopulation of white-tailed deer until special hunts were implemented in the early 1990s. Deer culls have become routine here and at other parks, resulting in recovery of native vegetation. The Upper Schooner Creek valley is flush with wildflowers and ferns, representative of the richness of this park.

Boardwalks and staircases take some of the difficulty out of the portion of the trail between Hesitation Point and the ravine of Upper Schooner Creek. Although the trail is well maintained, it gets less traffic than other trails in the park. It is busiest near the West Lookout Tower and around Ogle Lake.

From the West Lookout Tower, head east as the trail skirts the main park road about 10 to 20 feet down the side of the ridge. At 0.4 mile the trail intersects the inbound leg of Trail 8, which joins from the right (south). Stay straight (east) and continue on a course parallel to the main road for another mile, passing over two footbridges and behind the Tulip Tree Shelter Picnic Area.

At 1.5 miles Trail 8 turns right (south); before you make this turn, go left (north) and cross the main road to Hesitation Point. Soak up the views from a north-facing vista and then backtrack to the south side of the park road. Follow Trail 8 south for a little less than 0.25 mile to a wooden staircase with 153 steps leading down to Upper Schooner Creek (1.8 miles).

The Upper Schooner Creek valley is long and narrow, with an extremely steep bluff all along the south side. The bluff to the right side of the creek starts out equally steep but begins to flatten over the next 0.5 mile. Cross five footbridges as the trail switches from one side of the creek to the other.

Walk under a canopy of mature trees and cross a lengthy boardwalk to the trail juncture at 2.3 miles. Trail 8 turns north toward the West Lookout Tower. Instead go straight (south) to the parking lot west of Ogle Lake, one of two small lakes within the park boundaries.

Backtrack to the trail juncture at 2.4 miles; turn left (north) and climb a ridge point before the trail makes a steep drop to the left (west) into another valley. Cross the creek at the bottom of the ravine and head uphill again to reach the trail juncture with the outbound leg of Trail 8 at 3.1 miles. Turn left (west) and go 0.4 mile back to the lookout tower parking lot.

Miles and Directions

0.0 Begin at the trailhead.

0.4 At the Trail 8 juncture go straight.

1.5 Reach the Hesitation Point overlook.

1.8 Enter the Upper Schooner Creek valley.

2.3 At the trail juncture go straight (south) to Ogle Lake.

2.4 Backtrack to trail juncture and turn left (north).

3.1 At the trail juncture turn left (west) to return to the trailhead.

3.5 Arrive back at the trailhead.

46 Ogle Hollow Nature Preserve: Trail 5

An interpretive tree trail down and up a steep slope of a nature preserve inside Brown County State Park.

Location: Near Nashville in Brown County

Distance: 0.8-mile loop

Elevation change: 240 feet from the rim of the ridgetop to the bottom of the ravine

Approximate hiking time: 45 minutes

Difficulty: Strenuous

Jurisdiction: Indiana Department of Natural Resources, Division of State Parks & Reservoirs

Fees and permits: Park entry fee, higher for out-of-state vehicles; season passes available

Maps: USGS Nashville; Brown County State

Park brochure; Ogle Hollow Nature Preserve pamphlet

Special attractions: Yellowwood trees

Camping: Brown County State Park—404 individual campsites, from modern to primitive; rally and youth camping area; 204 sites in the horsemen's camp

Trailhead facilities: Water fountain and restrooms on the south edge of the rally campground parking lot; camp store located nearby

Finding the trailhead: There are two entry gates to Brown County State Park. From Nashville go 2.5 miles south on IN 46 to the West Gatehouse. Go 3.5 miles to a three-way intersection. Turn right (south) and go 1.5 miles to the Rally Campground parking lot. The trailhead is off the north side of the lot.

The other entry option is through the North Gatehouse. From Nashville go 0.2 mile east on IN 46/135 to the park sign. Turn right (south); pass through a covered bridge (9-foot-height, three-ton-weight vehicle restrictions) and go to the north gatehouse. Continue 2.2 miles to a three-way intersection. Stay left and go 1.5 miles to the Rally Campground parking lot.

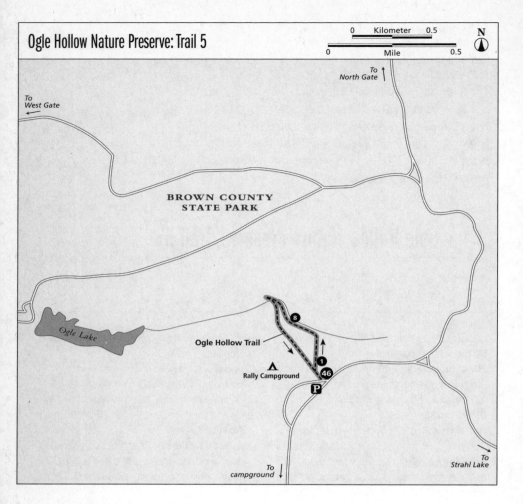

0   Kilometer   0.5

0   Mile   0.5

N

To
North Gate

To
West Gate

BROWN COUNTY
STATE PARK

Ogle Lake

Ogle Hollow Trail

8

Rally Campground

1

46

P

To
campground

To
Strahl Lake

The Hike

Few places escaped the hand of man during pioneer settlement of Indiana, when much of the landscape was stripped of timber and converted to pasture and farmland. Ogle Hollow is perhaps the best example of an area that survived. A small corner at the back end of the ravine was given state nature preserve status in 1970, making it the ninth site in a system that now includes about 230 sites across the state. Only forty-one acres in size, the Ogle Hollow Nature Preserve is a mere fraction of the 16,000-acre state park that is the largest in Indiana.

Trail 5 is short but demanding—almost vertical on the way down and the way back up. Because it is part of a state-protected nature preserve, it has been left undisturbed by human intervention other than the placement of signposts used to identify the twenty-two interpretive stations. The path is narrow but easy to follow, and it is not often a busy place.

The north-facing slope of the preserve, where Trail 5 is located, provides the moist environment necessary to support yellowwood, a tree found only in a few places in Indiana. Yellowwood is not a common tree anywhere, but it is found more often in the cool forests of southern Appalachia and the Ozarks. With little indication of reproduction, it is listed as a threatened species in Indiana. Two of the twenty-two interpretive signposts on Trail 5 identify the rare yellowwood, whose smooth gray bark is similar in appearance to a beech tree. The yellowwood is smaller, however, and grows at an angle, producing clusters of pealike flowers every other year.

Wildflowers and ferns also cover the hillside, but the numbered markers primarily identify trees, beginning with a black oak at Station 1. Other trees along the route are black gum, American beech, sassafras, red elm, wild black cherry, pawpaw, sycamore, black walnut, bitternut hickory, shagbark hickory, basswood, sugar maple, pignut hickory, white ash, red oak, and chestnut oak. Station 8 marks the location of two trees—an American beech and black maple—that have grown so closely together that they appear to come from a single trunk.

Also present in the preserve are flowering dogwood, redbud, spicebush, ironweed, Christmas fern, maidenhair fern, and narrow-leaved spleenwort. The first six stations are along the steep downhill leg, after which the trail follows a creek for six more stations before the grueling uphill stretch begins.

Miles and Directions

0.0 Begin at the trailhead and go right.

0.4 Reach the ravine bottom.

0.8 Arrive back at the trailhead at the ridgetop.

47 Twin Caves Trail

A trail through a nature preserve featuring virgin timber also passes several caves and sinkholes.

Location: East of Mitchell in Lawrence County
Distance: 2.5-mile loop
Elevation change: Minimal
Approximate hiking time: 1.5 hours
Difficulty: Moderate
Fees and permits: Park entry fee, higher for out-of-state vehicles; season passes available
Maps: USGS Mitchell; Spring Mill State Park brochure

Special attractions: Donaldson Woods State Nature Preserve, Twin Caves, Bronson Cave
Camping: Spring Mill State Park—187 modern and 36 primitive campsites; youth tent area
Trailhead facilities: Parking lot and a pit toilet at trailhead but no drinking water; water and restrooms also located elsewhere in the park

Finding the trailhead: From its intersection with IN 37 on the southwest edge of Mitchell, go 3.3 miles east on IN 60 to Spring Mill State Park. Turn left (north) and go 0.4 mile to the gatehouse, then another 0.1 mile to a three-way intersection. Turn right (northeast) at the intersection; go 0.2 mile and turn right (southeast). Go another 0.1 mile and turn right (south). The road ends at the Twin Caves parking area. The trail begins from the west edge of the parking lot.

Bronson Cave is one of several caves featured at Spring Mill State Park.

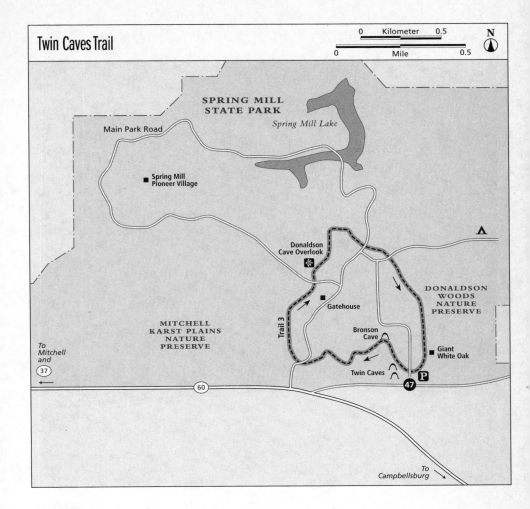

0   Kilometer   0.5

0   Mile   0.5

N

SPRING MILL
STATE PARK

Spring Mill Lake

Main Park Road

■ Spring Mill
Pioneer Village

Donaldson
Cave Overlook

Gatehouse

Trail 3

MITCHELL
KARST PLAINS
NATURE
PRESERVE

DONALDSON
WOODS
NATURE
PRESERVE

Bronson
Cave

To
Mitchell
and
37

Twin Caves

Giant
White Oak

47 P

60

To
Campbellsburg

The Hike

Karst topography is the geological name given to an area of limestone bedrock featuring caves, sinkholes, and underground streams. The Mitchell Plain, which stretches from the Ohio River north to central Indiana, is one of the best karst examples in the world. The area in which Spring Mill State Park is located has one of the highest concentrations of sinkholes in the United States, with an average of one hundred per square mile. Just down the road near Orleans, an amazing 1,022 sinkholes were counted in 1 square mile.

The funnel–shaped sinkholes vary in size but play an integral role in the development of cave systems like the one at Spring Mill. Groundwater mixed with vegetation creates a weak acid that dissolves the limestone. Over time cracks become caves, and when caves collapse they form exposed openings known as karst windows. Three

Two boats are moored at a pier near Twin Caves at Spring Mill State Park. Short boat trips are available into the caves.

examples—Twin Caves and Bronson Cave—are found on the Twin Caves Trail (also known as Trail 3).

The trail can be hiked in either direction but is described here as a clockwise loop that begins at a stone archway on the west edge of the parking lot. The archway leads to Twin Caves, where boat trips are offered from April through October, depending on water levels in the cave. Backtrack from Twin Caves to the stone archway and turn left (north) to pick up Trail 3. Go 0.1 mile to a wooden viewing platform near the mouth of Bronson Cave.

Go west from the cave on a winding course through a forest dotted with sinkholes for 0.5 mile to cross the main park road. After crossing the road, begin heading north for another 0.5 mile to a paved road. Cross the road and follow a gravel trail along the rim above Donaldson Cave, which is connected to the other caves. Go past the overlook above the Donaldson Cave and continue north, then south, crossing the first of two paved roads at 1.7 miles.

At 1.8 miles you will cross the second road and reach the Donaldson Woods State Nature Preserve. The sixty-seven-acre stand of virgin timber features several trees at least 300 years old, including one white oak protected by a split-rail fence near the south end of the preserve. The tree is believed to be between 400 and 500 years old. The preserve is named for George Donaldson, a wealthy Scotsman and nature lover who had a penchant for purchasing areas of unique beauty. Although he frequently hunted abroad, Donaldson zealously protected his property from disturbance of any kind.

Turn right (west) from the large oak tree to the Twin Caves parking lot.

Miles and Directions

0.0   Begin at the trailhead and go right.

0.1   Arrive at Twin Caves.

0.2   Come to Bronson Cave.

0.7   Cross the main park road.

1.2   Reach a paved park road; cross over.

1.5   Arrive at trail juncture on the left; go right (east).

1.7   Reach a paved park road; cross over.

1.8   Cross a paved park road.

1.9   Enter Donaldson Woods State Nature Preserve.

2.5   Arrive back at Twin Caves parking lot.

48 Spring Mill State Park: Village Trail

A trail to a cave canyon, through a pioneer village, and to a pioneer cemetery.

Location: East of Mitchell, Lawrence County
Distance: 2.0-mile loop, excluding optional tour of the village and cemetery
Elevation change: 150 feet
Approximate hiking time: 1.5 hours
Difficulty: Moderate to strenuous
Jurisdiction: Indiana Department of Natural Resources, Division of State Parks & Reservoirs
Fees and permits: Park entry fee, higher for out-of-state vehicles; season passes available

Maps: USGS Mitchell; Spring Mill State Park brochure
Special attractions: Donaldson Cave, Spring Mill Pioneer Village, Hamer Pioneer Cemetery
Camping: Spring Mill State Park—187 modern and 36 primitive campsites; youth tent area
Trailhead facilities: Parking for two dozen vehicles, picnic shelters, pit toilets, and a water supply at trailhead; water and restrooms located elsewhere in the park

Finding the trailhead: From its intersection with IN 37 on the southwest edge of Mitchell, go 3.3 miles east on IN 60 to Spring Mill State Park. Turn left (north) and go 0.4 mile to the gatehouse, then another 0.1 mile to a three-way intersection. Turn left (west) at the intersection and go 0.3 mile to the Donaldson Picnic Area parking lot on the right (northeast). The trail begins from the southeast edge of the parking lot.

The mill at Spring Mill Pioneer Village was originally built in the early 1800s and is still in operation.

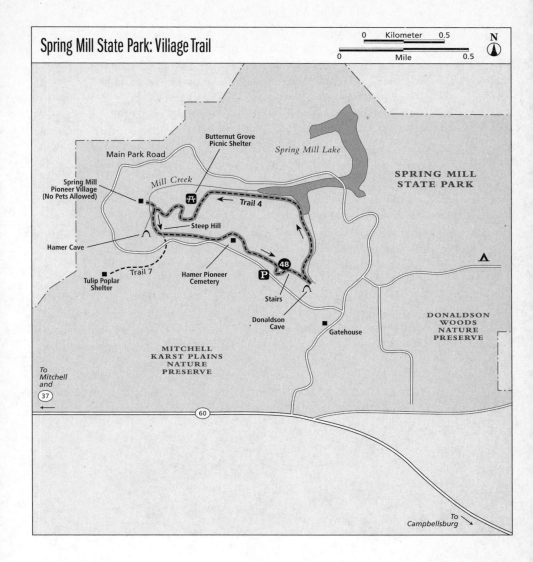

0   Kilometer   0.5

0   Mile   0.5

N

Main Park Road

Butternut Grove
Picnic Shelter

Spring Mill Lake

SPRING MILL
STATE PARK

Spring Mill
Pioneer Village
(No Pets Allowed)

Mill Creek

Trail 4

Steep Hill

Hamer Cave

Trail 7

Tulip Poplar
Shelter

Hamer Pioneer
Cemetery

P

48

Stairs

Donaldson
Cave

Gatehouse

DONALDSON
WOODS
NATURE
PRESERVE

MITCHELL
KARST PLAINS
NATURE
PRESERVE

To
Mitchell
and
37

60

To
Campbellsburg

The Hike

There are eight hiking trails in 1,358-acre Spring Mill State Park, including Trail 4.
History is the overriding theme of this trail, beginning with its most dynamic natural
feature—Donaldson Cave. Known as Shawnee Cave until George Donaldson purchased the area in 1865, the cave is part of a network that includes two other exposed
caves in the park. Professor Carl Eigenmann of nearby Indiana University began
extensive studies of Donaldson Cave in the early 1900s and discovered northern blind
cavefish, which has been placed on the state's endangered species list. The pinkish-

white fish with no eyes has adapted to the dark cave, as have other critters—the blind cave crayfish, the cave salamander, assorted spiders, and of course bats.

Other highlights that can be added to this hike are Spring Mill Pioneer Village and Hamer Cave. Trail 4 no longer leads through the Pioneer Village, but a spur provides access for a worthwhile visit. Pets are not allowed in the village.

The history of the village dates to the early 1800s, when Samuel Jackson Jr. capitalized on a spring-fed stream to build a small gristmill. A Canadian naval officer who served the United States in the War of 1812, Jackson sold the property in 1817 to two brothers—Thomas and Cuthbert Bullitt of Kentucky. The Bullitts built a three-story gristmill at the site, which is still in operation.

As a small village grew up around the prospering mill, ownership of the land changed hands several times. Hugh and Thomas Hamer purchased the mill and surrounding village in 1832, one year after its name was changed from Arcole Village to Spring Mill. The Hamer brothers had managed the mill for the previous owners for seven years. Under the brothers' ownership, the village thrived until the late 1850s. By 1898 it had been abandoned.

Envisioning a restored village as the centerpiece of a park, the state of Indiana began acquiring the land in the 1920s, and Spring Mill State Park was established in 1927. Besides the gristmill, which produces cornmeal for sale, there are nineteen other restored buildings in the village, including a post office, apothecary, blacksmith

The mill at Spring Mill Pioneer Village.

shop, tavern, distillery, and carpenter shop. Volunteers dressed in period costume bring the village to life by performing routine daily chores.

The trail is well marked and well traveled, especially around Donaldson Cave and the pioneer village.

Begin the hike at the east end of the parking lot by descending an elaborate wooden staircase to the stream running from Donaldson Cave. Turn right (southeast) to reach the mouth of the cave at 0.2 mile. Access to the cave may be restricted to protect bat populations.

From the cave follow the left (west) side of the stream, crossing a long boardwalk before curling west to the Butternut Grove Picnic Shelter at 1.0 mile and a pair of limestone picnic areas built by the Civilian Conservation Corps (CCC) in the early 1930s.

Turn left (south) and follow a winding course that reaches the optional spur trail to the Pioneer Village at 1.3 miles.

After exploring the village, backtrack to Trail 4 and turn right (south) to make a steep climb that will lead to Hamer Pioneer Cemetery at the 1.8-mile mark. The cemetery was established in 1832 and is typical of pioneer cemeteries—set on high ground to avoid flooding and as a way of putting the deceased closer to Heaven. Hugh Hamer, who established the cemetery, was buried here after he died of smallpox in 1872.

Continue east from the cemetery for 0.2 mile to the trailhead parking area.

Miles and Directions

0.0 Begin at the trailhead; descend the stairs and turn right (southeast).

0.2 Reach Donaldson Cave.

1.0 Arrive at Butternut Grove Picnic Shelter.

1.3 Reach spur to Spring Mill Pioneer Village.

1.8 Arrive at Hamer Pioneer Cemetery.

2.0 Arrive back at the Donaldson Picnic Area.

Southwest

The following hikes have been lumped into this region for lack of a better way to arrange them. They extend from Patoka Reservoir in south-central Indiana to Harmonie State Park on the Wabash River west of Evansville, and from Lincoln State Park near the Ohio River to McCormick's Creek State Park just west of Bloomington. They are listed in a clockwise sweep heading north from Evansville.

A few of the six trails—Patoka Lake and the two at McCormick's Creek, for instance—have interesting natural features. Others are singled out simply because they are nice hikes.

Patoka Lake is an 8,800-acre reservoir managed by the U.S. Army Corps of Engineers. The Indiana Department of Natural Resources manages the 26,000-acre recreational area surrounding the lake. The Main Trail passes several unique sandstone formations, the most dynamic being Totem Rock. The trail also skirts a peninsula that is a wintering home for bald eagles.

McCormick's Creek, Indiana's first state park, features a beautiful waterfall and canyon. Stone was quarried from the park to help build the first state capitol. North of the canyon and creek is Wolf Cave, which is 57 yards from one end to the other. The cave opening ranges from over 5 feet to a narrow 18 inches at the east end.

Harmonie and Lincoln State Parks have historical significance. Harmonie is located just south of New Harmony, the site of two utopian communities in the early 1800s. Lincoln State Park is situated near the pioneer farm where Abraham Lincoln spent his formative years, ages seven to twenty-one.

Shakamak State Park, south of Terre Haute, is a beehive on hot summer days as visitors take advantage of the popular park pool. The park and its three lakes are situated on abandoned coal mine property, which the citizens of Clay, Greene, and Sullivan Counties donated to the state in the late 1920s. The park owes its name to the Kickapoo, a Native American tribe that resided in the area. The Kickapoo called nearby Eel River *Shakamak*—meaning "river of long fish."

49 Harmonie State Park

A combination of loop trails through ravines and forest.

Location: About 25 miles northwest of Evansville in the southwest corner of the state
Distance: 3.0-mile loop
Elevation change: About 70 feet
Approximate hiking time: 2 hours
Difficulty: Moderate
Fees and permits: Park entry fee, higher for out-of-state vehicles; season passes available
Maps: USGS Solitude; Harmonie State Park brochure

Special features: Stream crossings, ravines, large trees, including one of the largest pecan trees in Indiana
Camping: Harmonie State Park—200 modern campsites; primitive youth tent area
Trailhead facilities: Picnic shelter and parking area but no drinking water at trailhead; water sources available at other park locations

Finding the trailhead: From New Harmony turn left (south) on IN 69 and go about 2.5 miles to IN 269. Turn right (west) and go 1 mile to the park gatehouse. From the gatehouse follow the main park road for about 4 miles; pass the pool and turn left (south) at the entrance to Sycamore Ridge Picnic Area. The trailhead begins about 15 yards off the main park road.

The Hike

Established in 1966, this park draws its name from the nearby town of New Harmony, the site of two failed experiments at developing a utopian community in the early 1800s. The first was a religious experiment led by Father George Rapp, a German immigrant, who sold the town in 1824 to Robert Owen, a Scottish industrialist. Owen sought to establish a community in which everyone shared the work and the profit. During Owen's short, two-year leadership, New Harmony developed the first free public school and first kindergarten in America, providing equal education for boys and girls, and the first free public library. The town has been restored as a tourist attraction, but few of those elements are reflected in the park other than the name.

The hike is typical of state park hikes—an up-and-down venture over ridges and ravines with a couple of slow-moving streams. Traffic on this well-marked, well-maintained trail is light compared to other routes in the park.

Take the hike in a clockwise direction by picking up the Trail 4 where it crosses the Sycamore Ridge Picnic Area access road (there is a trail marker). The trail parallels the main park road for less than 0.25 mile before swinging left (southwest) on a slight downward slope. At 0.25 mile it bends back to the right (north) and continues down and over an intermittent stream before rising on the other side to meet the main park road at the 0.4-mile mark.

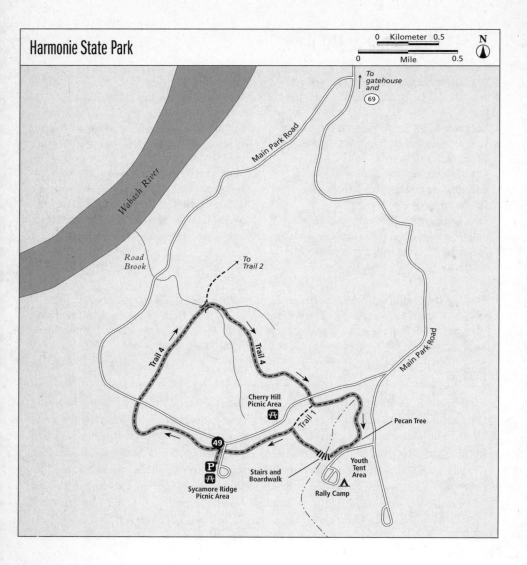

0   Kilometer   0.5

N

0   Mile   0.5

To
gatehouse
and
69

Main Park Road

Wabash River

Road
Brook

To
Trail 2

Trail 4

Trail 4

Cherry Hill
Picnic Area

Trail 1

Main Park Road

Pecan Tree

49

Stairs and
Boardwalk

Youth
Tent
Area

P

Sycamore Ridge
Picnic Area

Rally Camp

Cross the main road and pick up the trail on the other side. Immediately you will begin a long but gradual descent into another ravine. Walk up the opposite side of the ravine and drop down once more to where two streams converge near a small bridge at 0.7 mile. Cross the bridge and turn right (southeast) to climb out of the ravine, reaching the 1.0-mile mark near the top of the hill that in spring blossoms with Dutchman's breeches, violets, and other wildflowers.

Continue east and southeast along a ridgetop before dropping down slightly and then up to reach the main road near the Cherry Hill Picnic Area. Cross the road at 1.5 miles and pick up Trail 1, turning left (northeast). Trail 1 parallels the south edge of the park road for 100 yards before bending right (south) at a trail marker and cross-ing the back end of a ravine. As the trail reaches the back of the youth tent area at 2.0 miles, pass beneath one of the largest pecan trees in Indiana. Cross through the open area and follow the paved road, passing a latrine before turning right (north) at a Trail 1 marker. Enter one final ravine, this time on a wooden staircase designed to reduce erosion on the steep hillsides. After walking up the stairs on the other side, turn left (southwest) at a Trail 4 marker at 2.6 miles. Hike parallel to the main road for 0.4 mile west to the Sycamore Ridge access road and the trailhead.

Miles and Directions

0.0 Begin at the trailhead; go clockwise.

0.4 Cross the main park road.

0.7 Cross the bridge and turn right.

1.5 Cross main park road and connect with Trail 1; turn left (northeast).

2.0 Reach the youth camp area.

2.6 Connect with Trail 4 and turn left.

3.0 Arrive back at the trailhead.

50 Shakamak State Park

This trail loops around Lake Shakamak, the smallest of three lakes in the park.

Location: South of Terre Haute, southwest-central Indiana

Distance: 3.5-mile loop

Elevation change: Minimal

Approximate hiking time: 2 hours

Difficulty: Moderate

Jurisdiction: Indiana Department of Natural Resources, Division of State Parks & Reservoirs

Fees and permits: Park entry fee, higher for out-of-state vehicles; season passes available

Maps: USGS Jasonville; Shakamak State Park brochure

Special features: Backwater bays and boardwalks

Camping: Shakamak State Park—175 drive-in campsites and a youth tent area; 29 family or group cabins, including 2 ADA-accessible cabins

Trailhead facilities: Restrooms, nature center, swimming pool, and picnic area at trailhead

Finding the trailhead: Go 17 miles south on US 41 from Terre Haute to IN 48 and turn left (east). Go 9.5 miles to the park entrance on the west. After passing the gatehouse, turn right (west); go to the first intersection and turn left (west) to the nature center and swimming pool. The park's Trail 1 can be hiked in either direction by beginning at the parking lot. The best way is to begin at the nature center and head north of the parking lot alongside the swimming pool, hiking in a counterclockwise direction.

The Hike

Shakamak is the name Kickapoo Indians gave to nearby Eel River. The area is in the heart of Indiana's coal country, and the park is built on abandoned coal mines donated to the state in the late 1920s by Clay, Greene, and Sullivan Counties. Shakamak was established as a state park in 1929, and much of its development was done during the 1930s by the Civilian Conservation Corps (CCC).

There are four hiking trails in the park totaling 6.5 miles. Trail 1 begins in a bustling area with a swimming pool, picnic area, and nature center, but it does not take long to escape the hubbub along the wooded lakeshore. For the most part, the trail is easy to follow because it hugs the lakeshore, although it is slightly confusing near the family cabin area. Trail use is modest, due in part to the popularity of the swimming pool.

From the north side of the nature center, facing the lake, walk down a set of stone steps and turn right to follow a path that skirts the shoreline for the majority of the hike. Footbridges, staircases, and boardwalks dominate the early portion of the hike, providing easy passage over areas prone to wetness or erosion.

At 0.3 mile you will reach a floating boardwalk at the back of a bay that forms the first of the lake's four fingers. After crossing the boardwalk, turn left (west) and continue along the shore to complete the first finger at 0.6 mile. It is another 0.7 mile over more boardwalks and footbridges around the second finger bay. At the back end of the second finger, Trail 2 cuts off to the right (north) and leads to the youth camp area. Instead stay left (west) and continue on Trail 1 to the third finger of Lake Shakamak.

The back end of the lake's third finger is somewhat swampy, but a boardwalk, which

In 1929, Shakamak was established as a state park.

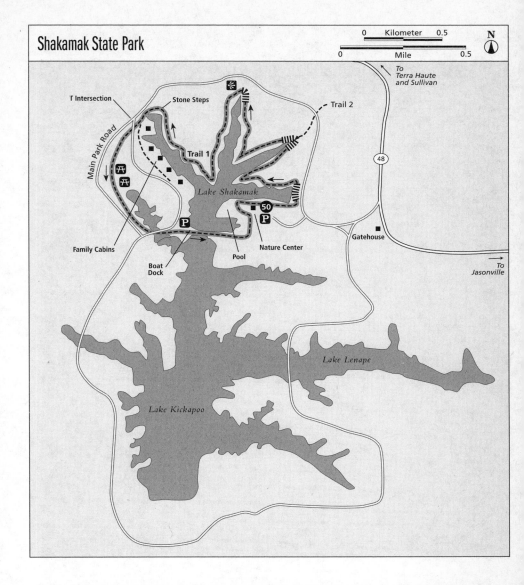

0   Kilometer   0.5

0   Mile   0.5

N

To
Terra Haute
and Sullivan

T Intersection

Stone Steps

Trail 2

Main Park Road

Trail 1

48

Lake Shakamak

50

P   P

Gatehouse

Family Cabins

Boat
Dock

Pool

Nature Center

To
Jasonville

Lake Lenape

Lake Kickapoo

includes a small viewing deck, zigzags through it. Exit the boardwalk at 1.8 miles and turn left (south) along the shoreline to a point directly across the lake from the pool.

After bending to the right (northwest) around that point, begin hiking the final finger. The family cabins are on the opposite (southwest) shore of this bay. At the back end of the bay, leave the lakeshore by hiking uphill via stone steps at 2.4 miles. Take a right (southwest) turn when the trail meets a T intersection; a left (south) turn goes to the family cabins. Walk through a stand of pine trees to the main park road at 2.7 miles.

A footbridge across one of the bays at Lake Shakamak.

The park road forks here; go directly across the left (east) fork and follow the trail through more pines and over small footbridges. Pass a pair of picnic shelters. At 3.0 miles reach a paved road that leads to the boat launch for Lake Shakamak. Turn left (east); pass the boat launch parking lot and pick up the paved pathway that leads over the earthen dam that separates Shakamak from the much larger Lake Kickapoo. After crossing the dam, turn left (north) to reach the parking area for the pool and picnic area.

Miles and Directions

0.0 Begin at the trailhead; turn right.

0.3 Cross a floating boardwalk and turn left to follow the lakeshore.

0.6 Complete the first finger bay.

1.8 Exit boardwalk and turn left (south).

2.4 Climb stone steps near the family cabins.

2.7 Cross the main park road.

3.0 Reach the boat ramp road. Go left, cross the dam, and turn left (north) to return to the parking area.

3.5 Arrive back at the trailhead.

51 McCormick's Creek State Park: Falls Canyon Trail

A combination of park trails through McCormick's Creek Canyon that leads from a canyon waterfall to the White River and back.

Location: West of Bloomington

Distance: 3.0-mile loop

Elevation change: About a 150-foot drop from the falls to the White River

Approximate hiking time: 1.5 hours

Difficulty: Strenuous

Jurisdiction: Indiana Department of Natural Resources, Division of State Parks & Reservoirs

Fees and permits: Park entry fee, higher for out-of-state vehicles; season passes available

Maps: USGS Gosport; McCormick's Creek State Park brochure

Special features: McCormick's Creek Falls, the White River, old stone quarry

Camping: McCormick's Creek State Park—190 modern electric and 32 primitive campsites; youth tent area

Trailhead facilities: Ample parking at the trailhead for Trail 3; restrooms, water, and other facilities spread throughout the 1,924-acre park

Finding the trailhead: From its intersection with IN 37 near Bloomington, go 15 miles west on IN 46 to the McCormick's Creek State Park entrance. Turn right (north) to reach the gatehouse. From the gatehouse follow the main park road just over 0.25 mile to the Canyon Inn entrance (the second left turn). Turn left (north) and go to the main parking lot. Begin the hike on Trail 3 at the east side of the parking lot.

The Hike

The Canyon Inn, near the starting point of this hike, rests on the original foundation of a sanitarium that became a turning point in the history of the area. The sanitarium was built more than a century ago by a physician, Frederick Denkewalter, who believed the tranquil canyon and cliffs provided an ideal setting as a resting place for the wealthy. The parklike surroundings also became a popular picnic and hiking spot for local residents. When Denkewalter died in 1914, the state and Owen County purchased the land and established Indiana's first state park in 1916.

McCormick's Creek State Park has grown to more than five times its original size of 350 acres. Some sections of this loop are rough because the trail follows the rocky creekbed. Other sections are steep climbs into and out of the canyon. The area near White River may be impassable during high water.

This hike combines parts of Trails 3, 7, 2, and 1. Begin northeast of the inn near the center of the parking lot, where a gravel trail leads to a Trail 3 marker. Signs along Trail 3 warn of hazardous areas along the cliffs overlooking the canyon. A stone stairway leads down to the canyon floor and the falls at 0.3 mile. McCormick's Creek is named for John McCormick, the first settler in the area, who homesteaded nearly one hundred acres along the creek and canyon. It is not a very big creek—at times no more than 3 feet wide—which makes the high-walled canyon it carved from the limestone bedrock all the more impressive.

Turn left (northwest) at the creek and follow its rocky banks for about 0.5 mile before passing an elaborate wooden staircase (Trail 5) that leads up the left (south) side of the canyon to a campground at 0.8 mile. Cross over to the right (north) side of the creek; continue less than 0.25 mile to a bend in the creek and cross back over to the left (south) side. Trail 7 joins from the left (south) at a steep wooden staircase at 1.0 mile. Cross once more to the right (north) side of the creek and turn right (north) to climb uphill on Trail 7 via another wooden staircase.

The trail passes over Trail 2 and continues north to a campground before curling left (west) along a gravel road that leads downhill to the White River. At 1.6 miles stop at the Cedar Point Overlook; a wooden shelter on a bluff to the right (north) of the road provides a nice spot from which to view the river. Gigantic sycamores punctuate the landscape near the river. Before reaching the river you will pass a water filtration plant that services the park and a pair of small stone buildings.

Turn away from the river and head southeast to an elevated boardwalk. Once off the boardwalk, continue east along the north bank of McCormick's Creek to Trail 2 at 2.3 miles. Turn right (southeast) onto Trail 2, crossing the creek to an old limestone quarry at 2.4 miles. Blocks of stone are piled by the site, from which limestone was taken for use in construction of the statehouse in Indianapolis.

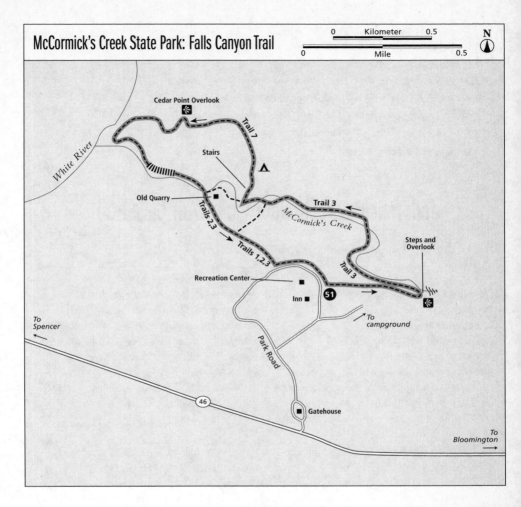

McCormick's Creek State Park: Falls Canyon Trail

Cedar Point Overlook

Trail 7

White River

Stairs

Old Quarry

Trails 2,3

Trail 3

McCormick's Creek

Trails 1,2,3

Steps and Overlook

Recreation Center

Trail 3

Inn

51

To Spencer

To campground

Park Road

46

Gatehouse

To Bloomington

Go right (southeast) from the quarry as Trails 3 and 2 merge on a steep uphill climb out of the canyon on a course to the southeast, joining with Trail 1 along the way. About halfway up the 100-foot ascent, Trail 7 cuts off to the left (northeast) and downhill. Continue uphill on Trails 3, 2, and 1 to pass the Trailside Shelter house and reach a paved road. Turn left (east) and follow the paved road about 0.25 mile back to the parking lot where Trail 3 began.

Miles and Directions

0.0 Begin at the trailhead at Trail 3 marker.

0.3 Reach the falls overlook and stone steps.

0.8	Arrive at the junction with Trail 5.
1.0	Reach the junction with Trail 7.
1.6	Arrive at the Cedar Point Overlook.
2.3	At the junction of Trails 7 and 2, turn right (south) and cross the creek.
2.4	Reach the old quarry at the junction of Trails 2 and 3.
2.6	At the junction with Trail 7, go straight (southeast) on Trails 1, 2, and 3.
2.7	Reach the park road; turn left (east).
3.0	Arrive back at the trailhead.

52 McCormick's Creek State Park: Wolf Cave Trail

A trail through a state nature preserve to an open cave.

Location: West of Bloomington
Distance: 2.0-mile loop
Elevation change: Minimal
Approximate hiking time: 1 hour
Difficulty: Moderate
Jurisdiction: Indiana Department of Natural Resources, Division of State Parks & Reservoirs
Fees and permits: Park entry fee, higher for out-of-state vehicles; season passes available

Maps: USGS Gosport; McCormick's Creek State Park brochure
Special attractions: Wolf Cave, Twin Bridges
Camping: McCormick's Creek State Park—190 modern electric and 32 primitive campsites; youth tent area
Trailhead facilities: Water available at several places in the park, including the stone restroom near the start of Trail 5

Finding the trailhead: From its intersection with IN 37 near Bloomington, go 15 miles west on IN 46 to the McCormick's Creek State Park entrance. Turn right (north) to reach the gatehouse. From the gatehouse follow the main park road past the Canyon Inn entrance (the second left turn). Continue in a counterclockwise drive that goes east, then west before reaching the Wolf Cave parking lot on the right (north) side of the road shortly before the park campground.

The Hike

Wolf Cave, the focal point of this trail, has a storied past. But which story is true? One legend tells of a young pioneer woman who was walking home after selling goods to flatboat operators at the nearby White River. Passing the cave, she encountered a pack of wolves. She was able to elude them by throwing off her gloves and bonnet as decoys. Another tale has her washing clothes at nearby Litten Branch when the wolves attacked. Less romantic is a third story, in which the last wolf in Owen County was killed near the cave in 1845.

Regardless of how it got its name, Wolf Cave is an example of how caves are formed by groundwater erosion of the limestone bedrock. The popularity of Wolf

Twin Bridges is a collapsed ceiling at the east end of Wolf Cave in McCormick's Creek State Park.

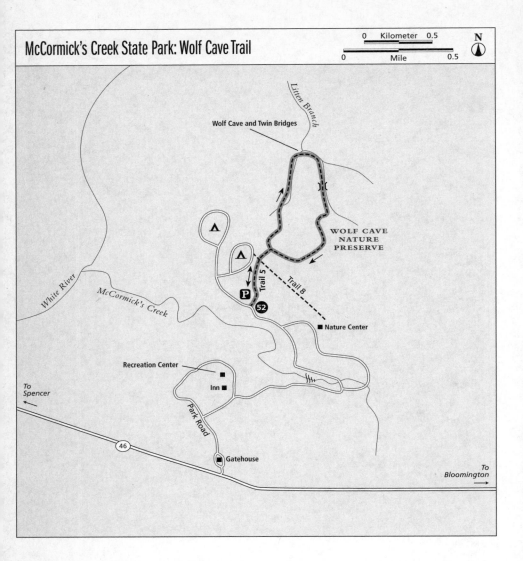

Cave, coupled with a new trailhead that eliminates crossing McCormick's Creek Canyon, makes this one of the busier trails in the park. Many visitors hike only to the cave and return the same way, skipping the eastern leg of the trail along Litten Branch.

To reach the cave, begin at the Trail 5 trailhead and walk north through a wooded area pockmarked with funnel-shaped sinkholes. At 0.3 mile Trail 5 intersects Trail 8, a paved path from the campground (left) to the nature center and pool (right). Continue straight and enter Wolf Cave Nature Preserve at 0.4 mile and cross a footbridge over Litten Branch. Cross the creek a couple more times before reaching Wolf Cave. You can follow the trail around the cave to Twin Bridges, but going through the cave may be prohibited to protect bats and their nesting habitat. If the cave is not marked as closed, the passageway is 57 yards long, with a narrow 18-inch opening at the far end. The cave is usually dry in summer but can be wet after extended periods of rain. Wear long pants and bring a flashlight. It is dark in the cave, plus the light helps in spotting critters, such as the cave salamander.

The cave opens at Twin Bridges, which was created when a roof section of Wolf Cave collapsed. Instead of backtracking, continue on Trail 5 and follow the east fork of Litten Branch south from Twin Bridges, crossing the creek once on a footbridge and then rock-hopping several more times over the next 0.5 mile. Near the 1.3-mile mark, the trail turns right (southwest) for a gradual uphill climb. Three benches are scattered along the trail, providing pleasant places to pause and enjoy the solitude of the surrounding forest. The beech tree is the dominant species in the preserve, but maple, sycamore, elm, walnut, tulip poplar, and elm trees are also present. Oak trees— red, white and chinquapin—prevail on the high ground, along with hickory trees.

At 1.7 miles cross Trail 8 again and continue on Trail 5 to the trailhead parking lot.

Miles and Directions

0.0 Begin at the trailhead.

0.3 Reach a juncture with Trail 8; go straight.

0.4 Enter Wolf Cave Nature Preserve.

1.0 Reach Wolf Cave and Twin Bridges.

1.7 Reach the Trail 8 juncture; stay straight on Trail 5 and return to the trailhead parking lot.

2.0 Arrive back at the trailhead.

Two young boys make their way through Wolf Cave in McCormick's Creek State Park.

53 Patoka Lake: Main Trail

This trail skirts the perimeter of a broad peninsula near the west end of Patoka Lake, the state's second-largest reservoir.

Location: Southern Indiana, about 9 miles south of French Lick
Distance: 6.5-mile loop
Elevation change: About 60 feet.
Approximate hiking time: 3.5 hours
Difficulty: Strenuous
Jurisdiction: Indiana Department of Natural Resources, Division of State Parks & Reservoirs
Special attractions: Totem Rock, Pilot Knob, other sandstone cliffs
Fees and permits: Park entry fee, higher for out-of-state vehicles; season passes available
Maps: USGS Cuzco and Birdseye; Patoka Lake hiking area brochure
Camping: Newton-Stewart State Recreation Area—445 modern and 45 primitive campsites; 7 backpacking sites
Trailhead facilities: Large parking lot at the trailhead; restrooms and water available at the solar-heated nature center; water also available at campgrounds

Finding the trailhead: From French Lick go 10 miles south on IN 145 to IN 164 and turn right (west). Go 1 mile to Crawford CR 27 and turn right (north). Go just over 1 mile to the gatehouse, then another 1.7 miles before turning left (west) and going 1 more mile to the nature center parking lot. The trailhead is off the northeast corner of the building.

The Hike

Archaeological evidence indicates prehistoric man inhabited this area as long as 10,000 years ago. Stone tools, pottery shards, and flint points have been discovered here. Early white settlers found petroglyphs of three turtles carved into a rock and on nearby trees. No explanation was ever determined, but speculation was that the artwork represented some sort of totem or "family mark" to native peoples. Consequently the site came to be known as Totem Rock. Although the carvings were destroyed more than a hundred years ago, the name stuck.

Totem Rock remains one of the highlights on this trail. The rock is located in the beginning portion of the 6.5-mile loop that traces a clockwise path around the edge of Newton-Stewart State Recreation Area on the western end of Patoka Lake. The 8,800-acre reservoir was created by the U.S. Army Corps of Engineers in the 1970s as a flood-control project for the Patoka River and more than a half dozen smaller creeks and rivers.

The Main Trail is one of three trails on the 1,000-acre peninsula that makes up the Newton-Stewart area. Various shortcuts and spurs cross the trail, but the Main Trail is simple to follow because of the prominent trail markings. Orange and white circles are painted on trees and are visible from both directions. Occasional signs also point the way, and mileage markers are posted at 0.5-mile intervals beginning just beyond

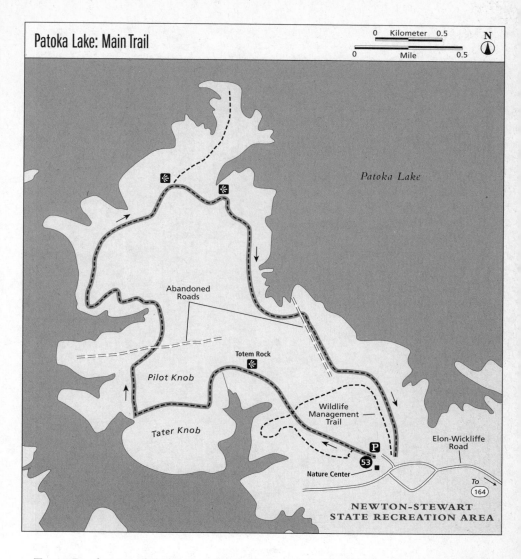

Patoka Lake: Main Trail

Patoka Lake

Abandoned
Roads

Totem Rock

Pilot Knob

Tater Knob

Wildlife
Management
Trail

Elon-Wickliffe
Road

Nature Center

P
53

To
164

NEWTON-STEWART
STATE RECREATION AREA

Totem Rock. Many hikers go no farther than Totem Rock before backtracking. Few hike the entire trail.

The outbound leg along the western side of the peninsula presents the most rugged aspects of the hike—a continuous series of gullies and rolling ridges decorated by sandstone outcroppings. The first evidence of the sandstone formations comes just past 0.1-mile mark when the Main Trail crosses the Wildlife Management Demonstration Trail. Turn right and make a short climb down to a rocky bluff that offers a prelude to what lies ahead.

But it is Totem Rock that is the most impressive formation on the trail. Arrive at the large rock overhang at 1.4 miles. The rock served as a gathering place for settlers

A hiker passes beneath the shadows of Totem Rock at Patoka Lake Main Trail. The sandstone formation has long been a drawing card for people.

for many years, either for church services or picnics. Local residents also called it Salt-peter Cave.

Head downhill away from Totem Rock, cross a creek, and head uphill to a meadow at Tater Knob. Cross the meadow on an uphill course to the northwest and reenter the woods before the 2.0-mile mark. Continue to pass through gullies and by rock ledges before coming to Pilot Knob at 2.5 miles. Go left (west) around the formation and head downhill. After passing another rock ledge on the right (east) side of the trail near the 3.0-mile mark, slip past one more gully and then hike a fairly flat stretch for more than 0.5 mile.

Cross an abandoned road at about 3.8 miles and pass through a small meadow. The trail reaches a juncture at 4.3 miles where a sign indicates that the lake is to the left (north); the Main Trail continues straight (east). Skirt the edge of two meadows, the second being the larger, as the trail crosses the north end of the peninsula, then turns south for the final 2.0 miles.

Almost half that distance is over a series of gullies that carry seasonal runoff. Beech trees dominate this area, but there is also a pine plantation along this side of the peninsula where bald eagles regularly nest in winter. A watchful hiker might be able to spot one.

Just past 5.7 miles the trail intersects with an abandoned road for 0.1 mile before dropping off left (east) into a broad ravine. After climbing out of the ravine, the final 0.5 mile is along a level grade above a stretch of sandstone bluffs to the left (east).

Miles and Directions

0.0   Begin at the trailhead and go left.
0.1   Cross the Wildlife Management Demonstration Trail and turn right.
1.4   Reach Totem Rock.
2.5   Arrive at Pilot Knob.
3.0   Pass a rock ledge on the right (east).
3.8   Cross an abandoned road.
4.3   Go right at the trail sign that reads TO LAKE/TRAIL CONTINUES.
5.7   The trail joins an abandoned road.
5.8   The trail leaves the abandoned road.
6.5   Arrive back at the trailhead.

54 Lincoln State Park

This hike combines several park trails over ground walked by Abraham Lincoln during his boyhood years.

Location: South of Dale in Spencer County
Distance: 5.2-mile double loop
Elevation change: Minimal
Approximate hiking time: 3 hours
Difficulty: Easy
Jurisdiction: Indiana Department of Natural Resources, Division of State Parks & Reservoirs
Fees and permits: Park entry fee, higher for out-of-state vehicles; season passes available
Maps: USGS Chrisney and Santa Claus;

Lincoln State Park brochure
Special attractions: Gravesite of Lincoln's only sister, Sarah; Sarah Lincoln's Woods Nature Preserve; Lincoln Lake; Lincoln Memorial Plaza
Camping: Lincoln State Park—150 modern and 89 primitive campsites; youth tent area
Trailhead facilities: Parking lot, restrooms, and water supply at trailhead; water and restrooms available at other locations throughout the park

Finding the trailhead: From Dale drive 5 miles south on US 231 to IN 162 in Gentryville. Turn left (east) and go 1.9 miles to the Lincoln State Park entrance, which is across from the Lincoln Boyhood National Memorial on the left (north) side of the highway. Turn right (south) to the park gatehouse and go 0.1 mile to the Lincoln Memorial Plaza parking lot. Turn left (east) into the parking area. The trailhead is on the north side of the parking lot.

The Hike

Born in Kentucky and elected from Illinois as the nation's sixteenth president, Abraham Lincoln spent his boyhood days here in Indiana. The Lincolns moved from Kentucky to this area in 1816, when Abraham was only seven and his sister, Sarah, was nine. Thomas Lincoln, their father, settled on 160 acres of dense forest.

Just a boy, Abe helped his father clear the land for a frontier farm that they worked for fourteen years before moving to Illinois. The actual farm site is across the highway from the state park at Lincoln Boyhood National Memorial, which is administered by the National Park Service. The gravesite of Lincoln's mother, Nancy Hanks Lincoln, who died in 1818 of "milksick" poisoning caused by white snakeroot, is also across the highway. The national memorial has a visitor center, a cabin site memorial, a living historical farm, and several short hiking trails.

Although farming occupied much of young Abe's life, he no doubt explored some areas of the state park that bears his name. It is known that he frequented the Noah Gorden mill.

Park management has been in the process of revising its trail system, and park brochures may not reflect the changes made to the trails. The following hike combines elements of Trails 1, 2, 3, and 5, which also have names—Lake Trail, John Carter Trail, Sarah Lincoln Grigsby Trail, and Mr. Lincoln's Neighborhood Walk, respectively.

From the Lincoln Memorial Plaza, hike north parallel to the main park road. Go about 0.1 mile before joining Trail 2; the John Carter Trail, named for a Lincoln family neighbor. Turn right (east) to enter a stand of pine trees. At 0.4 mile the trail angles to the northeast and makes the first of several crossings over Davis Enlow Ditch, a creek that trickles off to the northwest. There are several footbridges along the way.

Part of the trail is an old roadbed that runs parallel to railroad tracks within the park boundary. At 1.0 mile pass a couple abandoned coal strip mine pits, after which the trail turns to the west to go uphill slightly.

Turn south at the hilltop, following the park's east boundary for more than 0.5 mile over a couple of ridges. At 1.5 miles an unmarked trail joins from the right. Keep going straight (south), crossing more footbridges before reaching a concrete bridge at 2.0 miles. Cross the bridge and walk parallel to the creek that feeds Lincoln Lake. Trail 2 ends at the lakeshore, where it links with Trail 1 (Lake Trail) at 2.2 miles.

The gravesite of Sarah Lincoln, sister of Abraham Lincoln. The cemetery and Little Pigeon Primitive Church are located in the park.

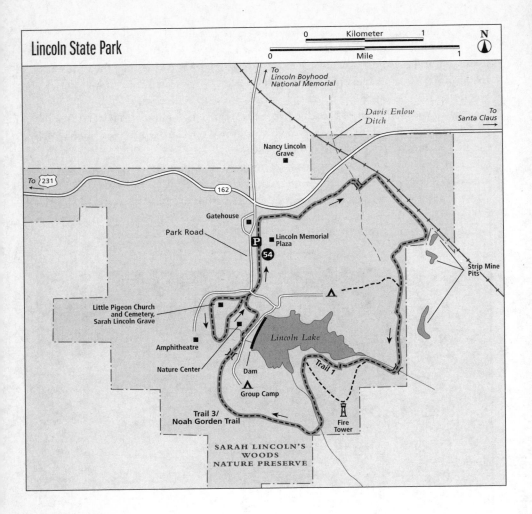

Turn left (south) onto Trail 1, passing two spur trails that lead to a fire tower, and continue for about 0.5 mile to where Trail 1 joins Trail 3 (Sarah Lincoln Grigsby Trail). Turn left onto Trail 3, which leads through Sarah Lincoln's Woods Nature Preserve, a ninety-five-acre area extending from the creek west over a ridgetop. The preserve has a variety of oak species—red, white, black, post, blackjack, and scarlet— plus many other common hardwoods like pignut hickory, sugar maple, white ash, and shagbark hickory.

Leave the west end of the preserve as the trail descends off the ridgetop to curl clockwise through a low spot. Cross a footbridge before exiting the woods just below the lake dam near the group camp area to reconnect with Trail 1 at 4.0 miles. Cross the dam on Trail 1 and intersect Trail 5 (Mr. Lincoln's Neighborhood Walk) off the north corner of the dam.

Turn left (west) onto a gravel path that leads to the Little Pigeon Primitive Baptist Church, the church the Lincolns joined when Abe was fourteen. His sister is buried in the graveyard behind the church.

Continue west on the gravel road past the church and turn left (south) to pass the site of Noah Gorden's mill and home at 4.5 miles. Turn left (east) at the homesite and curl back through the woods to complete the loop just east of the church at 4.8 miles. Turn right (east) and cross the paved road; turn left (north) to cross the main park road and go up a set of stone steps. Follow Trail 2, which runs parallel to the main park road, to return to the Lincoln Memorial Plaza parking lot.

Miles and Directions

0.0 Begin at the trailhead.

0.1 Turn right (east) at the Trail 2 juncture.

0.4 Cross Davis Enlow Ditch for the first time.

1.0 Pass abandoned coal mine pits.

1.5 Continue straight at an unmarked trail juncture.

2.0 Cross a concrete bridge.

2.2 At the trail juncture go left (west) on Trail 1 along lakeshore.

2.3 At the trail juncture go straight (west).

2.6 At the trail juncture go straight (south) to join Trail 3.

3.8 Reach the Lincoln Lake dam and reconnect with Trail 1; go left.

4.1 At the trail juncture, go left (west) on Trail 5, a gravel road to Mr. Lincoln's Neighborhood Walk.

4.2 Arrive at the Little Pigeon Primitive Baptist Church and cemetery.

4.5 Pass site of Noah Gorden's mill.

4.8 At the gravel road and Mr. Lincoln's Neighborhood Walk, turn right (east).

4.9 At the trail juncture turn left (north).

5.2 Arrive back at the trailhead.

Hoosier National Forest

From just south of Bloomington to Tell City on the Ohio River, the Hoosier National Forest forms a patchwork covering almost 200,000 acres. Despite its size, the Hoosier represents a mere 1 percent of the massive hardwood forest that blanketed Indiana before settlement by pioneers.

Lumber was a major commodity by the late 1800s, and Indiana led the nation in timber production in 1899 by harvesting more than one billion board feet, most of it prime hardwoods like white oak, black walnut, and tulip poplar. It is estimated that an average 800 million board feet of timber were cut annually from 1869 to 1903. By comparison, less than half that amount is being harvested in Indiana today, but hardwoods remain a vibrant commodity in an industry that has a $17 billion annual economic impact in the state.

In the 1800s trees documented as being 6 to 12 feet in diameter were chopped down and sold off. Most of the virgin forest was gone in 50 years. In addition, wildlife species that once roamed Indiana were gone, including white-tailed deer and wild turkey.

The demolition of forestland happened everywhere across the state, but the consequences seemed most wasteful in southern Indiana, where settlers learned a hard lesson. Land was cheap at $1 per acre, but the steep, rocky ground—now devoid of trees and depleted of nutrients—was prone to erosion and unsuitable for agriculture.

Small farms were failing, and the Great Depression only made matters worse. As farms were abandoned, the tax-delinquent land created a mounting fiscal problem for state and local governments. In 1934 Governor Paul McNutt sought help from the U.S. Forest Service, asking the agency to purchase land with the intent of establishing a national forest.

The first parcels were acquired in 1935, and in 1951 the Hoosier National Forest was established. In the meantime, the Civilian Conservation Corps (CCC) played a hand in reforestation efforts on the land. Although it does not match its presettlement glory, the forest has regrown and become the largest single landholding in the state. Within its scattered boundaries are some noteworthy sites.

The Charles C. Deam Wilderness, a 12,900-acre tract just south of Bloomington, is named for Indiana's first state forester. Granted wilderness protection by Congress in 1982, the Deam Wilderness borders Lake Monroe and contains forested ridgetops and ravines typical of southern Indiana.

Hemlock Cliffs is a box canyon carved out of sandstone by seasonal waterfalls. Eastern hemlock, an uncommon tree in Indiana, grows along the high cliffs of this canyon.

Pioneer Mothers Memorial Forest features the largest known stand of virgin timber in the state. The eighty-eight-acre property has been preserved since 1816.

There are countless other treasures in the Hoosier National Forest, including an abundance of wildlife. The deer and turkeys that were once absent have been restored, making the Hoosier a popular area for hunters, who can also pursue ruffed grouse, squirrels, and other game.

The Forest Service maintains a 260-mile trail system in the Hoosier National Forest, most of which are multiple-use trails for hikers, mountain bikers, and horseback riders. There are countless additional miles of abandoned trails, primitive roads, and forest service roads for the more adventurous explorer.

The trails in this chapter are presented south and southwest from Bloomington.

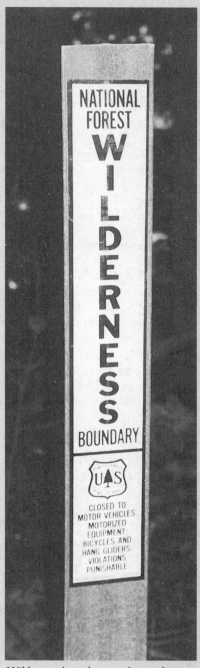

Wilderness boundary marker at the Charles C. Deam Wilderness in the Hoosier National Forest.

55 Cope Hollow Loop

This trail leads through the Charles C. Deam Wilderness of the Hoosier National Forest.

Location: South of Bloomington, south-central Indiana

Distance: 9.5-mile loop

Elevation change: A drop of 270 feet from the trailhead to the low point at Tanyard Branch; several other drops and rises along the way

Approximate hiking time: 6 hours

Difficulty: Moderate to strenuous

Jurisdiction: Hoosier National Forest, Browns-town District

Maps: USGS Elkinsville, Allens Creek, and Norman; *National Geographic/Trails Illustrated* map of Hoosier National Forest; Hoosier National Forest's Charles C. Deam Wilderness map

Fees and permits: No fees or permits required

Special attractions: Todd Cemetery, Tanyard Branch of Salt Creek, Dennis Murphy Hollow

Camping: Walk-in camping is permitted anywhere in the wilderness area, except within 100 yards of Tower Ridge Road, and is restricted to designated sites when within 100 feet of ponds, lakes, trails, or streams. Other wilderness rules on food and beverage containers also apply; group size is limited to 10 or fewer persons.

Trailhead facilities: There are two gravel parking lots on either side of Tower Ridge Road for about 16 vehicles, but no restrooms and no drinking water.

Finding the trailhead: From the intersection of IN 46 and IN 446 on the east side of Bloomington, go about 12 miles south on IN 446 to Tower Ridge Road. Turn left (east) and go 5.5 miles to the Grubb Ridge parking area. The trail begins on the north edge of the small parking area.

The Hike

It takes a degree of tolerance for horses to appreciate this hike. The trail is a multiuse venue, and it is hard to avoid horse traffic in the Hoosier National Forest. Only about 19 percent of the 260 miles of trails in the HNF are for foot traffic only, so hikers who want to see the area must share.

There is plenty to see on this hike, but it takes some effort to get to the highlights—Tanyard Branch and Dennis Murphy Hollow. Foot traffic is light, probably because horseback riders make heavy use of the trail. That makes for pretty rough trail conditions in certain spots, where the horses can turn most soil into a sloppy mess that retains water. When dried out, the stiffened mud can be hard on your ankles. The horse impact is less on the section south of Tower Ridge Road. Be alert to abandoned trails that occasionally join the main trail. Look for Forest Service trail markers—thin plastic markers about 3 feet tall—when uncertain.

Begin the hike at the Grubb Ridge trailhead by walking past the metal gate on the north side of the parking lot. This is the same starting point as the Peninsula Trail. At 0.1 mile turn left off the Peninsula/Grubb Ridge Trail to pick up the westbound leg of the Cope Hollow Trail. Pass a small pond and then cross over to the south side of Tower Ridge Road at 0.2 mile.

The trail does not wander far from the lightly traveled road over the next few miles. At 0.6 mile the trail splits. The left (south) path is the inbound leg of the Cope

The Tanyard Branch of Salt Creek on the south loop of the Cope Hollow Loop.

Hollow Trail. Go right (west) and continue with Tower Ridge Road to the right (north) and the back end of Dennis Murphy Hollow to the left (south). Pass an abandoned trail that joins from the left (south). Cross over to the north side of Tower Ridge Road at 1.1 miles.

Pass through a stretch of clearings in the forest as the trail curves toward the southwest. A series of deep ravines drop off to the right (north) over the next mile, but the trail keeps a relatively level course. The last of the ravines forms the east edge of Frog Pond Ridge, a 1.5-mile finger pointing almost directly north to Saddle Creek, which flows into Lake Monroe. Continue left (south), hugging Tower Ridge Road until coming to Todd Cemetery at the 3.0-mile mark. Pass along the west edge of the cemetery and make a fishhook turn to the northwest. Go another 0.5 mile to a trail split. Stay left, crossing Tower Ridge Road to the southwest at 3.5 miles.

Pass through a meadow and head downhill to connect at 4.0 miles with one of several feeder streams that form Tanyard Branch. The downward trend is so gradual that you will hardly notice the 150-foot drop from Tower Ridge Road. Along the way, three seasonal streams feed Tanyard Branch from the left (east) before Tanyard Branch spills into Little Salt Creek at 4.7 miles. At the third stream the trail turns left (northeast) into Cope Hollow.

After walking up the unnamed stream in Cope Hollow, begin a sharp uphill climb of more than 100 feet to a ridge forming the eastern boundary of the hollow. The next stretch of trail rises 100 feet over a span of about 1.25 miles, alternating between woods and meadows. Take a 0.25-mile trek uphill to a ridgetop; turn right (southeast) for 0.1 mile, then angle left (southeast) and drop into Dennis Murphy Hollow at 6.5 miles. After reaching the creek at the floor of the hollow at 7.1 miles, turn left (north). Follow the small stream through a fern–laden valley for 0.4 mile before turning right (northeast). Cross the creek and climb to a ridge that separates Dennis Murphy Hollow from Martin Hollow.

The ridge flattens out noticeably at the top as the trail passes through a couple of stands of pine trees before it intersects with the Hunter Creek Trail at 7.8 miles. Turn left (northwest) at the intersection and drop just below the ridgetop to meander around a series of gullies that tumble into Martin Hollow. Move back up to the ridgetop and follow a northward course before reaching a trail intersection at 9.0 miles. Turn left (west), passing a small pond on the left before reconnecting with the outbound leg of the Cope Hollow Trail near Tower Ridge Road at 9.3 miles. Turn right (northeast) and follow the trail back to the Grubb Ridge trailhead.

Miles and Directions

0.0 Begin at the trailhead.

0.1 Turn left at the trail juncture.

0.2 Cross to south side of Tower Ridge Road.

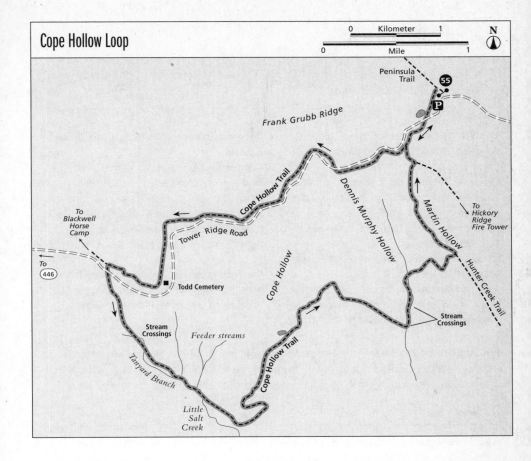

Cope Hollow Loop

- **0.6** At the trail intersection go right (west).
- **1.1** Cross to north side of Tower Ridge Road.
- **3.0** Pass Todd Cemetery.
- **3.5** Cross to south side of Tower Ridge Road.
- **4.0** Reach the Tanyard Branch of Little Salt Creek.
- **4.7** Reach Little Salt Creek.
- **5.0** Turn left (northeast) from creek and climb uphill.
- **6.5** Descend to Dennis Murphy Hollow.
- **7.1** Reach the creek in the bottom of the hollow.
- **7.8** Arrive at the Hunter Creek Trail juncture; bear left.
- **9.0** At the trail juncture turn left (west).
- **9.3** Return to Tower Ridge Road and cross over to north side.
- **9.5** Arrive back at the trailhead.

56 Peninsula Trail

This hike through Charles C. Deam Wilderness leads to a peninsula jutting into Lake Monroe, the state's largest lake.

Location: Hoosier National Forest, 16 miles southeast of Bloomington, south-central Indiana

Distance: 9.0 miles out and back

Elevation change: 300 feet from trailhead to lakeshore

Approximate hiking time: 5 hours or overnight

Difficulty: Moderate

Jurisdiction: Hoosier National Forest, Brownstown District

Fees and permits: No fees or permits required

Maps: USGS Elkinsville; *National Geographic/ Trails Illustrated* map of Hoosier National Forest

Special attractions: Peninsula campsite, Lake Monroe

Camping: Walk-in camping is permitted anywhere in the wilderness area, except within 100 yards of Tower Ridge Road, and is restricted to designated sites when within 100 feet of ponds, lakes, trails, or streams. Other wilderness rules apply; group size is limited to 10 or fewer persons.

Trailhead facilities: Two gravel parking lots on either side of Tower Ridge Road for about 16 vehicles; no restrooms or drinking water

Finding the trailhead: From the intersection of IN 46 and IN 446 on the east side of Bloomington, go about 12 miles south on IN 446 to Tower Ridge Road. Turn left (east) and go 5.5 miles to the Grubb Ridge parking area. The trail begins on the north edge of the small parking area.

The Hike

Although this trail is shared with horseback riders, it is a worthy stretch because of the destination—a backcountry campsite at the edge of a peninsula overlooking a sizable portion of Lake Monroe, the perfect setting from which to view spectacular sunsets. The area features two prominent ridges—Frank Grubb Ridge and John Grubb Ridge. The majority of the Peninsula Trail lies along the latter.

Established by Congress in 1982, the wilderness area covers nearly 13,000 acres. It is a well-used and well-marked area despite the wilderness designation, largely because lengthy portions of the trail followed abandoned roadbeds. Unlike other multiuse trails in the Hoosier National Forest, this one has minimal horse traffic.

From the trailhead hike 100 yards before reaching a trail split; the left (southwest) fork begins the Cope Hollow Loop. The right (northeast) fork is the beginning of the Grubb Ridge Loop and the Peninsula Trail; take this fork.

The trail, on an abandoned roadbed, curves through a forest of mixed hardwoods punctured by occasional stands of pine trees. Backcountry campsites can be located along the trail. Eventually the route straightens out on a northwesterly course along John Grubb Ridge. The ridgetop provides a reasonably level path, with occasional uphill stretches, but most of the topographic changes occur on either side of the

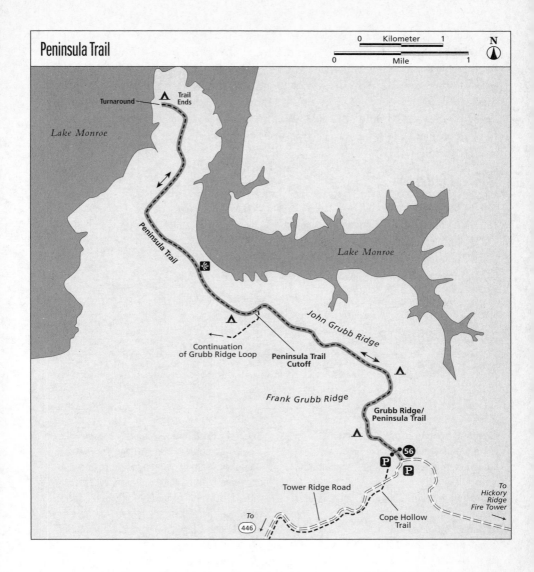

trail—gradual slopes to the left, sharper drops on the right toward Lake Monroe.

At 2.5 miles the trail splits and the Grubb Ridge Loop (Peninsula Trail cutoff) breaks to the left (southwest). Turn right (northwest) to continue toward the peninsula, passing through an area dotted with older hardwoods and little undergrowth. After 0.5 mile begin a descent of about 100 feet in elevation. Here, at 3.0 miles, the trail overlooks a very steep drop-off to the lake nearly 200 feet to the right (northeast). The remainder of the hike is a gradual descent in which scenery alternates through pine and hardwood stands, forest openings, cedar thickets, and patches of scrub brush.

Near the end of the trail, look for signs of old farmsteads—fence posts, rusted barbwire strands, perhaps an old pot or two, or remnants of an abandoned vehicle. Walk right to the rocky shores of Lake Monroe at 4.5 miles, a 10,750-acre reservoir created when the U.S. Army Corps of Engineers dammed up Salt Creek and several smaller tributaries—Clear, Sugar, Allens, Moore, and Saddle. The east side of the peninsula borders the Middle Fork State Wildlife Refuge, a haven for waterfowl.

To complete the hike, retrace the outbound path to the Grubb Ridge parking area at 9.0 miles.

Miles and Directions

0.0 Begin at the trailhead. Walk 100 yards and bear right at the fork.

2.5 Go right (northeast) at the trail junction.

3.0 Reach the Lake Monroe overlook.

4.5 Arrive at the peninsula campsite, your turnaround point.

9.0 Arrive back at the trailhead.

57 Sycamore Loop

A trail that leads along creek and to ravine overlooks of the Charles C. Deam Wilderness.

Location: Southeast of Bloomington
Distance: 6.3-mile loop
Elevation change: Gains and losses of 250 feet
Approximate hiking time: 3.5 hours or overnight
Difficulty: Moderate
Jurisdiction: Hoosier National Forest, Brownstown District
Fees and permits: No fees or permits required
Maps: USGS Elkinsville; *National Geographic/ Trails Illustrated* map of Hoosier National Forest

Special attractions: Sycamore Branch valley, a pioneer cemetery, Hickory Ridge fire tower
Camping: Walk-in camping is permitted anywhere in the wilderness area, except within 100 yards of Tower Ridge Road, and is restricted to designated sites when within 100 feet of ponds, lakes, trails, or streams. Other wilderness rules apply; group size is limited to 10 or fewer persons.
Trailhead facilities: Gravel parking area; no restrooms or drinking water at trailhead

Finding the trailhead: From the intersection of IN 46 and IN 446 on the east side of Bloomington, go about 12 miles south on IN 446 to Tower Ridge Road. Turn left (east) and go 8 miles to the Hickory Ridge fire tower parking area. The trail begins on the north edge of the parking area on the other side of the gate.

The Hike

Of the handful of hiker-only trails in the Hoosier National Forest, this ranks near the top. Difficulty is moderate, and the chance for solitude is superb.

The trail gets its name from the Sycamore Branch of Salt Creek and about a third of the hike follows the meandering rocky stream on an easterly course through a thick stand of towering white pines. But it is the tall sycamores near the headwaters that make it obvious how settlers came to name the stream that trickles east and then northeast into the South Fork of Salt Creek, which feeds nearby Lake Monroe, the state's largest lake.

The secluded stretch is popular for overnight campers at marked and unmarked campsites. The beginning and ending legs of this trail receive the heaviest traffic because of campsite locations and the cemetery.

Begin by hiking down the gravel road that leads to Terril Cemetery and will later serves as the inbound leg of this hike. At 0.25 mile turn right (east) off the roadway at a marked campsite and begin a gradual downhill walk along a ridgetop for another 0.25 mile. At the east tip of the ridge, the path becomes a little steeper and a series of switchbacks leads into a valley near the headwaters of Sycamore Branch.

While crossing the stream for the first time at the 1.0-mile mark, it is possible to hear traffic along Tower Ridge Road on the high bluff to the right (south). Continue to hop back and forth across stream several times over the next mile while hiking through a valley dominated by white pines and some tulip poplars.

One of the few hiking-only trails in the Hoosier National Forest passes through a stand of pine trees along Sycamore Branch.

The Hickory Ridge fire tower at the trailhead parking lot for the Sycamore Loop.

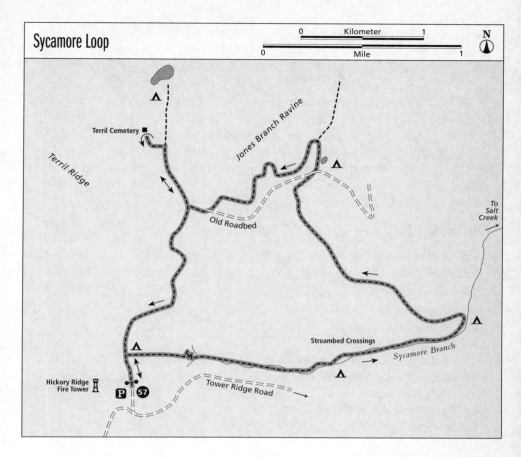

Sycamore Loop

0 — Kilometer — 1
0 — Mile — 1

N

Terril Cemetery

Jones Branch Ravine

Terril Ridge

Old Roadbed

To Salt Creek

Streambed Crossings

Sycamore Branch

Hickory Ridge Fire Tower

P 57

Tower Ridge Road

At 2.4 miles take an abrupt left (northwest) turn to begin an uphill stretch of trail that is almost leisurely in that it takes a full mile to climb 250 feet from the valley floor to the top of Terril Ridge. Along the way the forest switches from the thickly clustered pine trees of the valley floor to a mixture of hardwoods—oak, hickory, beech—and occasional pine trees.

At 3.2 miles turn right (northeast) onto an old roadbed and head downhill for 0.1 mile, then back uphill to where the roadbed turns right (southeast) at 3.3 miles. Go straight (north) and continue uphill. At 3.5 miles turn left (west) and wind west and south along a ledge that overlooks the Jones Branch ravine on the right (northwest) side of the trail.

At 4.3 miles reconnect with the gravel road and turn right (north). At 4.6 miles turn left (west) toward the Terril Cemetery, which can be seen from the roadway, or continue straight (north) for 0.25 mile to a remote pond that offers camping possibilities.

Grave markers in the small cemetery mark the final resting place for members of the Terril, Axsom, and Grubb families, whose legacies survive as place names in the Deam Wilderness—Terril and Grubb Ridges and the Axsom Branch of Salt Creek. The fading headstones give a clue to the harsh times the families endured while attempting to scratch out a living during the late 1800s and early 1900s. With rare exception, dates indicate that few lived beyond sixty years. Hezekiah and Alice Axsom have five children under the age of thirteen buried here, including four who died in one year—1931. The Whites lost a son who lived but two days.

Upon returning from the cemetery to the gravel road at 4.8 miles, turn right (south) and follow its winding path for about 1.5 miles back to the Hickory Ridge parking area at 6.3 miles. Before leaving, get an impressive view of the Hoosier National Forest and surrounding areas from the Hickory Ridge fire tower.

Miles and Directions

0.0   Begin at the trailhead.

0.25 At the marked campsite, turn right (east) off the gravel road.

1.0   Cross Sycamore Branch.

2.4   Turn left (northwest) and leave the valley on the climb to Terril Ridge.

3.2   At the old roadbed turn right (northeast).

3.5   At the trail juncture turn left (west).

4.3   At the gravel road turn right (north).

4.6   Take the left (west) turnoff to Terril Cemetery. (**Option:** Continue straight, north, for 0.25 mile for possible campsites.)

4.8   Return to the gravel road and turn right (south).

6.3   Arrive back at the trailhead.

58 Pioneer Mothers Memorial Forest

This linear trail passes through the largest known section of old-growth forest in the state.

Location: Just outside Paoli, south-central Indiana

Distance: 1.3 miles out and back

Elevation change: 180 feet from the parking lot to the memorial wall

Approximate hiking time: 45 minutes

Difficulty: Easy

Jurisdiction: Hoosier National Forest, Tell City District

Fees and permits: No fees or permits required

Maps: USGS Paoli; *National Geographic/Trails Illustrated* map of Hoosier National Forest

Special attractions: A white oak estimated to be 600 years old, Pioneer Mothers Memorial wall

Camping: No camping permitted

Trailhead facilities: Parking lot; no restrooms or drinking water at trailhead

Finding the trailhead: From the Paoli town square go west on IN 56 for 1 block to the first stoplight. Turn left (south) onto IN 37 and go 2 miles to a parking area on the left (east) side of the highway. The trail begins at the north end of the parking lot.

To reach the east entrance, from the Paoli town square go east 1.6 miles on US 150 to the first stoplight and turn right (south). There is a small parking area for two to three vehicles. Follow the paved road 0.4 mile to the Pioneer Mothers Memorial wall.

The Hike

Joseph Cox was the original owner of this property, and it was his decision in the early 1800s that preserved the ancient trees gracing an 88-acre section of this 250-acre property. It is the last virgin forest of this size known to exist in Indiana. When gazing at the massive oak and walnut trees in this small preserve, imagine what it must have been like when the state had more than nineteen million acres of forest like this.

Cox and his family managed to keep the woods untouched, despite numerous bids from timber companies. A community-wide effort to purchase the property from the Cox estate gained national exposure through the *Saturday Evening Post,* and the citizens were able to carry on Cox's pledge by raising the necessary $24,300. The U.S. Forest Service acquired the property in 1944 and designated it as a "natural area," which gave it federal protection while providing the Forest Service an area in which to study plant succession, tree growth, and forest conditions. The area was named a Research Natural Area in 1944.

The trail is unmarked other than at the entrance, but it is easy to follow for the short distance to the memorial wall and back. The area is not heavily visited.

From the west-end parking lot, locate the trail near an information marker. Enter the woods and begin a gradual downhill walk through a cathedral of enormous hardwoods.

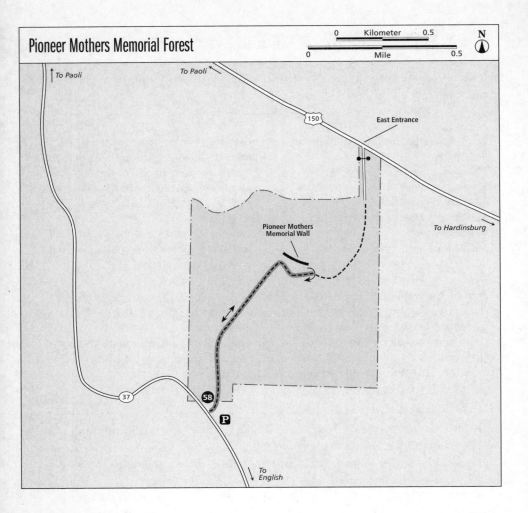

Pioneer Mothers Memorial Forest

Just before reaching the Pioneer Mothers Memorial wall at 0.65 mile, look for the remains of a white oak tree estimated as being more than 600 years old. The top of tree has broken off, but the base remains standing. From the memorial wall, backtrack along the trail to return to the west-end parking lot.

Miles and Directions

0.0 Begin at the trailhead.

0.65 Reach the Pioneer Mothers Memorial wall. Retrace your steps to the trailhead.

1.3 Arrive back at the trailhead.

59 Hemlock Cliffs National Scenic Trail

This trail leads through a box canyon draped with hemlock and featuring seasonal waterfalls and high sandstone cliffs.

Location: 7 miles south of English, south-central Indiana
Distance: 1.4-mile loop
Elevation change: 70 to 80 feet
Approximate hiking time: 1 hour
Difficulty: Moderate
Jurisdiction: Hoosier National Forest, Tell City District

Maps: USGS Taswell; *National Geographic/Trails Illustrated* map of Hoosier National Forest
Fees and permits: No fees or permits required
Special attractions: Two waterfalls
Camping: No camping permitted
Trailhead facilities: Gravel parking lot; no restrooms or drinking water at trailhead

Finding the trailhead: From the intersection of IN 37 and I-64, go north 2.7 miles to Crawford CR 8 and turn left (west). Go 2.5 miles to an unmarked gravel road. Take the gravel road 1.7 miles west and then north to a marked entrance for Hemlock Cliffs National Scenic Trail. Turn right (north) at the sign and take the gravel road (Forest Service 1134) to the loop at its end; park. The trailhead is east of the parking lot. From the new IN 37, brown signs lead the way to the trailhead along county roads. Follow these signs to the trailhead.

The entrance sign for Hemlock Cliffs National Scenic Trail.

Hemlock trees hang from the cliffs along Hemlock Cliffs National Scenic Trail.

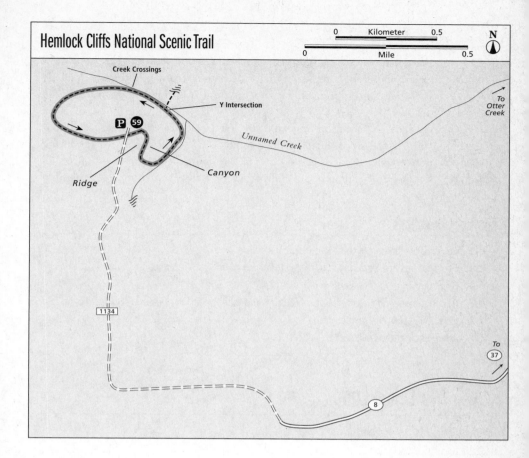

Hemlock Cliffs National Scenic Trail

Creek Crossings

Y Intersection

To Otter Creek

Unnamed Creek

Canyon

Ridge

1134

To 37

8

The Hike

This trail has more dynamic scenery packed into its short distance than many longer hikes. There are two seasonal waterfalls, steep-walled box canyons, a meandering creek, and hemlock trees dotting the sandstone cliffs.

The trail's remote location serves as a limiting factor on the area. The box canyons were popular with rock climbers, but visitation started to decrease when the Forest Service imposed a ban on rock climbing in 1996.

The trailhead marker is easily visible east of the parking area. Follow the crushed-stone walkway downhill to the trailhead and turn right (south). At 0.2 mile the trail turns left (east) and descends through a gap in the ledge. Wiggle through the opening to the left and descend a set of natural stone steps into the canyon. Its closed, bowl-shaped end to the right (south) is wet with a trickle of water even in the middle of summer.

The trail heads left (northeast) from the waterfall and crosses the small creek before reaching a Y intersection at the 0.6-mile mark. The right fork leads to another box canyon and small waterfall at 0.7 mile, which can be viewed from below or from a higher vantage point, depending on which side path is taken. Climbing or rappelling on the rock face of the box canyon and waterfall is prohibited by order of the Forest Service.

Return to the Y intersection and take the left (west) fork to resume the hike. Sheer cliffs and gradual slopes shadow the passage as the trail crosses a meandering creek four or five times before heading out of the ravine at 1.1 miles on an uphill walk through woodlands. The trail gradually levels off before returning to the parking lot at 1.4 miles.

Miles and Directions

0.0 Begin at the trailhead; turn right (south).

0.2 Descend into the box canyon to the waterfall via narrow gap in the cliff.

0.6 Bear right at the Y intersection.

0.7 Reach the second waterfall. Return to the Y and take the left fork.

1.1 Go uphill to exit the ravine.

1.4 Arrive back at the trailhead.

60 Two Lakes Loop

A double-loop trail around Celina and Indian Lakes.

Location: Northeast of Tell City, southern Indiana
Distance: 15.3-mile double loop
Elevation change: About 340 feet from high point to low point
Approximate hiking time: Overnight
Difficulty: Moderate to strenuous
Jurisdiction: Hoosier National Forest, Tell City District
Maps: USGS Branchville and Bristow; *National Geographic/Trails Illustrated* map of Hoosier National Forest

Fees and permits: Parking fee Apr 15 through Oct 15
Special attractions: Sandstone bluffs along the northeast shore of both lakes, historic Rickenbaugh House, two river crossings
Camping: 63 campsites at two adjacent locations near the east side of the property (rates vary per season and per site)
Trailhead facilities: Small gravel parking lot but no restrooms or drinking water at trailhead; drinking water, pit toilets and seasonal shower facilities available in the campgrounds

Finding the trailhead: From Tell City go about 18 miles northeast on IN 37, passing IN 145 and IN 70 to the marked entrance to Indian-Celina Lakes of Hoosier National Forest. Turn left (west). From the gatehouse go about 2.5 miles to the trailhead parking lot on the left (south) side of the main road.

The Hike

Restricted to hikers only, this trail is as easy to follow as those in state parks, but without the traffic. There are several stream crossings, including two over the Anderson River and Tige Creek that can be knee deep or deeper. Take along a pair of thick-soled beach booties or water socks for these two short water crossings. Although there is an elevation difference of nearly 350 feet between the high and low points on the trail, there are few elevation changes of more than 100 feet at one time.

Begin at the designated main trailhead. There are other entry points, but the main trailhead provides the option of taking the hike as a whole or in two halves by using a connector trail that bisects the overall hike into almost equal parts that can each be handled without difficulty in a few hours.

From the parking lot go southwest on the connector trail, looking for markers that designate the path as part of the American Discovery Trail (ADT). Markers are varied on the trail—white paint blazes on trees, white plastic Forest Service tags, tin tags, ADT tags, and brown plastic Forest Service posts. Confused? Actually, all markers follow the same course. The only differences worth noting are the orange markings on the Forest Service brown posts that designate the connector trail.

The connector trail moves quickly into a stand of pine trees; look for a pond downhill to the left (east). After reaching the pond, join the main trail at a T intersection at

Celina Lake, one of the two lakes on the trail in Hoosier National Forest.

0.9 mile. A right (west) turn leads to Indian Lake; a left (east) turn goes to Celina Lake. Take the right option and head uphill toward a noticeable knob. Upon passing the knob, veer to the left (southwest) and continue toward another knob—the high spot of the Indian Lake loop at 775 feet elevation, or about 275 feet above the lake.

A saddle leads to another knob, but the trail bends before reaching the peak and takes a counterclockwise path around the knob while beginning a gradual descent toward Indian Lake. The north-facing slopes are a good location in spring to see toothwort, trillium, and dogtooth violet. Round a stand of white pine trees and catch a glimpse of Indian Lake through the trees.

At 2.1 miles exit the woods to begin a stretch through ankle-deep grass that goes over Indian Lake Dam. The dam forms the 150-acre Indian Lake by controlling the flow from Anderson River and Tige Creek. At the west edge of the dam, turn right (north) and walk the west shore of Indian Lake, aptly named since it parallels an old Indian treaty boundary. The terrain is noticeably different here as the trail rolls over small ridges and through shallow gullies for about 1.0 mile. The landscape is punctuated by the presence of large rocky outcroppings above and to the left (west) of the trail.

After crossing a seasonal stream at 3.5 miles, begin climbing as the trail bends uphill toward the northwest and away from the lake. Reach a clearing near the top of the hill and connect with an abandoned roadway at a T intersection at 4.3 miles. Turn right (north) and follow the gravel road downhill to another T intersection, crossing a small concrete bridge over a stream. The gravel road turns left (northwest), but the trail turns right (southeast). Go 0.1 mile to cross another creek by hopscotching over the rocks. The trail is not well marked in this area, but the path can be located without much trouble on the other side of the creek.

Pass a stand of pine trees near the northeast corner of the lake—a stretch that can be muddy at times. In contrast, however, are some beautiful sandstone cliffs about 50 yards inland from the lakeshore. At 5.6 miles, before you reach the northeast corner where Anderson River and Tige Creek flow into the lake, turn left (northwest) and head uphill. Daffodils bloom in abundance on this hillside in springtime. Near the top of the hill, pass through another pine plantation before sliding down off the ridge to Anderson River at 6.5 miles.

There is no bridge here and no shallow patch of rocks over which to hop, but the water is shallow enough under most circumstances to wade the 20-foot distance from bank to bank without getting wet above the calf. It is a good idea to remove your hiking boots before fording the river—no need to get them wet when you have another creek to cross and miles to go before completing the hike. The river bottom is gravel and rock, so take care to avoid cutting or injuring your feet if you did not bring the recommended beach booties or water socks.

Once on the other side, walk along a flat stretch that bends around the point of a ridge separating Anderson River from Tige Creek. After rounding the point, link up with Tige Creek and walk its bank for a less than 0.25 mile before having to cross

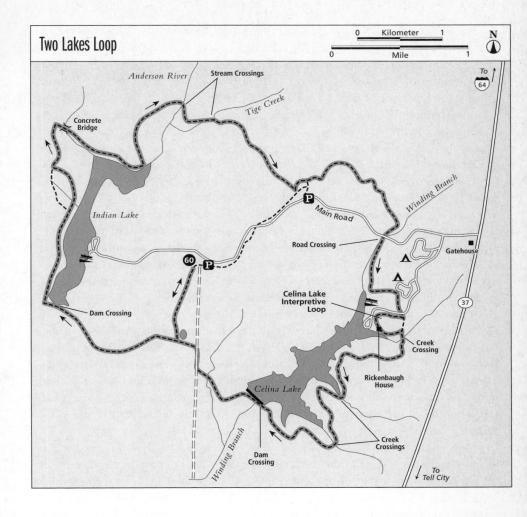

the creek at 6.8 miles. Again, this may require removal of hiking boots, depending on the depth of the water. It is shallow enough at times to cross without having to change footwear.

After crossing the creek, enter a stand of tall pine trees. At the other end of the pines, turn right and head uphill for 0.75 mile to intersect the orange-marked connector trail at 7.6 miles. You can take a 1.0-mile shortcut from here back to the main trailhead parking lot. Or you can turn left (east) to add the remaining mileage around Celina Lake—a loop that begins by descending part of the way into a broad ravine and then climbing the other side to a pine plantation. A marked crossroad provides another chance to head back to the trailhead parking lot. Turn left instead to continue toward Celina Lake, heading northeast around the base of a knob that peaks at 815 feet in elevation.

The trail itself levels off around 700 feet and then heads down to Winding Branch at 9.1 miles; this is the main tributary that feeds Celina Lake. Before you reach the creek, however, you will pick up an old roadbed and follow it on a southwest course to the main road. Turn left (southeast) at the road and walk about 100 yards before crossing the road at 9.2 miles to pick up another old roadbed. This goes south along Winding Branch for about 0.5 mile before the trail makes a sharp left (east) turn at 9.7 miles and heads uphill just as Celina Lake comes into view.

Go uphill away from the lake, passing the campgrounds and crossing the paved road leading to the boat ramp at 10.1 miles. Turn right (west) and follow the Celina Lake Interpretive Loop, which leads to the historic Rickenbaugh House at 10.6 miles. Jacob Rickenbaugh and his family settled on the shore of Celina Lake in the 1870s, largely because bark from the abundant oak trees provided tannin for his trade as a master hide tanner. He paid three Belgian stone masons $3 a day to build the sandstone block house, which took one year to complete. It served as the local post office and church meetinghouse until a church was constructed at Winding Branch, a small town now beneath the waters of Celina Lake. The interpretive loop also passes sandstone cliffs that provided shelter for Native Americans.

When the interpretive loop rejoins the main trail, turn right (south) and head downhill to cross a small stream. There is no need to change footwear here or at the last stream crossing. After crossing the second stream, go up over a ridge and drop into another ravine. Go up the other side of the ravine as the trail closes in on Celina Lake. Continue along the east shore of the lake with minor elevation changes, hiking in and out of a series of fingerlike coves that become increasingly larger, except for the last one. The first two coves require dropping down off the ridges to cross small streams before going back uphill.

After rounding the final, smaller cover, exit the woods at the southeast corner of the earthen dam at 13.5 miles. After crossing the dam, the trail turns slightly to the left (southwest) below a ridge and crosses one last stream. This one is filled with larger rocks and is easy to get over. Head uphill from the stream to where the trail turns right (north) along an abandoned road at 13.8 miles. Go about 300 yards before turning left (north) off the road. Go another 300 yards to intersect the orange-marked connector trail at 14.4 miles. Turn right (north) and it is about 0.9 mile back to the main trailhead parking lot.

Miles and Directions

0.0   Begin at the trailhead.

0.9   At the trail juncture go right (west) to travel the loop in a clockwise direction.

2.1   Leave woods to cross the Indian Lake dam.

3.5   Cross a seasonal stream.

4.3   Reach a trail juncture at a logging road; turn right (north) onto the road.

5.0 At the trail juncture turn right (southeast) onto the trail.

5.6 The trail changes direction; go left (north) and uphill.

6.5 Wade across Anderson River.

6.8 Ford Tige Creek.

7.6 At the trail juncture go left (east) to continue Two Lakes Loop. (**Option:** Follow the orange-marked connector trail for 1.0 mile back to the trailhead.)

9.1 Reach Winding Branch and turn right (south).

9.2 Cross the main road; turn left (east) onto the gravel road and then turn right (south).

9.7 Turn left (east) and go uphill.

10.1 Cross the paved boat ramp road and turn right (west) onto the Celina Lake Interpretive Loop.

10.6 Visit the Rickenbaugh House (open seasonally).

11.1 The interpretive loop rejoins the main trail; turn right.

13.5 Reach the Celina Lake dam.

13.8 Turn right (north) onto the abandoned road.

14.4 Reach the trail juncture; turn right (north) to return to the trailhead parking lot.

15.3 Arrive back at the parking lot.

61 Tipsaw Lake Trail

A trail around Tipsaw Lake.

Location: Northeast of Tell City in southern Indiana

Distance: 6.0-mile loop

Elevation change: About 80 feet

Approximate hiking time: 3 hours

Difficulty: Moderate

Jurisdiction: Hoosier National Forest, Tell City District

Fees and permits: No fees or permits required for trail access; entry fee to access the campgrounds or boat ramp Apr 15 through Oct 15

Maps: USGS Bristow, Gatchel, and Branchville; *National Geographic/Trails Illustrated* map of Hoosier National Forest; Hoosier National Forest map

Special attractions: Tipsaw Lake shoreline

Camping: Tipsaw Lake—48 campsites plus two group camp areas; open mid-Apr to mid-Oct

Trailhead facilities: Parking lot and water fountain at the trailhead; restrooms available at the Tipsaw Lake Recreation Area campgrounds (gate fee)

Finding the trailhead: Go north from Tell City for 17 miles on IN 37 to the TIPSAW LAKE RECREATION AREA sign. Turn left (west) and go 2 miles to the trailhead parking lot on the left (south) side of the road.

The Hike

Tipsaw Lake, formed primarily by Sulphur Fork Creek, Massey Creek, Snake Branch, and one other unnamed stream, is one of four small reservoirs within this area of the Hoosier National Forest, all of which are circled by a trail. This may be the easiest of the four trails—a flat course except for a series of modest climbs at the outset that traverse the hillside between the boat ramp/picnic area and the campground. Otherwise this is hardly a challenge; nevertheless, it is a pleasant hike.

Although the trail also is open to mountain bikes, it does not suffer from overuse. Hikers have the right-of-way over bikers. The trail is clearly marked with yellow diamond tags on trees, plus brown plastic marker posts. The yellow tags have black diamond directional arrows. Ticks can be troublesome along the meadow and dam portions of the trail.

To begin, head southwest from the small trailhead parking lot on a crushed-stone pathway with stands of pine trees on one side and tulip poplars on the other. The trail continues on a southwest course between the main road to the right (north) and Sulphur Fork Creek to the left (south). At 0.7 mile turn right (north) to cross the main road and hike up the wooded hillside, turning left (northwest) on a meandering stretch that works up and down the hill while crossing a footbridge and a couple of small streams.

Return to the lake at 1.4 miles and hug the shoreline around a fingerlike bay pointing to the northwest. At the back end of the bay, cross an unnamed creek at 1.8 miles and continue south, then southwest, crossing several more small seasonal creeks. Exit the woods at 2.0 miles to enter a shoreline meadow leading to the earthen dam at 2.4 miles. Hike across the dam to enter a stand of pine trees whose fallen needles help cushion the trail.

Cross a small creek at 3.0 miles. The trail then hugs the shoreline of another fingerlike bay, following an old roadbed for 0.5 mile. Pass a metal barricade at 3.5 miles; cross another small stream and briefly follow a gravel road that serves as a back entrance to the property. Turn left (north); cross Snake Branch at 3.6 miles and come to a T intersection at 3.7 miles. Go left (west) for 0.2 mile before leaving the road and heading north at 3.9 miles.

The trail again follows the shoreline, first along the bay formed by Snake Branch and then turning northeast along the southeast shore of the main lake. Move up and down over small gullies and ridges for about 0.5 mile before coming to a large meadow that is managed as a wildlife clearing through a cooperative program of the U.S. Forest Service and the Indiana Department of Natural Resources. The clearing is a good place to see deer or other woodland wildlife, so approach quietly.

At 5.9 miles the trail makes a hairpin turn to the left (northwest) and crosses Sulphur Fork Creek before returning to the trailhead parking lot.

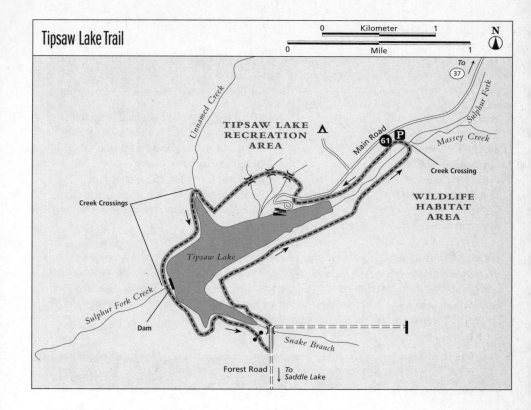

Miles and Directions

0.0   Begin at the trailhead.

0.7   Turn right (north) and cross the main road.

1.4   Return to the lake and hug the shoreline.

1.8   Cross an unnamed creek.

2.0   Exit the woods and enter a shoreline meadow.

2.4   Cross the dam.

3.0   Cross a small creek.

3.5   Reach the metal barricade and gravel road.

3.6   Cross Snake Branch.

3.7   Reach the T intersection and turn left (west).

3.9   Turn left off the road.

4.4   Reach the wildlife clearing.

5.9   Cross Sulphur Fork Creek.

6.0   Arrive back at the trailhead.

62 Saddle Lake Loop

A short, scenic walk along the shores of Saddle Lake.

Location: North of Tell City
Distance: 2.2-mile loop
Elevation change: Minimal
Approximate hiking time: 1+ hour
Difficulty: Moderate
Jurisdiction: Hoosier National Forest, Tell City District
Fees and permits: No fees or permits required

Maps: USGS Gatchel; *National Geographic/ Trails Illustrated* map of Hoosier National Forest; Hoosier National Forest map
Special attractions: Lake views
Camping: Limited to 13 sites; no fees
Trailhead facilities: Parking area, boat ramp, beach, and pit toilets at trailhead; no drinking water

Finding the trailhead: From Tell City go 10 miles northeast on IN 37 to the marked Gatchel exit. Turn left (northwest) and go 0.2 mile to a T intersection with Old IN 37. Turn right (northeast) and go 0.5 mile through Gatchel to a gravel entry road (Forest Service 443) to Saddle Lake. Turn left (north) and go about 1 mile to a paved parking lot near the lake's boat ramp. Trail markers are located on the north side of the parking lot at the boat ramp.

Butterfly and wildflower.

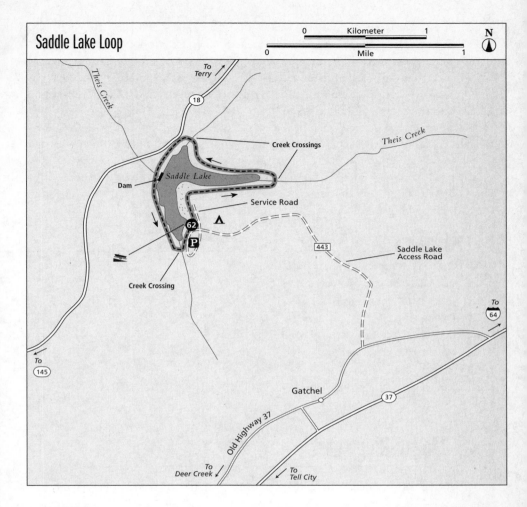

Saddle Lake Loop

Kilometer

0 1

Mile

0 1

N

To Terry

Theis Creek

18

Creek Crossings

Theis Creek

Dam

Saddle Lake

Service Road

62

P

443

Saddle Lake Access Road

Creek Crossing

To 64

To 145

Gatchel

37

Old Highway 37

To Deer Creek

To Tell City

The Hike

This trail can be hiked in either direction but is described here counterclockwise. The well-maintained trail appears to get little use.

Begin at the boat ramp and walk through a wooded area to a service road at 0.1 mile. Turn left (north) and head up a slight incline past a service shed to an amphitheater-like structure overlooking the beach. After passing this area, enter the woods and continue along the southeastern lakeshore. Rocky outcrops punctuate the hillside to the right (east), and wildflowers dot the pathway.

Make the first creek crossing at 0.7 mile and enter a stand of large pine trees whose trunks are 2.5 feet in diameter. Make a slight climb out of the pines and back into hardwood forest to begin an up-and-down stretch over a series of moderate humps.

Cross a culvert at 1.0 mile and walk uphill again to a section of beech trees. Descend from this hump into a gully and the second creek crossing. Once more, go uphill and come close to a county road (Perry CR 18) before dropping back downhill to cross the lake's earthen dam at 1.4 miles. In spring and summer, wildflowers along the dam—bergamot, milkweed, butterfly weed, Queen Anne's lace, black-eyed Susan—attract an array of butterflies.

At the other end of the dam, follow a stretch of trail along the southwest shore of the lake that slips across two gullies. After the second gully, the trail is a straight shot on flat terrain about 30 feet above the lakeshore to another stand of pine trees. Drop off the flat at about 1.8 miles to make another creek crossover. The boat ramp is visible from here. Cross one last creek at 1.9 miles; go uphill and follow the gravel path back to the parking area.

Miles and Directions

0.0 Begin at the trailhead.

0.1 Turn left (north) onto a service road.

0.7 Reach a creek crossing.

1.0 Cross a culvert.

1.4 Cross the Saddle Lake dam.

1.8 Make another creek crossing.

1.9 Make the last creek crossing.

2.2 Arrive back at the trailhead.

63 Mogan Ridge East

A trail through abandoned farm field, over a narrow ridge, and across a shallow creek.

Location: Northeast of Tell City, near Derby

Distance: 6.4-mile loop, with new connector trail

Elevation change: 390 feet difference from Kuntz Ridge to Clover Lick Creek

Approximate hiking time: 3.5 hours

Difficulty: Strenuous

Jurisdiction: Hoosier National Forest, Tell City District

Fees and permits: No fees or permits required

Maps: USGS Derby; *National Geographic/Trails Illustrated* map of Hoosier National Forest; Hoosier National Forest map

Special attractions: Kuntz Ridge, Clover Lick Creek

Camping: No camping permitted

Trailhead facilities: Parking area for about a half dozen vehicles; no drinking water or restroom facilities

The cross-country American Discovery Trail (ADT) winds it way through southern Indiana.

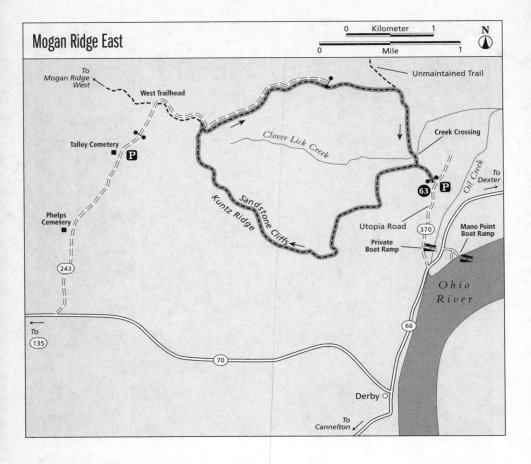

Mogan Ridge East

Finding the trailhead: Go 1 mile north on IN 66 from its intersection with IN 70 in Derby. Turn left (north) onto Perry CR 370/Utopia Road and pass the private boat ramp as you head uphill. The trailhead parking lot is on the right (east) side of the road, 0.7 mile from IN 66.

Alternate route: Because high water on the nearby Ohio River can flood access to the east trailhead, there is an alternate entry point. Go 2.9 miles west on IN 70 from the intersection with IN 66 in Derby to Perry CR 243/Ultimate Road. Turn right (north) and go 1.3 miles to a small gravel parking lot on the right (east) across from the Talley Cemetery. It is a 0.5-mile walk up the dirt road to a connector spur that joins the Mogan Ridge East and Mogan Ridge West Trails.

The Hike

It requires a little history lesson to understand how Mogan Ridge East got its name, considering the fact that no part of the trail is within a mile of Mogan Ridge. Once part of a larger multiuse trail, Mogan Ridge East has been set aside exclusively for hikers. Mogan Ridge West, which in part traverses Mogan Ridge, is an 11.0–mile trail that is open to hikers, bikers, and horseback riders. The two trails are connected by a 0.5-mile spur. Although only half as long, Mogan Ridge East is just as challenging as its counterpart.

The trail is marked with white diamonds and is easy to follow. Orange diamonds mark the new connector trail. Traffic typically is light.

Both the Mogan Ridge East and West Trails are part of the American Discovery Trail. Mogan Ridge East is a prime spot for wildflowers, especially in spring when the path is festooned with splashes of sweet William, self-heal, daisy fleabane, wild geranium, Jacob's ladder, Virginia bluebell, and Virginia waterleaf.

To hike the Mogan Ridge East Trail from its east end, begin in the parking area off Utopia Road and cross the gravel road. Pass the metal gate and slip through a gap between a pair of knoblike hills. Go downhill to a trail juncture at 0.4 mile. Turn left (southwest) and go through a meadow to the 0.6-mile mark, where the trail turns left (south) and goes uphill to the eastern tip of Kuntz Ridge.

At 1.8 miles swing clockwise around the base of a triangular-shaped ridgetop. Curl to the right (west) and pass a very narrow backbone with sandstone cliffs dropping steeply off to the right (north) side of the trail. Continue along Kuntz Ridge, gradually turning northwest.

At 3.0 miles go downhill briefly before climbing again to a gravel road at 3.5 miles. This is the connector spur to Mogan Ridge West. Turn right (east) and continue along the Mogan Ridge East Trail as it follows the gravel road for about 0.5 mile. The surface of the road changes to dirt at a metal gate. Go straight (east), heading uphill briefly before descending to the edge of a meadow. Continue downhill, passing a stand of pine trees to a T intersection at 5.2 miles. Turn right (south) on a downhill course to Clover Lick Creek, which is at 6.0 miles.

The rocky stream has an intermittent flow and is easy to cross most of the time. Go uphill for 0.1 mile from the creek to complete the loop at the trail junction at 6.1 miles. Turn left (southeast) and go 0.3 mile to return to the parking lot.

Miles and Directions

- **0.0** Begin at the trailhead.
- **0.4** Reach a trail juncture and turn left (southwest).
- **0.6** The trail turns left (south).
- **1.8** Arrive at Kuntz Ridge and the sandstone cliffs.
- **3.5** Reach a trail juncture and turn right (east) (*Note:* Left goes to Mogan Ridge West Trail).
- **5.2** Turn right (south) at a T intersection.
- **6.0** Cross Clover Lick Creek.
- **6.1** Reach the trail juncture and turn left (southeast) to return to the trailhead.
- **6.4** Arrive back at the trailhead.

64 German Ridge Lake Trail

A short loop trail past sandstone cliffs overlooking the lake.

Location: Perry County in southern Indiana, east of Tell City
Distance: 1.0-mile loop
Elevation change: Minimal
Approximate hiking time: 45 minutes
Difficulty: Easy
Jurisdiction: Hoosier National Forest, Tell City District
Maps: USGS Rome; *National Geographic/Trails*

Illustrated map of Hoosier National Forest; Hoosier National Forest map
Fees and permits: No fees or permits required
Special attractions: Moss-covered sandstone cliffs
Camping: German Ridge Campground—20 campsites
Trailhead facilities: Shelter house with pit toilets

Finding the trailhead: From Tell City go east on IN 66 through Cannelton to Rocky Point. Go 6.4 miles east on IN 66 from Rocky Point to Perry CR 3 and turn left (north). Go 0.75 mile to a gated entrance to German Ridge Recreation Area. After passing the gate, take the right fork to the picnic area. Locate the shelter house to the left (north) side of the parking lot. The trailhead is on the opposite (north) side of the shelter house.

The Hike

The German Ridge Recreation Area of the Hoosier National Forest is primarily devoted to horseback riding, but hikers get to see a slice of it with this loop trail, described here in a clockwise direction. The trailhead behind the picnic shelter is marked with a brown plastic post and white diamonds. The trail is a wide path and easy to follow. German Ridge was developed in the 1930s by the Civilian Conservation Corps (CCC).

It doesn't take long to get to the focal point of this brief hike. After crossing a footbridge at 0.1 mile, the striking sandstone cliffs are almost immediately visible. Even on the hottest of summer days, the tree-shaded cliffs can be a cool setting. At 0.3 mile a feeder trail to the horseman's camp connects from the left (southeast). Be sure to take the path to the right (south) that leads in a clockwise direction. The cliffs rise on the left (south), while glimpses of the lake can be seen through the trees below and to the right (north). At 0.6 mile reach another feeder trail that connects to the horseman's camp to the south. Stay right (west and north) and walk downhill away from the cliffs to a T intersection near the lake's edge. Turn left and circle the lake to the beach near the parking lot and trailhead.

Hoosier National Forest maps will show a one-mile outer loop, but it's a stone-covered forest road that is absent any distinguishing features and not worth the extra effort.

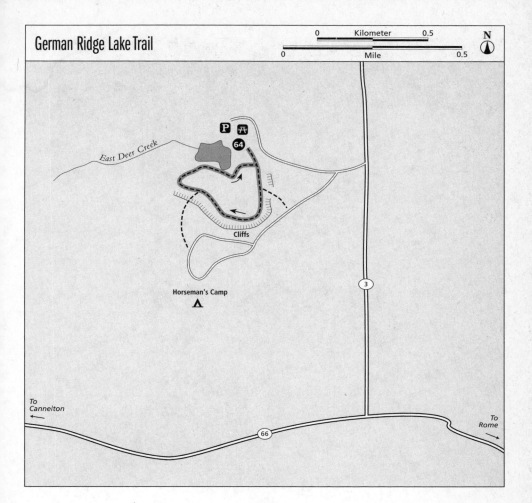

German Ridge Lake Trail

East Deer Creek

Cliffs

Horseman's Camp

To Cannelton

To Rome

Miles and Directions

0.0   Begin at the trailhead.

0.1   Cross a footbridge.

0.3   Reach the sandstone cliffs.

0.6   At the trail juncture stay right.

0.8   Come to a T intersection; turn left.

1.0   Arrive back at the trailhead.

Exposed sandstone cliffs guard the trail at German Ridge.

Knobstone Trail

Hikers do not have to leave Indiana to get a taste of the Appalachian Trail.

A much shorter but more than adequate replica can be found in southeast Indiana along the state's most distinctive geographic feature—the Knobstone Escarpment. The escarpment appears like a fortress rising 300 to 400 feet above the Scottsburg lowlands to the east as it meanders for more than 100 miles from the Ohio River northwest toward Martinsville.

The Knobstone Trail (KT) follows the spiny ridges and deep ravines for 58 miles, beginning at Deam Lake State Recreation Area and ending at Delaney Park. It passes through 40,000 acres of public forestland. The area is richly diverse, with abundant fauna and flora.

The KT was first opened in 1980 and at the time measured only 32 miles. The Indiana Department of Natural Resources is exploring ways to extend the trail farther through the Jackson–Washington State Forest, the Hoosier National Forest, and Morgan–Monroe State Forest and along private-land corridors. By the time it is finished, the KT may be double its present length. It already is the longest trail in the state.

Multiple trailhead locations along the way shorten the legs to between 5 and 12 miles, making it a popular trail not only for long-distance hikers but also for day hikers opting to tackle the KT in shorter pieces.

Backcountry camping is permitted along the KT as long as campsites are on public land and are at least 1.0 mile by trail away from all roads, recreation areas, and trailheads.

The KT is well marked with white blazes. Most locations where the various legs intersect are further marked with signs. All trailheads are marked with 4- by 4-inch KT posts on the access roads and large trailhead signs.

Water supplies along the trail are limited, so many hikers stash supplies at the trailheads. Many of the streams and creeks that the KT crosses are seasonal, so do not count on them for water.

Whether in pieces or as a whole, the KT has earned its nickname as "the little Appalachian Trail."

The trail is described in linear sections on a northwest course from about 20 miles north of Louisville, Kentucky, toward Salem, Indiana.

65 Deam Lake to Jackson Road

The shortest leg of the Knobstone Trail, this is a good warm-up for more challenging legs of the trail.

Location: Between Borden/New Providence and Sellersburg, Clark County
Distance: 5.0-mile shuttle
Elevation change: Two climbs of more than 150 feet
Approximate hiking time: 4 hours
Difficulty: Strenuous
Jurisdiction: Indiana Department of Natural Resources, Division of Outdoor Recreation
Fees and permits: No fees or permits required unless you park at Deam Lake State Recreation Area, which has an entry fee, higher for out-of-state vehicles; season passes available
Maps: USGS Henryville and Speed; Indiana Department of Natural Resources Knobstone Trail brochure

Special attractions: Bowery Creek, Bartle Knobs
Camping: Deam Lake State Recreation Area—116 campsites plus 68 sites in the horsemen's campground. Camping is permitted on public ground along the Knobstone as long as the campsite is at least 1 mile by trail from all roads, recreation areas, and trailheads and as long as the camp is not visible from the trail and all lakes.
Trailhead facilities: Only parking areas at the Deam Lake and Jackson Road trailheads; drinking water and restrooms located at Deam Lake State Recreation Area

Finding the trailhead: From the Scottsburg exit off I-65, go south 0.8 mile on IN 311 to IN 60. Turn right (west) and go 8 miles to the DEAM LAKE STATE RECREATION AREA sign at Waggoner Knob Road. Turn right (north) and go 0.8 mile to Wilson Switch Road near Miller Cemetery. Turn right (east) and go 1.4 miles to the Deam Lake trailhead on the left (north) side of the road. A 4- by 4-inch wooden post with a KT symbol on the right (south) side of the road marks the location.

The Hike

Deception is the best way to describe the opening leg of the Knobstone—it might not seem all that difficult at first. Once you hike a few miles in, however, you will know firsthand the kinds of challenges you will encounter along the remainder of the trail. Trail traffic may be high near the Deam Lake trailhead because of its proximity to the state recreation area.

The trail, marked by white blazes, begins east of Deam Lake with a gradual climb of about 120 feet over the first mile and then drops into a ravine before intersecting a gravel road at 1.9 miles. Cross the road, turn right (southeast), and continue downward to Bowery Creek at 2.2 miles.

From here the Knobstone is anything but easy. Over the next 1.5 miles, go uphill along a series of round hilltops named Bartle Knobs. From the creek to the highest

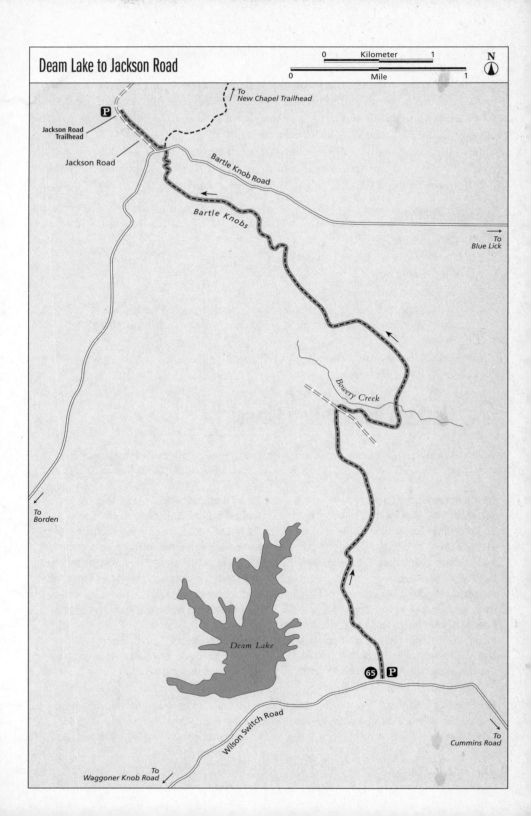

Deam Lake to Jackson Road

To
New Chapel Trailhead

P

Jackson Road
Trailhead

Jackson Road

Bartle Knob Road

Bartle Knobs

To
Blue Lick

Bowery Creek

To
Borden

Deam Lake

65 P

Wilson Switch Road

To
Cummins Road

To
Waggoner Knob Road

Kilometer

Mile

N

knob, there is an elevation change of 400 feet, which is typical of what the next 50.0-plus miles are like.

After peaking out at Bartle Knobs, slide down the back end of the Berry Run ravine and climb up once more to reach Bartle Knob Road just short of 5.0 miles. Cross the road to continue the trail, or turn left and then right to follow the gravel road for 0.4 mile to reach the Jackson Road trailhead.

By going straight, the trail skirts another knob before dropping into a ravine and connecting with a spur trail on the left at about 5.2 miles. The spur is a strenuous uphill stretch of about 0.5 mile to the Jackson Road trailhead.

Miles and Directions

0.0 Begin at the trailhead.

1.9 Cross the gravel road; turn right (southeast).

2.2 Cross Bowery Creek.

3.3 Hike over the Bartle Knobs.

4.8 Reach Bartle Knobs Road; turn left (west) to the Jackson Road trailhead. (**Option:** Continue straight (north) to skirt another knob and connect with strenuous spur to the trailhead.)

5.0 Arrive at Jackson Road trailhead.

66 Jackson Road to New Chapel

A demanding stretch of the Knobstone Trail along ridgetops and through ravines.

Location: Clark State Forest

Distance: 12.0-mile shuttle

Elevation change: Multiple climbs of more than 250 feet

Approximate hiking time: 8 hours or overnight

Difficulty: Strenuous

Jurisdiction: Indiana Department of Natural Resources, Division of Outdoor Recreation

Fees and permits: No fees or permits required

Maps: USGS Henryville; Indiana Department of Natural Resources Knobstone Trail brochure

Special attractions: Round Knob, Virginia Pine–Chestnut Oak Nature Preserve

Camping: Deam Lake State Recreation Area—116 campsites plus 68 sites in the horsemen's campground. Camping is permitted on public ground along the Knobstone as long as campsite is at least 1 mile by trail from all roads, recreation areas, and trailheads and as long as camp is not visible from the trail and all lakes.

Trailhead facilities: Parking available at the Jackson Road and New Chapel trailheads; no restrooms or drinking water

Finding the trailhead: To reach the Jackson Road trailhead, go left (east) from the Deam Lake trailhead on Wilson Switch Road for 0.5 mile to Flower Gap Road. Turn right (south) and go 0.2 mile to Cummins Road. Turn left (east) and go 1.3 miles to Crone Road. Turn left (northeast) and

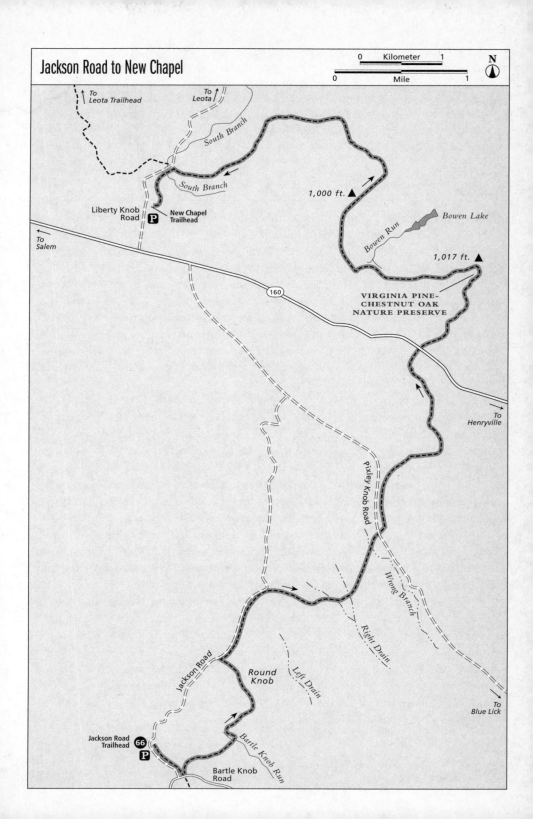

0   Kilometer   1

0   Mile   1

N

To
Leota Trailhead

To
Leota

South Branch

South Branch

Liberty Knob
Road

New Chapel
Trailhead

P

To
Salem

1,000 ft. ▲

Bowen Run

Bowen Lake

1,017 ft. ▲

VIRGINIA PINE-
CHESTNUT OAK
NATURE PRESERVE

160

To
Henryville

Pixley Knob Road

Wrong Branch

Right Drain

Left Drain

Jackson Road

Round
Knob

To
Blue Lick

Jackson Road
Trailhead

66

P

Bartle Knob Run

Bartle Knob
Road

go 1.1 miles to Beyl Road. Turn left (northwest) and go 1 mile to Bolling Road. Turn right (northeast) and go 1 mile to the intersection of Mayfield Road. Go straight (northwest) onto Bartle Knob Road and continue for 3.9 miles to Jackson Road, a gravel road on the right. Turn right (northeast) onto Jackson Road and go 0.3 mile to the Jackson Road trailhead on the left (west).

To reach the Jackson Road trailhead from I-65, go northwest from exit 16 on Pixley Knob Road to Blue Lick. Turn left (southwest) onto Reed Road and go about 1.4 miles. Bartle Knob Road turns right (northwest). Go 3 miles to the entrance of Jackson Road Trailhead parking on the right (north).

The Hike

Bartle Knobs, Bartle Knob Road, Bartle Knob Run—in short order, the trail touches all three before coming to one of the toughest challenges in the full 58.0-mile hike—a steep, 360-foot climb up Round Knob. Traffic is generally not significant along the middle legs of the trail, but the area is open to hunting during regulated seasons.

This is the longest leg of the KT, and it all starts after crossing Bartle Knob Road and angling down the north-facing side of a ravine to Bartle Knob Run and the creek that wanders through the ravine. Turn left (northwest) along the creek before heading uphill to Round Knob at 1.2 miles. The climb starts somewhat gradually, but the final 150-foot rise is covered in less than 0.25 mile. The view from Round Knob is spectacular, especially to the southeast. On a clear day it is possible to see downtown Louisville, Kentucky, more than 20 miles away.

After leaving Round Knob, cross a saddleback that leads to Jackson Road at 1.6 miles. Turn right (northeast) and walk along the gravel road for nearly 1.0 mile before turning right (southeast) at 2.5 miles to hike through the Right Drain ravine. Yes there is a nearby ravine named Left Drain, and the trail soon crosses Wrong Branch, which later joins Right Branch. Cross the Wrong Branch and Pixley Knob Road at 4.0 miles and turn left (north) to parallel the road a short ways while going up a narrow ridge point. You have made a 350-foot climb by the time you reach the top.

Go from one knob to another before a sharp downhill maneuver to the crossing of IN 160 at 6.3 miles. Cross the road and go uphill on an old logging road to the Virginia Pine–Chestnut Oak Nature Preserve. The twenty-four-acre hilltop site is dominated by a native stand of Virginia pine, an uncommon tree in Indiana except in the Knobstone region. Chestnut oaks control the lower slopes.

After leaving the preserve, come to the highest point on the Knobstone Trail—a knob at 1,017 feet above sea level. Turn left (west) from here and follow a long, narrow ridge descending about 200 feet to Bowen Run at 8.8 miles. This stream feeds Bowen Lake, which is about 0.5 mile to the northeast. Cross the creek a couple of times before heading uphill to another knob that is 1,000 feet above sea level. Swing northeast, then northwest along a string of knobs before descending into a ravine and the South Branch of Big Ox Creek. The New Chapel trailhead parking lot is about 0.25 mile southwest and uphill from the trail.

Miles and Directions

0.0 Begin at the trailhead.

1.2 Reach Round Knob.

1.6 At Jackson Road go right (northeast).

2.5 The trail turns right (southeast) off Jackson Road.

4.0 Cross Wrong Branch and Pixley Knob Road and turn left (north).

6.3 Cross IN 160.

7.3 Reach the Virginia Pine–Chestnut Oak Nature Preserve.

8.8 Arrive at Bowen Run.

12.0 Reach the New Chapel trailhead; go left (south) to the parking lot.

67 New Chapel to Leota

This part of the Knobstone Trail features long stretches along ridgetops, with occasional drops into ravines, including scenic North Branch Valley.

Location: Clark State Forest, Scott County

Distance: 9.0-mile shuttle

Elevation change: Multiple changes of 250 feet or more

Approximate hiking time: 6 hours

Difficulty: Strenuous

Jurisdiction: Indiana Department of Natural Resources, Division of Outdoor Recreation

Fees and permits: No fees or permits required

Maps: USGS Henryville, South Boston, and Little York; Indiana Department of Natural

Resources Knobstone Trail brochure

Special attractions: North Branch Valley

Camping: Camping is permitted on public ground along the Knobstone as long as campsite is at least 1 mile by trail from all roads, recreation areas, and trailheads and as long as camp is not visible from the trail and all lakes

Trailhead facilities: Parking available at the New Chapel and Leota trailheads; no restrooms or drinking water

Finding the trailhead: To reach the New Chapel trailhead, go left (east) from the Jackson Road trailhead for 3.9 miles to Mayfield Road. Turn left (northeast) and go 1.3 miles to Blue Lick Road. Turn left (northwest) and go 0.5 mile and continue right (northeast) on Blue Lick Road. Go 1.5 miles to Beers Road. Turn left (northwest) and go 1.8 miles to a T intersection with IN 160. Turn left (west) and go 4.7 miles to Liberty Knob Road. Turn right (north) and go 0.4 mile to the New Chapel trailhead parking lot on the right (east) side of the road.

To reach the New Chapel trailhead from I-65, go 5.7 miles west on IN 160 to Liberty Knob Road. Turn right (north) and go 0.4 mile to the trailhead parking lot on the right (east) side of the road.

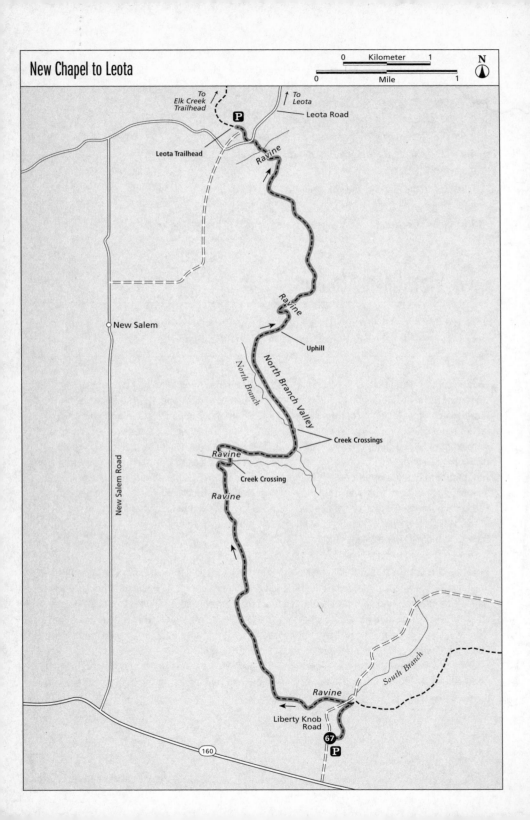

Kilometer

Mile

N

To
Elk Creek
Trailhead

P

To
Leota

Leota Road

Leota Trailhead

Ravine

Ravine

Uphill

New Salem

North Branch

North Branch Valley

Creek Crossings

Ravine

Creek Crossing

Ravine

New Salem Road

Ravine

South Branch

Ravine

Liberty Knob
Road

67

P

160

The Hike

Unlike the earlier segments of the Knobstone Trail (KT), where the highlights were knobs, the main attraction on this 9.0-mile stretch is the North Branch Valley—a narrow, high-sided ravine rich with wildflowers, ferns, and some of the biggest trees on the KT. Traffic is generally not significant along the middle legs of the trail, but the area is open to hunting during regulated seasons.

The first half of the New Chapel–to–Leota leg wanders along the edge of the forest and rolls along ridgetops, occasionally dipping across the back end of ravines. Near the 3.0-mile mark, drop into a ravine and cross the creek. Then climb the other side, cross over a narrow ridge, and make a steep descent into a side ravine of North Branch Valley at 4.5 miles. For those keeping track, this is about the 20.0-mile mark of the full KT.

Turn right (east) to round a point and then left (north) for a 1.0-mile walk through the lush ravine. Climb up the right (east) side of the ravine, cross the ridgetop, and descend into another ravine.

Go uphill again and follow the ridgeline north for 1.5 mile before turning northwest to traverse one last ravine. Cross the creek at the ravine bottom and head uphill to cross Leota Road at 8.9 miles. Continue up for 0.1 mile to the Leota trailhead parking lot. The parking area is along a utility corridor.

Miles and Directions

0.0 Begin at the trailhead.
3.0 Drop into a ravine and cross a creek.
4.5 Reach the North Branch Valley.
8.9 Cross Leota Road.
9.0 Reach the Leota trailhead.

Fungus sprouts from a fallen log near the Knobstone Trail.

68 Leota to Elk Creek

Three hills and several ravines lead to scenic lake.

Location: Between Salem and Scottsburg
Distance: 7.0-mile shuttle
Elevation change: Climbs of 250 to 350 feet, descents of 150 to 250 feet
Approximate hiking time: 5 hours
Difficulty: Strenuous
Jurisdiction: Indiana Department of Natural Resources, Division of Outdoor Recreation
Fees and permits: No fees or permits required
Maps: USGS Little York; Indiana Department of Natural Resources Knobstone Trail brochure

Special attractions: Vic Swain Hill, Elk Creek Public Fishing Area
Camping: Camping is permitted on public ground along the Knobstone as long as camp is at least one mile by trail from all roads, recreation areas, and trailheads, and as long as it is not visible from the trail and all lakes.
Trailhead facilities: Parking available at the Leota trailhead; parking and latrines available at the Elk Creek trailhead

Finding the trailhead: From the New Chapel trailhead parking lot, turn left (south) onto Liberty Knob Road and go 0.4 mile to IN 160. Turn right (west) and go 1.8 miles to New Salem Road. Turn right (north) and go 3.4 miles, passing through New Salem. At the 3.4-mile mark, turn right (east) onto Leota Road and go 1.7 miles to an unmarked gravel road on the left (north). Turn onto the gravel road and go 0.1 mile to the Leota trailhead entrance. Turn left (east) and go 0.1 mile to the parking lot and trailhead.

To reach the Leota Trailhead from I-65, go approximately 7.5 miles west on IN 160 to New Salem Road. Turn right (north) and drive 3.4 miles to New Salem—Finley Knob Road. Turn right (east) and go 1.7 miles to an unmarked county road. Turn left (north) and proceed 0.1 mile to the trailhead parking lot.

The Hike

The trail from Leota to Elk Creek begins at an opening on the north side of the parking lot near a small pond. Descend from the Leota trailhead along a ridgeline that leads to Vic Swain Hill at 1.2 miles. The hill marks a departure from the mostly northward direction that the Knobstone Trail (KT) has followed until now. From here the trail heads west for the next 5.8 miles over a series of ridges and ravines.

After an especially steep climb near the 4.0-mile mark, spend the next mile dropping into Monroe Hollow before going back uphill approximately 200 feet to another ridgetop.

From there descend into McKnight Hollow and skirt the south edge of Elk Lake. After crossing Smith Hollow, make a 300-foot climb to a knob overlooking the lake. Turn southeast to cross a saddle to another knob, then go downhill into Frank Garrett Hollow. Near the west tip of Elk Lake, reach a trail juncture. Go left (west) up Nowing Hollow to continue the KT or right (northeast) to reach the Elk Creek trailhead.

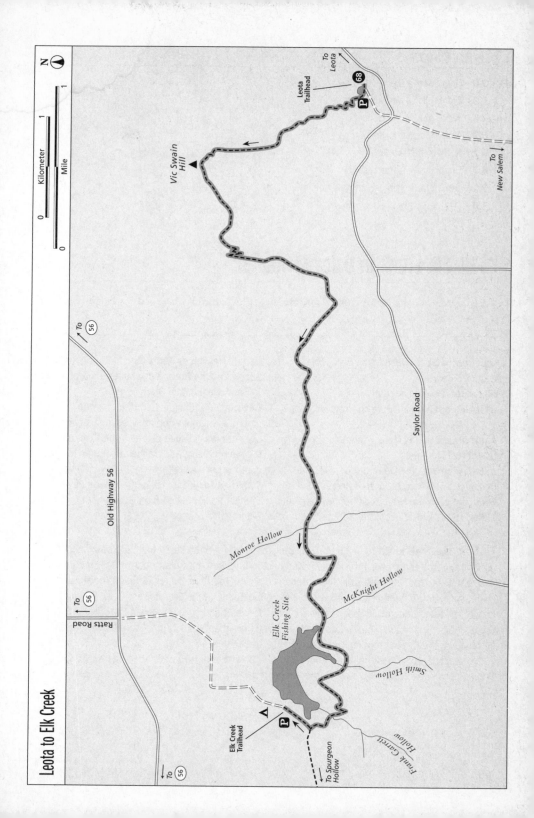

Leota to Elk Creek

N

0   Kilometer   1

0   Mile   1

To 56

Old Highway 56

Ratts Road

To 56

To 56

Elk Creek Trailhead

Elk Creek Fishing Site

Monroe Hollow

McKnight Hollow

Smith Hollow

Frank Garrett Hollow

To Spurgeon Hollow

Saylor Road

Vic Swain Hill

Leota Trailhead

68

To Leota

To New Salem

Miles and Directions

0.0 Begin at the trailhead.

1.2 Climb Vic Swain Hill.

4.7 Arrive at Monroe Hollow.

5.7 Cross McKnight Hollow.

6.2 Reach Smith Hollow.

6.7 Cross Frank Garrett Hollow.

6.9 Turn right (northeast) at trail junction.

7.0 Reach the Elk Creek trailhead.

69 Elk Creek to Oxley Memorial

This section of the Knobstone Trail crosses ridgetops, ravines, and roads, plus offers optional segments at its north end.

Location: Jackson-Washington State Forest east of Salem

Distance: 5.5-mile shuttle

Elevation change: Multiple changes between 150 and 250 feet

Approximate hiking time: 4 hours

Difficulty: Strenuous

Jurisdiction: Indiana Department of Natural Resources, Division of Outdoor Recreation

Fees and permits: No fees or permits required

Maps: USGS Little York; Indiana Department of Natural Resources Knobstone Trail brochure

Special attractions: Backcountry area of Jackson-Washington State Forest

Camping: Camping is permitted on public ground along the Knobstone as long as campsite is at least 1 mile by trail from all roads, recreation areas, and trailheads and as long as camp is not visible from the trail and all lakes.

Trailhead facilities: Parking and latrines at the Elk Creek trailhead; only parking at Oxley Memorial trailhead

Finding the trailhead: To reach the Elk Creek trailhead from the Leota trailhead parking lot, turn left (south) and go 0.1 mile to the paved Leota Road. Turn left (east) onto Leota Road and go 1.1 miles to the first paved road (an unmarked county road) on the left. Turn left (north) and go 1.2 miles to a T intersection with Bloomington Trail Road. Turn left (northwest) onto Bloomington Trail Road and go 1.8 miles to IN 56. Turn left (west) and go 2.8 miles to the sign for Elk Creek Public Fishing Area. Turn left (south) onto Ratts Road and go 1.8 miles to the fishing area entrance. At the KT post turn left (west) to the Elk Creek trailhead.

To reach the Elk Creek Trailhead from I-65, go 8.3 west from I-65 at Scottsburg on IN 56 to Elk Creek Road. Turn left (south) to reach the trailhead parking lot at Elk Creek Public Fishing Area.

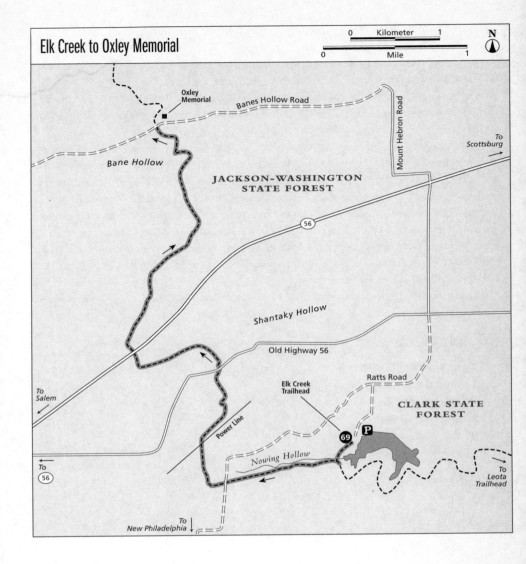

Oxley
Memorial

Banes Hollow Road

Mount Hebron Road

To
Scottsburg

Bane Hollow

JACKSON–WASHINGTON
STATE FOREST

56

Shantaky Hollow

Old Highway 56

To
Salem

Elk Creek
Trailhead

Ratts Road

CLARK STATE
FOREST

Power Line

69 P

Nowing Hollow

To
56

To
Leota
Trailhead

To
New Philadelphia

The Hike

From one of the most remote stretches (Leota to Elk Creek), the Knobstone Trail (KT) switches to perhaps its least spectacular sections between Elk Creek and Spurgeon Hollow to the northwest. A half dozen road crossings, a power line corridor, and occasional logging operations interrupt the natural setting.

This part of the trail is not without challenges, however. There are several steep knobs to be climbed, although the severity of the elevation change is only 150 to 250 feet, unlike the 250- to 400-footers on the KT's southern sections. Traffic generally is not significant along the middle legs of the trail, but the area is open to hunting during regulated seasons.

Beginning at the Elk Creek campground, go south down the connecting trail to the main trail. Turn right (west) to walk through Nowing Hollow for about 0.5 mile before climbing a ridge. Make the first road crossing just past the 1.0-mile mark, beyond which the trail drops into a ravine and climbs on a northeast slant along a south-facing slope.

Atop the ridge at 1.6 miles, connect with a power line corridor for about 0.3 mile before dropping off the left (north) side into a ravine. Climb the other side and cross Old SR 56 at 2.3 miles. Cut across the back end of Shantaky Hollow and work uphill to a knob that at 974 feet above sea level is the high point of this KT section. Descend over 200 feet to cross IN 56 at 3.2 miles, then head back uphill to follow a ridgeline for about 1.0 mile as the KT enters the Jackson-Washington State Forest.

On a northward course over the next 2.0 miles, the KT crosses two roads and traverses several ravines, including Bane Hollow, to reach the John Stuart Oxley Memorial trailhead on Banes Hollow Road.

The memorial is in honor of John Stuart Oxley, an avid hiker and KT supporter who died in 1998.

Miles and Directions

0.0 Begin at the trailhead; walk down connector and turn right (west) onto the KT.

1.1 Cross a gravel road.

1.6 Reach a power line corridor.

2.3 Cross Old SR 56.

3.2 Cross IN 56.

5.5 Reach Banes Hollow Road and Oxley Memorial trailhead.

70 Oxley Memorial to Spurgeon Hollow

This section of the Knobstone Trail crosses ridgetops, ravines, and roads, plus offers optional segments at its north end.

Location: Jackson-Washington State Forest, east of Salem
Distance: 8.5-mile shuttle with optional route ending at 6.5 miles
Elevation change: Multiple changes between 150 and 250 feet
Approximate hiking time: 4 or 5 hours, depending on route taken
Difficulty: Strenuous
Jurisdiction: Indiana Department of Natural Resources, Division of Outdoor Recreation and Division of Forestry
Fees and permits: No fees or permits required

Maps: USGS Kossuth and Little York; Indiana Department of Natural Resources Knobstone Trail brochure
Special attractions: Backcountry Area of Jackson-Washington State Forest
Camping: Camping is permitted on public ground along the Knobstone as long as campsite is at least 1 mile by trail from all roads, recreation areas, and trailheads and as long as camp is not visible from the trail and all lakes.
Trailhead facilities: Parking at the Oxley Memorial and Spurgeon Hollow trailheads

Finding the trailhead: To reach the Oxley Memorial trailhead from the Elk Creek trailhead parking lot, return to IN 56 and cross to the north side of the highway. Turn left (west) at Mt. Hebron Road and then right (north) at a Y intersection onto Rutherford Hollow Road. Go about 0.5 mile to where the road curves left and intersects Banes Hollow Road. Turn left (west) and go 2 miles to the Oxley Memorial trailhead on the right.

To reach the Oxley Memorial Trailhead, go 8.3 west on IN 56 from I-65 in Scottsburg to Elk Creek Road. Turn right (north) and take the first left, Mt. Hebron Road, and go to a Y-intersection. Turn right (north) and drive 0.5 miles to Banes Hollow Road. Turn left and go 2 miles to the trailhead parking lot.

The Hike

Take your pick. This stretch of the Knobstone offers two options near the midpoint— a 3.0-mile leg that is relatively easy hiking through a valley or a 5.0-mile leg of rugged hiking from ridgetop to ridgetop. Both cut through the Backcountry Area of Jackson–Washington State Forest and are marked by DNR Division of Forestry blue blazes along with the white KT blazes.

You will have a few miles of hiking from the Oxley Memorial trailhead to make up your mind on the options.

From the trailhead go north and uphill to pass over a ridge that drops into Herron Hollow at the 1.0-mile mark. From Herron Hollow, go uphill for 0.5 mile and cross Pull Tight Road. Continue uphill another 0.25 mile and the KT turns left (west) to Arnold Creek. Hike up and down along a ridgeline to cross at West Point Road.

Oxley Memorial to Spurgeon Hollow

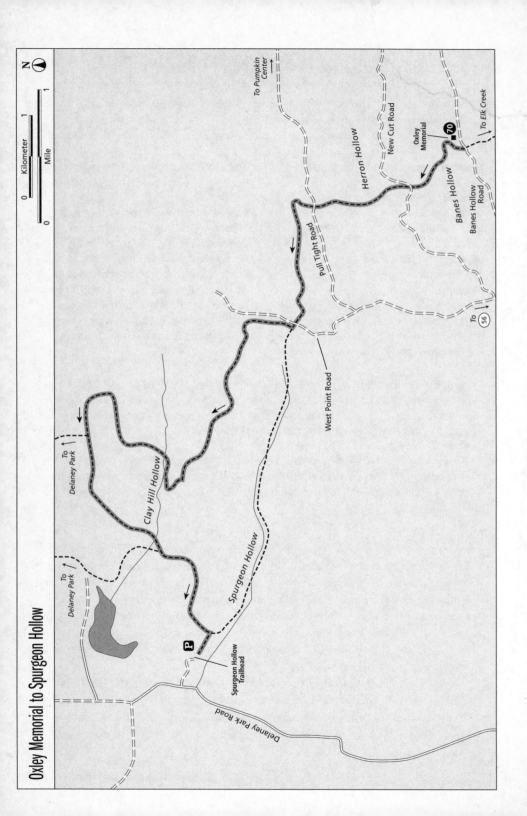

Just across the road, the KT splits: Go left (west) for the shorter route to Spurgeon Hollow trailhead or right (north) for the slightly longer (and hillier) option. The shorter option is fairly easy as it passes through Spurgeon Hollow, with more than half the distance squeezed within a steep-walled ravine.

The longer option is more rugged and in places is marked with blue blazes. It also intersects twice with the Delaney Park loop. The longer option begins with a lengthy trek along a ridgeline before descending into Clay Hill Hollow. Turn right (east) at the bottom of the ravine and cross the creek to start a 250-foot climb on a very steep grade. Follow the trail along the ridge for about 1.5 miles before turning south for a return trip into Clay Hill Hollow. Cross the creek and go uphill 200 feet; pass over a broad, flat ridge and descend sharply to rejoin the shorter option of the KT. Turn right (west) and go 0.25 mile to the Spurgeon Hollow trailhead.

Miles and Directions

0.0   Begin at the trailhead.

0.9   Reach and cross New Cut Road.

1.5   Cross Pull Tight Road.

1.8   Reach Arnold Creek; turn left (west)

3.5   Trail juncture; go right (northeast) for the long link to Spurgeon Hollow. (**Option:** Go left [west] instead for shorter link ending at 6.5 miles.)

8.5   Arrive at Spurgeon Hollow trailhead.

71 Spurgeon Hollow to Delaney Park

This section of the Knobstone Trail features ridgetops and ravines.

Location: Jackson-Washington State Forest, between Salem and Brownstown.
Distance: 6.0-mile shuttle with an optional 2.0-mile shortcut
Elevation change: Three 200-foot climbs on long option; one 200-foot climb on short option
Approximate hiking time: 4 hours
Difficulty: Strenuous
Jurisdiction: Indiana Department of Natural Resources, Division of Outdoor Recreation
Fees and permits: Entry fee for Delaney Park
Maps: USGS Kossuth; Indiana Department of

Natural Resources Knobstone Trail brochure.
Special attractions: Scenic ridgetop overlooks
Camping: Overnight camping plus several cabins at Washington County–owned Delaney Park. Camping is permitted on public ground along the Knobstone as long as campsite is at least 1 mile by trail from all roads, recreation areas, and trailheads and as long as camp is not visible from the trail and all lakes.
Trailhead facilities: Only parking available at the Spurgeon Hollow at Delaney Park trailheads; water, restrooms, and a restaurant at Delaney Park

Finding the trailhead: To reach Spurgeon Hollow from the Elk Creek trailhead turnoff at IN 56, turn left (west) and go 10.2 miles to its intersection with IN 135 in Salem. Turn right (north) and go 8.4 miles to Plattsburg. Turn right (east) onto Rooster Hill Road and go 1.7 miles to a T intersection with Winslow Road. Turn right and go 0.6 mile to a T intersection with Delaney Park Road. Turn right (south) and go 0.5 mile to the Spurgeon Hollow trailhead.

To reach Delaney Park from the Spurgeon Hollow trailhead, turn right (north) onto Delaney Park Road and go 0.7 mile to the Delaney Park entrance. Continue 0.5 mile to the gatehouse and then 0.5 mile more to the Delaney Park trailhead parking lot.

To reach the Spurgeon Hollow trailhead from Salem, take IN 135 north for 3.6 miles to East Delaney Park Road. Turn right (east) and go 1.8 miles to Delaney Park Road. Turn left (north) and go 4.0 miles to the entrance to Spurgeon Hollow trailhead.

The Hike

Delaney Park is the north terminus of the Knobstone Trail (KT) . . . for now. Plans are being evaluated to extend the KT along the Knobstone Escarpment toward the Tecumseh Trail south of Martinsville.

There are two ways to get to Delaney Park from Spurgeon Hollow—one short and one long. Both begin by heading east from the Spurgeon Hollow trailhead for 0.25 mile to an intersection with the two KT segments from the Oxley Memorial trailhead.

Turn left (north) and go up and over a ridge into Clay Hill Hollow. At 1.2 miles the trail splits. The left (north) fork is the shorter route to Delaney Park trailhead,

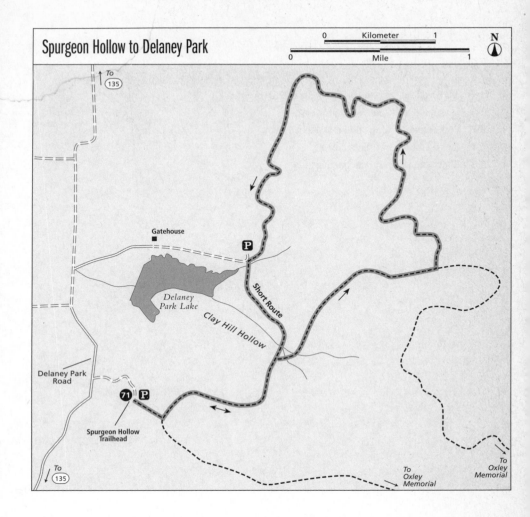

0   Kilometer   1

0   Mile   1

N

To 135

Gatehouse

P

Delaney Park Lake

Short Route

Clay Hill Hollow

Delaney Park Road

71   P

Spurgeon Hollow Trailhead

To 135

To Oxley Memorial

To Oxley Memorial

leading along the pine-forested eastern shore of Delaney Lake. The right (north) fork, described here, retraces an inbound portion of the Oxley Memorial–to–Spurgeon Hollow route before turning left (north) at 2.4 miles to wander over flat ridgetops and into a couple of ravines.

After traveling north through two ravines, turn left (west) for 1.0 mile, curling along the back end of a ravine. The trail bends sharply left (south) for the stretch run to the Delaney Park trailhead. Descend one steep hill to a creek that runs through Mandy Hollow and then climb up and over a ridge to another creek.

At the second creek turn right (west) and go 0.25 mile to the Delaney Park trailhead.

Miles and Directions

0.0   Begin at the trailhead.

1.2   Reach the trail intersection. Go right (north) for the longer leg to Delaney Park. (**Option:** Go left [west] for the shorter leg ending at 2.0 miles.)

2.4   Turn left at a trail intersection.

5.6   Cross creek that runs through Mandy Hollow.

5.75 Turn right (west) at second creek.

6.0   Reach the Delaney Park trailhead.

Appendix A: Suggested Reading

Allen, Durward. *Our Wildlife Legacy* (New York: Funk and Wagnalls, 1962).

Baker, Ronald L. and Marvin Carmony. *Indiana Place Names* (Bloomington: Indiana University Press, 1975).

Deam, Charles C. and Thomas E. Shaw. *Trees of Indiana* (Indianapolis: Indiana Department of Conservation, 1953).

Goll, John. *Indiana State Parks* (Saginaw: Glovebox Guidebooks, 1995).

Indiana Department of Natural Resources. *Directory of Indiana's Dedicated Nature Preserves* (DNR Division of Nature Preserves, 1991).

Jackson, Marion T. *The Natural Heritage of Indiana* (Bloomington/Indianapolis: Indiana University Press, 1997).

Jordan, Christopher and Ron Leonetti, photographers. *The Nature Conservancy's Guide to Indiana Preserves* (Indiana University Press/Quarry Books, 2006).

Lindsey, Alton A. *Natural Features of Indiana* (Indianapolis: Indiana Academy of Science, 1966).

McPherson, Alan. *Nature Walks in Northern Indiana* (Indianapolis: Hoosier Chapter Sierra Club, 1996).

———. *Nature Walks in Southern Indiana* (Indianapolis: Hoosier Chapter Sierra Club, 1991).

Runkel, Sylvan T. and Alvin F. Bull. *Wildflowers of Indiana Woodlands* (Ames, Iowa: Iowa State University Press, 1994).

Seng, Phil T. and David J Case. *Indiana Wildlife Viewing Guide* (Helena, MT: Falcon Publishing, Inc., 1992).

Thomas, Phyllis. *Indiana: Off the Beaten Path,* 9th edition (Guilford, Connecticut: Globe Pequot Press, 2007).

Appendix B: Additional Resources

Federal Agencies

Indiana Dunes National Lakeshore
1100 North Mineral Springs Rd
Porter 46304
(219) 926-7561

Muscatatuck National Wildlife Refuge
12985 East US 50
Seymour 47274
(812) 522-4352
www.fws.gov/midwest/muscatatuck
E-mail: Muscatatuck@fws.gov

U.S. Fish & Wildlife Service

Bloomington Ecological Services Field Office
620 South Walker St
Bloomington 47403-2121
(812) 334-4261
E-mail: MidwestNews@fws.gov

Northern Ecological Services Field Office
P.O. Box 2616
Chesterton 46304-5716
(219) 983-9753
E-mail: MidwestNews@fws.gov

Hoosier National Forest

Supervisor's Office and Brownstown Ranger District
811 Constitution Ave
Bedford 47421
(812) 279-5987; TTY: (812) 279-3423

Tell City Ranger District
248 15th St
Tell City 47586
(812) 547-7051; TDD: (812) 547-6144

Indiana Department of Natural Resources

Executive Office
402 West Washington St, Room W256
Indianapolis 46204
(317) 232–4020
www.in.gov/dnr

Division of Fish & Wildlife
402 West Washington St, Room W273
Indianapolis 46204
(317) 232–4080

Division of Forestry
402 West Washington St, Room W296
Indianapolis 46204
(317) 232–4105

Division of Nature Preserves
402 West Washington St, Room W267
Indianapolis 46204
(317) 232–4052

Division of Outdoor Recreation
402 West Washington St, Room W271
Indianapolis 46204
(317) 232–4070

Division of State Parks & Reservoirs
402 West Washington St, Room W298
Indianapolis 46204
(317) 232–4124

Local Agencies

Allen County Parks & Recreation Department
7324 Yohne Rd
Fort Wayne 46809–9744
(219) 449–3180

Tippecanoe County Parks Department
4449 SR 43 North
West Lafayette 47906-5753
(765) 463-2306

Conservation and Hiking Organizations

ACRES Land Trust, Inc.
1802 Chapman Rd
Huntertown 46748
(206) 637-2273
www.acreslandtrust.org
E-mail: acres@acreslandtrust.org

Carroll County Wabash & Erie Canal Association
1030 North Washington St
Delphi 46923
(765) 564-6572
www.wabashanderiecanal.org
E-mail: mccain@carlnet.org

Hoosier Hikers Council
P.O. Box 1327
Martinsville 46151
(765) 349-0204
www.hoosierhikerscouncil.org
E-mail: hikers@scican.net

Merry Lea Environmental Learning Center
Box 263
Wolf Lake 46796
(260) 799-5869
www.goshen.edu/merrylea
E-mail: merrylea@goshen.edu

The Nature Conservancy
Indiana Chapter
1505 North Delaware St, Suite 200
Indianapolis 46202
(317) 951-8818
www.nature.org/wherewework/northamerica/states/indiana/

Index

Adventure Hiking Trail, 140–43
Beach Trail, 26–29
Bicentennial Woods: Eagle Trail, 37–39
Big Walnut Creek Nature Preserve: Tall
    Timbers Trail, 122–24
Boy Scout Trail, 82–85
Brown County State Park: Trail 8, 164–67
Central Plain, 102–24
Chain O'Lakes State Park, 44–47
Charlestown State Park, 137–39
Clifty Falls State Park, 132–37
Cope Hollow Loop, 202–5
Cowles Bog, 20–22
Crooked Lake Nature Preserve, 39–41
Deam Lake to Jackson Road, 236–38
Delphi Canal Trails, 91–93
Dune Succession Trail, 17–19
Dunelands, 13–35
Edna W. Spurgeon Woodland Nature
    Preserve, 48–50
Elk Creek to Oxley Memorial, 246–48
Fort Harrison State Park: Fall Creek Trail,
    106–8
Fox Island Park, 64–66
German Ridge Lake Trail, 232–34
Glacial Lakes, 36–61
Harmonie State Park, 179–81
Hathaway Nature Preserve at Ross Run,
    88–90
Hemlock Cliffs National Scenic Trail,
    215–18
Heron Rookery Trail, 30–32
Hill Country, 153–77
Hoosier National Forest, 200–234
Jackson Road to New Chapel, 238–41
Kekionga Trail, 71–75
Knob Lake Trail, 150–52
Knobstone Trail, 235–54

Kokiwanee Nature Preserve, 85–87
Leota to Elk Creek, 244–46
Lincoln State Park, 196–99
Little Calumet River Trail, Bailly
    Homestead, and Chellberg Farm,
    22–25
Long Lake Loop, 14–16
McCormick's Creek State Park: Falls
    Canyon Trail, 185–88
McCormick's Creek State Park: Wolf
    Cave Trail, 188–91
Merry Lea Environmental Learning
    Center, 41–44
Mogan Ridge East, 228–31
Morgan–Monroe State Forest: Low Gap
    Trail, 154–57
Morgan–Monroe State Forest: Three
    Lakes Loop, 158–61
Mounds State Park, 103–5
Mount Baldy Trail, 32–35
Muscatatuck National Wildlife Refuge,
    127–29
New Chapel to Leota, 241–43
Ogle Hollow Nature Preserve: Trail 5,
    167–69
Olin Lake Nature Preserve, 51–53
Ouabache State Park, 67–70
Oxley Memorial to Spurgeon Hollow,
    249–51
Patoka Lake: Main Trail, 192–95
Peninsula Trail, 206–8
Pine Hills Nature Preserve, 108–10
Pioneer Mothers Memorial Forest, 213–14
Pokagon State Park, 54–59
Portland Arch Nature Preserve, 99–101
Saddle Lake Loop, 226–28
Salamonie Reservoir: Bloodroot Trail,
    76–79

Salamonie Reservoir: Switchgrass Marsh and Tree Trails, 79–82

Scarce O'Fat Trail, 161–63

Shades State Park: Pearl Ravine, 115–18

Shades State Park: Ravine Trails, 111–15

Shakamak State Park, 181–85

Shaw Lake Loop, 144–46

Southeast, 125–52

Southwest, 178–99

Spring Mill State Park: Village Trail, 174–77

Spurgeon Hollow to Delaney Park, 252–54

Starve Hollow State Recreation Area, 146–49

Sycamore Loop, 208–12

Tipsaw Lake Trail, 223–25

Turkey Run State Park, 119–21

Twin Caves Trail, 170–73

Two Lakes Loop, 218–23

Versailles State Park, 130–32

Wabash Heritage Trail, 94–98

Wabash Valley, 62–101

Wing Haven Reserve: Trillium Woods Trail, 59–61

About the Author

Phil Bloom is a native Hoosier and lifelong resident of Indiana. He joined the Indiana Department of Natural Resources as communications director in 2007 after a thirty-three-year newspaper career, including eighteen years as an award-winning outdoors editor at the *Fort Wayne Journal Gazette.*

Bloom is an active member of the Outdoor Writers Association of America and served as the group's president from 2008 to 2009. He is an Eagle Scout and an Indiana Certified Master Naturalist. He lives in Fort Wayne.